MW01202248

BARRIERS TO LOVE

EMBRACING A BISEXUAL IDENTITY

MARINA PERALTA

with Penelope James

BARRIERS PRESS

Los Angeles

BARRIERS TO LOVE
Embracing a Bisexual Identity

Author: Marina Peralta
Co-author: Penelope James

Notice of Rights
No part of this book may be reproduced or transmitted in any form or by any means, electronic or mechanical, including photocopying, recording, or by any information storage and retrieval system, without prior written permission from the publisher.

Notice of Liability
The author shall not have any liability to any person or entity with respect to any loss or damage caused or alleged to be caused directly or indirectly by the content contained in this book.

Author's Note
This story is substantially as I remember it, drawn from memories of people and experiences that took place over a lifetime. To respect the privacy of the individuals portrayed, I have changed identities and certain details and features about them.

Published by
Barriers Press
Los Angeles

ISBN 978-0-9899007-0-6

9 8 7 6 5 4 3 2 1

Cover and Book Design: Marty Safir, Double M Graphics

The time has come, I think, when we must recognize bisexuality as a normal form of human behavior... we shall not really succeed in discarding the straitjacket of our cultural beliefs about sexual choice if we fail to come to terms with the well-documented, normal human capacity to love members of both sexes.

– Margaret Mead (1975)

Table of Contents

PART III
THE
STRAIGHT
LIFE

PART IV
JULIA

PART V
MARINA

.

PART I
MAMI

BARRIER ONE
Consequences of Past Actions

My car draws up outside my house. I turn off the lights, but I don't get out. I'm still high from the exhilaration of the dance. My body vibrates, and the rhythm of funky jazz beats in my ear. For an hour I had kept the tempo—moving, twisting, swaying, bending, grinding, and kicking. Lost myself in the motions. Entered another dimension and touched the infinite. Dancing is my way of praying, or a ritual cleansing after giving six hours of family therapy and listening to the problems of others.

I didn't stop until the teacher's voice broke into my trance. Her "Marina!" brought me back to the reality of the studio and the other, younger students staring at me with something like awe. A girl asked if I was a professional dancer. "In my dreams," I told her. Another said, "I can't believe a woman your age can move like that." I smiled at her. "Since long before you were born."

Reality taps me on the shoulder. My underwear is sticking to my skin. The sweet-sour smell of physical exertion is on me. I should go inside, take off my sweaty clothes, and shower.

The phone is ringing as I enter. My daughter, Gabriela, usually calls in the evening. I sink into a chair and grab the receiver.

"Guess who contacted me?" she asks and not waiting for a reply, "Karla, my half-sister."

Maybe a few seconds go by, but half a lifetime flashes through my mind. "Karla? Our Karla?"

"Yes, Mom, our Karla, from when we lived in Mexico City."

"Where is she?" I glance at my door as if expecting her to turn up here.

"In New York. She lives there."

Karla. My lost child. Thoughts swirl in my head, old feelings unearthed, twisting, turning, and gathering speed, the past a callous dance come back to lure me into it.

2

"How did she find us?" My voice reflects my wonder and dismay. Why so long? Several years before, Gabriela and I searched for her online and found no trace.

"On Facebook. She wants to get to know us."

"After thirty-five years?" For all that time we knew nothing about her. Not how she grew up or where she was or what she was doing. Or if she was alive. She came into our lives and left her mark, then disappeared into another.

"We *are* her family," Gabriela says.

We *were* her family, but I don't correct her. Karla was its youngest member. Daughter of my heart. My lover's daughter. My husband's daughter. What a mess we made of her young life.

As Gabriela prattles on, I listen with half a mind. The other half is filled with a memory I've stored in the back of it for many years, like an old suitcase I hadn't thrown away in case I might use it again. Now it's been hauled out and brought to me to assess its worth.

I sent Karla away—a child I had nurtured as my own. Legally, I had no claim to her. If I'd kept her with me in Mexico, it would have been the equivalent of kidnapping, removing her from her biological mother. No choice but to send her to a crazy woman.

My son Armando begged me, "Please keep her here. She's our little sister. Or let me go with her so I can bring her back."

His offer brought tears to my eyes. My body felt as fragile as an autumn leaf crushed under the weight of my decision.

"She's going to Spain to live with her mother," I told him. "But she's part of our family, and I promise she won't be gone for long." A promise not mine to keep, but caught in a tangled wire of deception, what else could I tell him?

I saw little Karla off at the airport. A three-year-old, with short black hair, upturned nose, and her mother's full lips. She had a trembling smile of anticipation over the plane flight ahead, but confusion lurked in her dark eyes. Why did she have to leave her sister, her brothers, and her home? Armando had told her how lucky she was to be going on this long plane ride, and how he wished he could go as well, and that helped, but in her child's way, she seemed to know she didn't belong.

She wore her favorite dress, a navy blue with red piping around the sleeves and skirt. She insisted on wearing dresses. "No pants for me," she'd say. "Pants are for boys like my brothers."

I went down on my knees and hugged her sturdy little body so tightly that she pulled away. "Remember, I love you." I tried to hide the sob in my voice.

"When is Oki coming back?" she asked, referring to herself in the third person.

"In a few months," I said. Another false promise. "We'll miss you very much." A last hug, and the flash of a thought—I'd pretend the flight had been cancelled, take her home and keep her forever. I may not have given birth to her, but Karla was also my creation, my daughter.

I let her go, watched her disappear into the tunnel leading to the plane, her short legs in their red socks and navy blue shoes spinning to keep up with the woman holding her hand, a friend who would see her safely to Madrid.

A hollow place opened inside me, and its emptiness grew until I relegated her to the land of lost persons.

Excitement oozes from Gabriela's voice. "Karla has a daughter, nineteen."

"Really?" I say, my mind elsewhere. "What about her mother?" A question I've asked myself often.

"Claudette? She's living in Switzerland."

"Does Karla see her?"

"I don't know. Karla said they don't get on well."

Memories hit me of gorgeous Claudette belting out a love song; fun-loving Claudette playing with the kids; glazy-eyed Claudette covered in blood; and Claudette's naked body on our last evening. Lost in the emotional damage she had heaped on me. Why would I want to see her again? Yesterday's problems are no more, and we're no longer young, and she must have changed. Or a hint of the love we once had exists to rediscover in our waning years.

Gabriela says, "I'm going to invite Karla to come here to San Diego and meet all of us."

I think of the little girl walking away into the unknown. "It's a great idea," I say. I want to see her with all my heart, but I hesitate to reopen that door. Too late. Already it has opened, and a wave of memories rolls in, turning the past into the present again.

BARRIER TWO
A Hidden Memory

Claudette's fingers brush my cheeks with feathery lightness and trace the outline of my jawbone, seeking the contours of my face. They move across my lips, playing and stroking them into fullness. They renew their exploration to the tender place under my earlobes and then dance lightly over my neck, from one side to the other, until I writhe in response. They circle each of my breasts. Ripples of feeling run through me as they mark a path down my body. Her fingers besiege every part of my being, and I allow them to find their way.

We embrace and our bodies blend into the same movement.

Her breast is full, its dark areola sharp, as she moves it against me, back and forth, exciting me to fulfillment. Then ... a disturbing image fills my mind.

A breast like a large, squishy balloon with a raisin on top is rubbing me between my legs in the place where I do pee-pee.

I'm four years old and I'm under a bed. This space smells of dust, and sweaty feet, and sour old clothes, and it's dark except for a ray of light on the side next to the window. The floor beneath my bare behind is cold. Our maid, a young girl with a pretty face, coaxed me to hide here with her.

I don't mind what her breast is doing to me. What's more, I like the sensation it gives me, sort of ticklish in a good way that makes me tingle all over and want it to go on. I can see her face with her mouth open, and she's breathing hard, and her eyes are glassy like my doll's. She moves her breast up and down so that the raisin pushes at my pee-pee as if wanting to get inside.

I cry out. What she's doing makes me feel that I've gone to heaven and the angels are kissing me.

"Shush!" she says, and I remember thinking I'd angered her.

I push Claudette off me. "I can't go on." I huddle at the end of the bed, my arms around my bent legs, like a scared child. For that is what I feel like— scared and shocked and bewildered. I'm thirty-two years old, having sex with a woman, experiencing only pleasure, and it's ruined by this flashback.

With sudden clarity, I remember.

I see myself in my pink dress with navy blue dots staring up at a pretty young girl in her twenties, a maid in our household, who has asked me to play a game with her. "We have to get under the bed," she tells me. It's fun to get under the bed, like being in our own world where no one can see us, like playing hide-and-seek. She pulls down my panties and pushes up my dress. "Now for the best part of the game," she says, and kisses her fingers and rubs them round and round my pee-pee place until I scream, and then she shows me how to do it to her.

I like this game so much that we play it every day.

"You can't tell anyone," she says. "It's our little secret. You have to swear on my medal."

But I'm not used to keeping secrets. Why do I have to promise not to tell anyone about our game? Because we hide and she makes me feel good in my pee-pee place.

Someone comes into the room and sees the maid's legs sticking out from under the bed and asks, "What are you doing there?" The maid lies, says she's searching for a brooch she dropped. She crawls out, but I'm quiet; I don't want to be caught.

The maid comes for me when nobody is around. She hisses at me: "Shhh. We don't want anyone to find out about our game." Her face wrinkles like the wicked witch's, and she pinches my arm so hard it makes me cry out. "If you tell, *el cuco* (the boogeyman) will take you in the middle of the night."

I'm so scared I don't want to go to bed. I ask my grandmother, Nona, can I sleep with her because I don't want *el cuco* to get me.

"Who told you that?" she asks. I shake my head and say I can't tell, it's a secret, but she insists. I can't keep secrets from her. As she listens her eyes cross, and I've never seen them cross before, or her face with such a fierce look on it. She says my pee-pee place is my private part and I shouldn't let other people touch me down there.

The next day the maid goes away and never comes back.

Our little game fades from my mind.

Or I block it out.

BARRIER THREE
Loss of My King

Mazatlán, Mexico
1946

On a spring morning my father takes me to the place where he works. He holds my hand tightly as we walk through the main plaza in the city center. I skip a little to keep up with him, even though he isn't walking fast, but he takes such long steps—one for every two or three of mine. He's a tall man, taller than almost anyone else, and many have to look up at him.

The air is fresh before the heat smothers it, and it has the fragrance of bougainvillea and the promise of spring in this hot coastal Mexican city. Early-morning cooking smells waft over from the vendors' stalls, and my nostrils fill with a haphazard collection of sizzling oil, carbon, mashed fruit in the *aguas frescas*, and the fierce odor of our local coffee brewing. Overlying everything is the eternal odor of cigarettes—the harsh, throat-grating Delicados.

My hand fits into my Papi's palm as if it belongs there, as if it is indeed a part of him. At six, I reach his waist, but I hold my head up as high as I can so that everybody can see me walking at the side of the most handsome man in the world. In his white suit and with his fair hair glinting in the sun, he could be a king in one of my fairy tale books. In real life, the people act like he is one. Why else would they bow or drop their heads or tip their hats to him? Why do they come up and say how wonderful he is and, "Thank you, Don Marcos," for doing so many good things to help them? All kinds of people— men wearing sombreros and *huaraches*, old women in gray shawls, young women carrying or dragging little children, shop owners, stall vendors, the man who sells Coca Cola and 7-Up, men in dark suits, others who are dirty and disarrayed and smell like the *cantina*—come to him, and from their expressions I see how they respect him.

My Papi is not a real king, and he wears a hat instead of a crown, but Mami has told me he represents law and justice in our city. We're going to his palace; I'm wearing my best dress, navy blue with a white lace collar and cuffs, and white shoes to match, and Mami pinned a big white bow on top of my blond curls.

I am his Princess and he never lets me forget it, never lets go of my hand, which should show everyone how important I am to him. But they don't care; they keep on stopping us, grasping his arm, asking for his attention, and begging for his help. Why does he have to share our day with them?

He must sense my impatience as, with a chuckle, he bends over and lifts my chin so that I can look right at him. "You, *mi Princesa*, are the most important person in the world to me, but I must tend to others as well. It is my duty."

I nod, but I can't help being sulky. "Does your duty matter more to you than me?"

He's about to answer when a woman appears in front of us and holds out her hands in a pleading gesture. Her face is lined and cracked, and her clothes are black, the color of sadness. "Don Marcos, how can I ever repay you for helping my son?" Tears roll down her cheeks. "You gave him justice and saved him from those *verdugos* in jail."

I gaze up at my father; he wrinkles his brow as if trying to remember.

"His name is Juan Alvarez," she says. "They accused him of abusing a rich man's daughter, even though he was somewhere else. You didn't believe their story and ordered that the true culprits be found and sent to jail."

He nods, smiling at her, and his green eyes soften to a light color. "I only did what was right," he says. "Your son shouldn't have to pay for someone else's crime."

She wipes away her tears with the back of her hand. "God bless you, Don Marcos, and may the Virgin watch over your little girl."

His hand tightens on mine; he's telling me that he will protect me. As we walk on, I ask, "Why did she cry when she thanked you?"

He turns and his eyes hold a different softness—a tenderness meant just for me. Not for my brothers or for Mami. Just me. "Because I was the only one who believed in his innocence."

Eagerly I climb the twenty steps, counting them one by one, that lead up to the Municipal Palace. I'm going to see the place where Papi rules over the people.

*

In the evening when Papi comes home I sit on his lap and tell him about my day. He has his own scent, like fresh, sweet lemon. I run my fingers through his wavy fair hair and find a white one. "Pull it out," he says. "We'll show it to Mami." I close my eyes and tug, and it tightens, and then it's a wisp in my hand.

"Mami, Papi has a white hair," I tell her.

She makes a face of annoyance. "You're only thirty-six," she says to him. "Too young to be going gray. It's all those problems that people pile on your shoulders."

"Carmen, my work means a lot to me," he tells her. "As a judge, it's my duty to help people and do the right thing for them."

"What about me, Papi?"

"My little Marina, you're my *Princesa*, and you're very precious to me."

I lean back against him, safe and secure in the crook of his arm.

*

The phone rings late at night. A harsh, forbidding sound that wakes me. I hear Mami scream. Once, but somehow I know she's covered her mouth so as not to wake me or my brothers. Something terrible has happened. I'd go and find out, but my eyes are closing. I fall back asleep.

Next day Mami tells us my grandmother, Nona, is having some friends over, and they will both be busy attending to them. My aunt is coming and she will take care of us.

I watch from an upstairs window as people arrive. Rather than eager and excited about a party, they are serious. They all wear black, and women wear veils like in church. I sneak downstairs for a closer peek. The living room is full of people. They don't seem to be having a good time; many are chanting, "*Ave Maria.*" Praying the rosary. At a party? I see Mami sitting with my aunts, but they aren't talking, and Mami's face has a distant expression as if she's somewhere else.

I move closer to a group of ladies so I can hear bits of conversation.

"What will Carmen do?" a woman asks. "How will she manage with five small children?"

Another says, "Poor little ones. They're too young to understand."

Why are we poor? My eyes search the room as a horrible suspicion forms in my mind. I go into the living room and walk up to Mami.

"Where's Papi?" I ask.

Everyone becomes quiet, even the ones saying their rosary.

"Papi has gone away," Mamá says and points a finger upwards—to the ceiling, to the sky, to Heaven. "Jesus called him to his side to help all the needy people in Mexico. It was too much for him to do here on Earth."

"It's not true," I shout and stamp my foot. "We need him more than they do." I turn and see all the faces staring at me, and I have to get away from them.

I run outside to search the sky for a sign, any sign. Seeing none, I send Papi a message. *Please come back to us. I need you. We need you. Much more than all those other people.*

My aunts pull me back indoors, give me a tea to "calm" me, and put me to bed. I cry myself to sleep. Later, I hear that my little brother who's three picks up Papi's picture and talks to it for hours, telling it that we miss him and to please come home soon.

When I'm older I find out that Papi was killed in Mexico City while there on business. At the end of a long day, in his hotel room, he got stomach cramps from indigestion. He went out to the pharmacy on the other side of the street to buy some salts to settle his stomach. On his way back, he was crossing over when a taxi came at full speed, hitting him so hard he died on the spot.

"Why did Jesus have to take him from us?" I keep asking.

"*Si te toca, te toca*," Nona recites the Mexican quote that means, "If it's your turn to go, you go." Fate, destiny, that moment, an unexpected happening.

If it is his turn, it might as well be mine.

I think and think about it. Then I go out to the street and wait until I see a car coming. I step off the pavement right into its path—only to be snatched back. "What are you doing?" my cousin screams, grasping my arms from behind.

"I want to go join my Papi in Heaven." I struggle in her hold. It isn't fair. She's ten, and I'm only six. I wriggle like a lizard, but she's stronger. "You can't stop me," I yell. "My mind is made up." She half drags me away from the curb, and other people, hearing my screams and her shouts, come out and help her carry me, resisting all the way, back into the house. She warns my mother and my aunt to make sure I don't try it again. My aunt puts me to bed and gives me a spoonful of *Passiflorina*, a calming drug. It takes the fight out of me and makes me sleepy. From then on Mami makes sure that someone watches me closely.

They can't hold me back forever. *Someday, Papi, I will find you again.*

My father's family offers to help us out, but Mami would rather be independent. But how can she manage with five children, six years to three months old? My maiden aunts, who have a large home here in Mazatlán, suggest that my little brother who is a toddler of two live with them until my mother gets settled. She agrees—for the time being.

We go to live in Tijuana in a house next to Nona, my father's mother, and Mami partners with one of my uncles in a pharmacy business.

Nona is the one who takes care of me while Mami manages the pharmacy. Nona understands what is going on inside my heart. She attends to all of our family members as well, moving around her house, slender, tall, and straight. Her gentle features hide her strong character. Proudly genteel, she's a gracious hostess. Friends, politicians, important people, and servants all admire her perceptive mind, which my Papi had inherited from her.

"Your father was a fair and just man," she says as she brushes my hair. "He believed in treating everyone, rich or poor, in the same way. He would not rule in favor of the rich, or take bribes, or let the wealthy blame others for their misdeeds."

*

I go up to the attic in my aunt's house to search for the books that belonged to him. His signature is on the inside page. I touch them, smell them, and hold them against my chest, trying to find his essence in their pages. They are heavy, bound in red leather with the title in gold letters. I spell out the letters: L-E-G—the last one isn't easy because sometimes it has a soft "huh" sound and other times it's more like a growl. "Ga." I make out the word, "Le-gal." I heard him say it often, so I know it has to do with his work.

"Did Papi use those books to rule over the people?" I ask my aunt.

"No, *mi amor*, they were your father's books when he was a law student."

Papi, what were your thoughts when you read these books? I imagine you as a student, hunched over them, reading late at night. I want to be like you, to read, to learn, to be what Mami calls "an intellectual." I want to follow in your steps and help the poor the way you did.

After he's gone, so suddenly, I often think how life owes me because his stay here was so brief. I move on, but in my mind, I'm still his *Princesa*. My king has deserted his princess and his realm before we're ready to go on without him. All I can do is try to live up to his standards and learn what he knew so that, like him, I can help people.

.

BARRIER FOUR
A Symbiotic Relationship

Mazatlán, Mexico 1946
Veracruz, Mexico 1939

A few days after Papi dies, Mami takes me to sleep with her in the big bed she shared with him. "I don't want to be here alone," she says. We fall asleep, her back to me and my arms around her. When I awake, she's on the other side of the bed. I snuggle up to her. She stirs, opens her eyes, and gives a little start. "Oh, Marina, you startled me. I forgot you were here with me." I give her a kiss and try to cuddle, but she sits up and stretches her arms. "It's my first good night's rest since your Papi died. It helped to have you share my bed."

Pure joy fills me. Because of me, Mami got to rest. I helped her.

"This bed is too large for just me," she goes on. "You should sleep here every night." I throw myself at her and give her a big hug. For the first time since Papi left us I'm happy.

At six, I believe I'm my mother's confidante, friend, and protector. And she is my protector who, like a battling angel, will defend me from all the hurtful things in life.

The next nine years we will sleep together in the same bed. When I'm little, I think it's because she needs me to be there in my father's place. And I need her to need me—and to protect me. As I get older, I realize it's more like a practical solution. My three brothers sleep in the other bedroom.

*

Sometimes when Mami and I lie in bed she tells me stories. I like them more than the ones in my picture books because she makes them sound real. She has a way of taking me into her story and making me feel I'm there, watching everything that happens.

"Tell me how you met Papi," I ask her.

She sighs. "Ay, Marina, you want to hear that story again?"

"Yes, because you always make it sound new."

She rests her head on her hand as if thinking. "This story starts when a handsome young prince with fair hair and green eyes came to work in a city called Veracruz. Every girl in town wanted to snare him, and their mothers hatched plots to win him over. Most of them didn't stand a chance; his family belonged to the elite in this country."

"What does 'elite' mean?"

"High society, a family of noble ancestry," she says. "Rulers."

"Why didn't the girls stand a chance?"

"Because they didn't come from a high-class family."

"Is that fair?" I don't understand. If that's true, Cinderella wouldn't have a chance to marry Prince Charming.

"Yes, that's how it's always been. The more educated people rule the uneducated and marry other people like themselves."

"So if a poor person wants to become high-class, can they?"

"If they marry into a good family."

"And you did?"

"My father was an important man in our city," she says in an indignant voice.

"Nona says the people loved Papi because he didn't choose between the rich and poor."

"Let's get on with my story," Mami says.

Her story unwinds like a fairy tale in which the dashing prince meets his beautiful bride, sweeps her off her feet, and carries her away—though not to live happily ever after. The thought of Papi makes me want to cry, but I don't want Mami to stop, so I swallow my tears and listen.

"Veracruz is a big port," she starts, "and it gets very hot and humid in summer. People stay indoors during the day and go out in the early evening to cool down. Once upon a time, a girl called Carmen lived there, and she and her mother liked to walk in the town plaza, where tall palm trees swayed in the sea breeze, and the air was fresher."

I know Carmen is Mami, though she tells it as if Carmen were another person.

"As they approached, Carmen could hear music from a block away." Bright colored lights gave the plaza a festive appearance, and musicians on a raised covered dais with wrought-iron railings played romantic melodies. The air filled with the odors of frying tortillas in pans, and roasted nuts, but on a warm night, Carmen preferred to choose an *agua fresca* from the display of fruit waters in large glass jars—pinky-red watermelon, amber tamarind, creamy white rice, or purple hibiscus. Vendors went by selling cold drinks, ices, and cotton candy. She tried to ignore the stands where crowds of men were gathered, and the strong smell of alcohol wafting from them. Her mother gave them a dirty look. "Some of those men will have to go to confession tomorrow," she said and gestured toward the darkened cathedral that stood at one side like a disapproving elder overseeing its flock.

Traditionally, young people promenaded around the plaza, girls in one line and men in another across from them. The girls were decked out in their best dresses to show off to friends and meet future husbands. Carmen was wearing her new dress, dark green with a nipped-in waist, a gold-buckle belt, and a long ballerina skirt that swirled around her legs. No other girl had a dress like hers—she'd ordered it from a grand store in Mexico City.

"Where did you buy that dress?" the other girls asked, and, "It's the style of the American actress who dances," and, "How many meters of material in that skirt?"

Her mother joined the other mothers, all seated on carved stone benches where they could supervise the young people and gossip about the goings-on.

At nineteen it was time for Carmen to find a husband, though the ultimate decision as to whom she would marry belonged to her parents. She didn't flirt like other girls; she knew her worth and that she was the prettiest girl in town—her pearly white skin made her stand out from darker complexions—and people found her funny and witty, whereas most girls had little to say.

Carmen linked her arm with her best friend's and they walked around the plaza. They made a turn just as a man in the opposite line passed them. His eyes met Carmen's for a second—or maybe two. He tipped his hat and went on.

"How handsome he is," her friend said. "He's that lawyer from Mexico City. I heard he has a high position in the oil company, and he's not married."

Carmen nodded. "*This one is mine,*" she told herself.

"The battle was on," Mami said. "No, it was war among the girls as to which one would land him. I gave him a big smile whenever I saw him, but they all did." Mami's smile is magical. I've seen how it draws everyone to her, offering fun and delight in her company.

"Your Papi smiled back at me. Only me. Not at the other girls. The next round he asked my name and told me his. My mother, who was watching us like a hawk, called out, 'Carmen, who are you talking to?' I took him over and introduced him to her, and he asked for her permission to walk with me. She didn't hesitate to give it. Imagine the talk when people saw us together. Then he requested the honor of calling on me, and, of course, my mother agreed. He was the biggest catch in the town, and she was the envy of all the other mothers. And you know what happened after that."

"You were married and came to live here in Mazatlán, and I was born, and since I was the oldest, you and Papi loved me more than my little brothers."

"That's not true," she says, laughing her special laugh. "We love— he loved—all of you the same." Her voice trembles, and she's silent for a moment, as if considering this. "But you, Marina, are my great comfort in these dark days."

Left on My Own

TIJUANA, MEXICO, AND MEXICO CITY
1950

My grandmother, Nona, has a proud expression as she sits at the head of the table for our Sunday family meal. It's a tradition for my uncles and aunts and cousins to get together on this day each week in Nona's house in Tijuana. My brothers and I come over to see her whenever we like; all we have to do is cross her big garden from where we live at the back.

This is not a usual Sunday meal. Although everyone is boisterous and laughing, there's an undercurrent of sadness.

I can't remain quiet anymore. At ten-and-a-half I have to voice what is on everyone's mind. "Mami, do we have to move to Mexico City? Can't we stay here?" I ask this on purpose because the rest of the family is present, and they can persuade her to change her mind.

Why move away from this enchanted home where my uncle and aunt and cousins live? Away from the garden with the big trees that we climb, and the tree house my uncle built for us to play in? I like driving over the border every day to school in San Diego. What I don't like is that mean, goggle-eyed Sister Mary Ann, who grabs me by the shoulders and shakes me for talking in class.

Everyone at the table stops eating and stares at Mami. She holds up her hands to indicate she has no choice. "This family and you, Nona, have become more my family than my own. But since our pharmacy business failed, I have to find a way to provide for my children."

"Surely you can find something to do here, Mami," I say, and several people nod.

"Like what? Tijuana is a small city that lives off tourism. I can't work in a hotel or restaurant in a demeaning job. Mexico City is much larger—I think it has almost 3 million inhabitants, and my sister who lives there says there are many opportunities for someone like me. Besides, your father's friends have promised to help me find work and obtain scholarships to good schools." I know that tone well. She's made up her mind and she won't change it.

One of my uncles says, "I'm sure we can look after you and the children here. Living in Mexico City will be quite a struggle for you."

Mami sticks out her jaw and shakes her head. "Thank you but no."

I've never noticed Nona's wrinkles before, but now I see solid lines across her forehead, and little ones around her mouth make it droop. When she smiles the corners don't lift, as if it hurts, and it seems like she's suddenly old and tired.

"Well, Carmen," she says, her voice cracked and halting. "I'm deeply saddened to lose you, but I think you're making the right decision. We'll all miss the children very much." She glances at me. "The most important thing is to do what is best for them."

*

Is this what is best for our family? This gloomy apartment where we're living in Mexico City? My whole world has been switched around. I've been taken away from the people, home, places, school, and friends I love, and expected to settle for this in exchange. Worst of all, I've lost Mami as well.

She's never at home. Always at work or out with her friends.

She's an executive secretary for Pemex, the national oil company. When we get home from school, only the maid, Teresa, is here to give us our meal. She's supposed to watch us, but she's in the kitchen, listening to soap operas on the radio. My brothers are my only companions. I fight a lot with Pepe, who is nearest to my age, a year younger; he's nine. We hit each other until Roberto, who's seven and more sensitive, begs us to stop. We're all unhappy about coming here. Pepe is more aggressive; Roberto cries a lot; and little Fabian, who's only four, is confused, missing everyone who fussed over him. I'm the only one who pays attention to him, but he's getting too big and wants to be more like his brothers. We all go out to the street and make friends with other kids on the block.

At the end of the day I wait by the window for Mami to come home. Although she gets off work at three in the afternoon, she's never here to greet us when we get home at five after a two-hour ride in the school bus all over the city. Instead, she goes out with her friends and often comes home so late that I'm asleep. Why does she want to be with them rather than with us? It's as if she doesn't want to see us anymore except on Sundays. We still share the same bed, which is comforting, but she's too tired to talk much. She's very busy, she says, with her job and going out with those "good contacts," who will help her get ahead in the world and help us when we are older, as she constantly reminds us. But I think she leaves me on my own because she likes being with them more, especially her friend Iris, who also works at Pemex.

Whenever I try to give her a kiss or a hug or cuddle, she shoos me away, telling me, "Marina, you're always on top of me." Yet she's affectionate with other people.

One day she comes home early from work and brings Iris for dinner. Mami told me that everyone calls her La Güera because of her long blond hair, which she wears in a coil. But when she comes to our apartment, she undoes it so that I can see how long her hair is—all the way down to her waist. I touch it and it's like straw. I think she paints it, but since nice ladies don't paint their hair, everyone pretends it's her true color. Iris and Mami have lunch together every day. So why do they also go out with each other in the evening? For that reason, I don't like Iris, though she's nice and invites me and Mami to Sanborns, where I eat a big slice of chocolate cake. I glare at her, hoping she will realize she's taking Mami away from me.

I keep on waiting at the window for Mami to come home, and sometimes I see her climbing the steps. But mostly I'm disappointed; it's as if she's abandoned me since we came to Mexico City, leaving me alone to fend for myself.

*

Teresa's food isn't agreeing with me. It's nothing like the delicious, carefully prepared food in Nona's house. I can see the grease sitting on top of my chicken broth or glistening on the red rice she makes daily. My tummy aches in the evening. At first it's a dull pain, but it gets more intense. Even if I lie down, it doesn't go away. Mami comes home earlier than usual to find me crying out loud from the sharp pain. The next day she doesn't go to work and takes me to the doctor. I have colitis, and he orders a light diet of chicken broth, cream soups, and mushy foods that I don't have to chew on. No candy or chocolates. No *pan dulce*—sweet bread—until I'm better. I'm being punished for some unknown sin.

The light diet isn't working. My tummy aches don't go away. Then rashes break out on my eyelids, under my knees, in my armpits, and in my private parts. I can't stop scratching myself. Pepe teases me. "You're like a dog with fleas." Maybe I do have fleas, as I feel little mites crawling all over me. At school I can't go outside for gym or recess because the sun makes my rashes worse.

Again, Mami takes me to the doctor. He prescribes lotions and creams for the itching, and they help for a while. The rashes come back. The doctor says to use baby soap when I bathe, as I must have very sensitive skin.

Mami is so worried that she finds another doctor. He says, "Children who move from one place to another often show symptoms that have no reason for being. This may be a physical reaction to an emotional problem. Once she adjusts, the rashes will go away."

They do go away, though they return at odd intervals, usually when I'm stressed or unhappy. My mysterious stomach problems persist well into my later years.

*

My brothers and I make friends with a group of boys on our block. I'm the only girl, which makes me feel very important. Since I'm a good athlete, I can keep up with them and run as fast.

They all like me a lot because I let them kiss me. Real kisses.

It starts when José, who's funny and has a mischievous face, says, "Let's kiss like they do in the movies." We stick our lips together for a few seconds.

"What's so great about that?" I say when we become unstuck. We try again to see if it will give us the crazy feeling people get in the movies after kissing, like Gene Kelly in *Singin' in the Rain*.

"I guess it's all made up," he says. The next day, he comes back and tells me that we didn't do it right; his older brother told him to stick his tongue into my mouth. That sounds icky. I don't want to try it, but he says he'll buy me an ice cream if we get it right. So he sticks his tongue in my mouth, wiggles it a bit, and that's all. An easy way to earn an ice cream. He goes and tells his friend Luis, who also wants to do it, and then the other boys as well. All the boys kiss me, and they like me a lot, more than Pepe, and they're all around me, leaving Pepe on his own, so he goes off to sulk by himself.

I don't mind most boys' kisses, though some are slimy. A few stick their tongues in so far I almost choke. A couple slush their tongues around my mouth as if they were cleaning it out, and there's one I call "the Hose" because he leaves so much spit in my mouth that I won't let him kiss me again. I like José most because he's learned how to move his tongue the way I enjoy. And Luis because he's tall and bends when he kisses me, and makes me feel protected.

Pepe is so jealous of all the attention I'm getting that he tells Mami what I'm doing. She goes sort of crazy, shrieking and throwing up her arms, and shouting that her daughter is not a *cualquiera*, and if she finds me playing with the boys again, even roller-skating, she will tell my uncle to call the police on them.

"No wonder you have so many things wrong with you," she says in front of Pepe. "Don't you know that people's mouths are full of germs? Young boys especially. They put all kinds of dirty things in them, and if they kiss you, you're bound to catch their germs and get sick. You'll have sores on your mouth, and everyone will know you've been up to no good, and nice girls won't want to be friends with you."

How would I know that kissing boys would have such terrifying consequences?

*

All my life, a whiff of Chanel No. 5 reminds me of my mother and the elegance of a time when she always dressed up and her perfume lingered long after she had left for work.

Even when I find out her friends, society women in Mexico City, also wear it, it is still *her* perfume to me. On them it smells overdone, like their makeup. On her it seems to be part of her personality, giving her an aura of charm and sparkle. Years later she confides it was never the perfume of her choice—too heavy and vaguely oppressive—and I'm as let down as if she had disowned her closest friend. But as a social newcomer, she has to follow the trend in order to be accepted in upper-class circles.

"I still wear Chanel No. 5," she tells me years later. "I got used to it."

Everything she does helps fulfill a purpose—to be accepted in Mexico City society. Not an easy task for a woman from a provincial town to enter that tight-knit group. She changes the way she dresses and expresses herself and acquires new manners. She's not the same Mami as before. Her work and her society friends come first.

I treasure the moments that belong just to Mami and me. There are so few of them.

Early in the morning, for a few minutes, she's herself before she turns into that other person who isn't really Mami. That person getting ready to go to work.

She wears a suit; it gives her a serious appearance, she says, and social category, and she can also wear it to after-work engagements. Her favorite is navy blue with a slim waist and straight, calf-length skirt, like the ones in fashion magazines. She chooses a deep red, Italian silk blouse, a color she likes because it shows off her curly black hair and the compelling black eyes that I inherited. I hope to learn to stare people down the way she does, aiming them at someone so they feel forced to respond to her.

She puts on a string of pearls and pearl earrings that Papi gave her when I was born. "Not like the cheap baubles the other secretaries wear," she says. She believes it's important to dress like the lady she is. "We may not have much money," she tells me, "but our family has *abolengo*—lineage, and we should never forget that. Even though I have to work to support us."

I'm losing Mami to her work and those new friends of hers. I've heard them tell her how they admire her courage and determination, how she's a valiant widow struggling to support her four small children—my little brother is still living with my aunts. I've heard them call her "*La Simpática*" because she's so charming and funny.

"Why do you go out so often with your friends?" I ask.

"I'm doing PR for you kids," she tells me. "I have to move up in this world and meet important people and make good contacts that will benefit you in the future."

"What are good contacts?"

"People in positions of power or authority."

"Why them?"

She hesitates as if considering my question. "Because they are important to me ... and someday, to you."

I wish she wasn't so impressed by them, especially my father's family. She acts like they are her real family instead of her own parents. She tries to fit in, speaking the way they do, agreeing with everything they say, sharing their opinions as if they were her own, and constantly seeking them out instead of her own family.

"Knowing the right people can help you get ahead," she says. She tells my brothers: "Boys, make friends who have well-placed parents who can help you get ahead later on. Marina, I want you to marry a man from a good family, someone who will take care of you and your children so that you'll never have to go out to work to support your children."

BARRIER SIX
Interrupted Sexual Development

The doorbell rings once, twice, and again after several minutes. It's late afternoon, and Teresa must be listening to her soap operas. I sigh as I go to see who it is.

"Miguel, what a surprise," I say to my cousin, a tall teenager who's never come by the house. "My mother isn't home."

His goggle eyes remind me of nasty Sister Mary Ann. "I've come to see your brothers." It surprises me that Miguel, who at fifteen is much older, would bother with kids like them. He has the kind of slouching swagger boys are copying from James Dean in *Rebel Without a Cause**, as if to show the world they are worth noticing.

My brothers don't seem excited to see him—he's never paid attention to them before. I go back to my bedroom and to reading my book. After a while I hear the front door bang.

I'm sitting on my bed when he appears in my doorway. "I gave them five pesos to go buy some candy," he says. "Told them to take their time."

What can I say to him? We barely know each other, and he's five years older, but he's paying attention to me. His plump, piggy lips open in what I suppose is a smile but is more like a leer. "You look nice in your school uniform."

What? It's a brown and white skirt and beige blouse.

He sits on the bed and says, "Marina, you like to play, don't you?"

I nod, but why would an older boy want to play with me?

"Games?" I ask. "Like Monopoly?"

"No, older kids' games. I'll show you." He moves closer. "It goes like this." In one swift movement, he slides his hand up my leg, hooks his fingers under the elastic on my panties, and starts rubbing my crotch—my dirty, private part. Why there?

I shrink back and stare at him, wide-eyed. I don't know what to do. He said this was a game, and I don't want to seem too young to play it.

His fingers touch a tender spot, and my tummy gives a wallop and turns over. I don't move or say anything, just sit there like a doll and let his fingers stroke me.

An inner voice tells me to make him stop, this isn't right. But I don't want to. It's as if some place in me that has long been hidden is suddenly blooming. My body undulates to an unknown rhythm and shakes when the throbbing below increases to an almost unbearable strength. I moan not from pain but from pleasure. He pulls down my panties, and I spread my legs and will him to go on and invade me, to satisfy this roaring need inside me. I moan again and whimper, but I can't hold back a cry of sheer delight.

He grabs my hand and claps it to my mouth. "They mustn't hear us," he says in a rough whisper. When the urge to cry out is too strong, I dig my teeth into my hand.

Voices call: "Marina, Miguel, we're back."

"My brothers." I push away his hand and jump off my bed. Miguel is slower to react, his other hand moving up and down inside his trousers. "Hurry," I say, and I see his reluctance as he takes out his hand and stands there, breathing heavily. As I pull up my panties and straighten my skirt, I let out little gasps from the continuing sensation like an itch in my private parts. "You go out," I say. "I have to use the bathroom."

I wish I could put ice on my crotch to soothe it, but cold water will have to do. I fill the wash basin and sit in it, hoping it won't get unstuck and fall with my weight. The cold water helps diminish the sensation until I'm ready to join the boys.

I go out and eat some of my brothers' candy because Miguel tells them to share it. He'll come by again, he says, and give them money to buy more. He doesn't pay any attention to me, and soon I leave and go to my room. I try to concentrate on my book, though all I can think is, what did he do to me? I wouldn't mind him doing it again.

He does. About twice a week he comes to our home and we play. I get better and better at his game, and he also does it to his Thing.

One afternoon he says, "We're going to play another way." He pushes me against the wall and, with jerky movements, lifts my skirt and pulls down my panties, almost ripping them in his haste. He pulls out his Thing. I've never seen one this size before—must be as long as my forearm. Where was he hiding it? He wiggles it like a puppet so I can see the ugly red mushroom top with its pee hole. Then, holding my shoulders, he tries to drive it into my crotch. It hurts and I yell, "No!" and shove him away from me.

He comes back fast, trying again to force his big Thing into me. I shriek—a piercing sound even to my ears—and he takes a step away from me.

"Go away," I shout, "leave me alone!" But he won't. His eyes are set, like a zombie's, and he comes forward and pushes his Thing, like a weapon, at me.

I dodge under him, and since I'm much smaller and he's big and clumsy, I'm able to get away.

I pull up my panties and run out of the room, out of the apartment, out to the street. Anywhere to get away from him and that Thing of his. I hide behind a neighboring wall until I see him leave. Only then do I return to my home, to my bedroom, where I close the door and lie there weeping for hours. I go to the bathroom, where I see in the mirror how my face is red and bumpy from crying, and I wash it in cold water, which doesn't help much.

When Mami comes home I pretend to be asleep, but something makes her suspicious. "Marina, I know everything about you," she says, "even your breathing pattern. You can't hide from me." She taps my shoulder and I don't move. I hear her walk around the bed and feel her breath on my cheek. "I know you're awake, so stop playing the Sleeping Beauty."

Reluctantly, I do as she says, the same as I always do. I have to obey her. She studies my face. "Did one of your brothers hit you?"

"No."

"You were crying. What are you hiding?"

"Nothing." I can't tell her what Miguel did to me.

"I don't believe you."

I bury my head in my pillow, but Mami is relentless and she goes on until I answer. "Miguel ... he tried ... to put ... his Thing ... inside me." My words come out in sobs.

She's going to scold me, tell me it's my fault, and I should have known better than to let my fifteen-year-old cousin come into our bedroom.

Instead, it's as if someone had lit a firecracker under her. She raises her hands, curling her fingers as if she would gouge out his eyes. "That filthy boy did a filthy thing to you and ..." She shrieks words I've never heard before; they must be very bad words to match her anger. Then she marches outside and two blocks away to where Miguel lives with his mom, Gladys.

When she returns, all she tells me is she's forbidden him from setting foot in our home again.

According to her, that's the end of it, never to be talked about or mentioned. A veil of secrecy is dropped over the incident. It's better to ignore or forget such a shameful thing.

*

The word "filthy" remains in my mind. I'm filthy, and what he did to me was filthy. Even filthier is my own secret—I enjoyed his little "game" and played along with it—something my mother doesn't suspect. The worst is that I want him to do it to me again. I dream about the way his fingers made me feel. Even thinking about it makes the urge come back.

My fingers explore, and I find that touching myself can take me to the edge of intensity. By moving them as he did, I can stimulate myself almost as much as he did to me. I don't need him or anyone to excite me down there.

At first I'm relieved to find a solution on my own. Then I want more, so I satisfy myself again. And again. Until I'm sated and wet and wishing I'd never learned to do this. I can't stop.

How can I want to do something that makes me feel as filthy as the dirtiest beggar in the street? I'm so filthy that nothing in the world can cleanse me.

*

In May, we go to stay with my grandmother. Nona takes me to the cathedral to offer flowers to the Virgin. I've participated in this religious ritual since I was the smallest girl here. Now I join the throng of little girls wearing long white dresses and carrying baskets full of flowers, and I'm the tallest. At ten, it's my last year to take part in this ceremony.

The enormous chandeliers are lit and the choir sings "*Ave Maria*" as we march down the aisle, the little girls in the front and the older ones in the back, to leave our offerings at the altar.

Always before, I enjoyed this ritual. As one of the Virgin Mary's chosen, I'm special and sainted for this day.

No, after what happened with Miguel, I'm not one of her chosen anymore. I study her statue, her Immaculate Heart, her beautiful face, and beg her to make me pure again. But there's no response, no answer to my confusion. I see all the other girls in their white dresses, and they're whispering among themselves, saying things they don't want me to hear. Could be *manchada*—stained. Or it might be *malvada*—bad, but I have to get out of here, away from them, away from the Virgin Mary, and away from this holy place where I don't belong. I run outside and stand on the steps, panting with fear that everyone seems to notice how dirty I am inside.

Nona comes after me, loving and concerned.

"I don't want to offer flowers to the Virgin anymore," I tell her. Let her think it's because I consider myself too old to do it anymore.

When I accompany her to Mass, the priest talks in his sermon about how easy it is to give in to temptation and fall from grace. "Do you have any idea of what happens to sinners?" He asks and points his finger at all of us in the congregation. I cringe in my seat, making myself as small as I can so that his pointed finger will not single me out as a sinner.

"They burn in the eternal flames of hell," he says. "Do any of you know how that must feel? Take a candle and hold your finger over the flame, and you'll see."

Everyone is quiet. People's faces show interest, and some look scared, but it's nothing like the terror inside me. Will God punish me for what I did? Why would he show me any mercy?

*

I don't play with the boys again. I won't go anywhere near them. I know what they really want—to stick their Things inside me. When a boy so much as touches me, I shriek and run away. If I see a group of boys, I run away. If a boy seems interested in me, I run away. I'd rather stay home, do my schoolwork, and read my books.

What I can't understand is why, when I think about what Miguel did to me, the same sensation comes back—the one that made me gulp with pleasure. I get the urge to reach down and touch myself there until I scream. The same filthy feeling that oozes like mud from between my legs, dirtying me, and my body.

I'm so filthy that nothing in the world can cleanse me.

BARRIER SEVEN
Sexual Feelings Are Wrong

Mexico City
1955-57

"Please come to my party," my best friend, Adriana, says. "There'll be music and dancing and lots of nice boys."

I don't care for her new group of friends—the ones she's seeing a lot of since she turned fifteen. Maybe it's because I'm still fourteen and they're several years older, in their late teens.

"You'll enjoy yourself," she urges me. "You need to go out more, come out of your shell. All you want to do is stay at home reading books."

"My books are my companions," I tell her. Why can't she understand? We used to share our thoughts and hopes and books. Intimate things as well. I run my fingers through her gorgeous, sheer black mane, and caress each lock.

One afternoon when I was at her house and we were lying on her bed, talking, she said, "I wonder what it's like to kiss someone."

Without thinking, I leaned over and kissed her on the lips. "Like this?"

She giggled, and said, "No, more like this." She pressed her lips to mine, and we stayed like this for a full minute.

"That's not the proper way to do it," I told her. "For a real kiss, you have to open your lips and let your tongue play with mine."

We experimented until we got it right. Kissing a girl was more enjoyable than kissing a boy. She had softer lips, and didn't push as hard, and gave pleasure rather than take it.

We don't have any more long talks, and all she can think about are the boys she likes and how to attract them. She's not interested in books anymore or in kissing me, because she says it was all childish make-believe. Now she can get the real thing. "I'm having such a great time," she says, preening as she shows off to me about all her newfound knowledge.

My idea of a good time is to spend the evening with a Corín Tellado* romance novel; the heroine always finds her man and lives happily ever after.

Or, after reading Erich Fromm's *The Art of Loving*,* I got interested in human behavior, and I've gone on to read Freud and Maslow. I'd rather tackle Freud than meet some silly boy. But I prefer to dance and for everyone to see how good I am at it, so I agree to go to the party.

I put on a green taffeta dress with a flounced skirt that swishes when I move. Mami helps me fix my hair in gracious waves falling to my shoulders, and she allows me to put on lipstick. If a boy asks how old I am, I'm going to say I'm fifteen.

When I enter Adriana's living room—cleared of furniture for the party—I see that other girls are all dressed up, some with ballerina skirts and crinolines and others in tight, form-fitting dresses with whalebone girdles underneath. Many appear to have spent the afternoon in the beauty parlor, flaunting beehive and glued bouffant hairdos, and lots of eye makeup. Adriana wears her hair loose, like mine.

"You're like a film star in that dress," I tell her. She's wearing a red-and-black Italian silk print that she had made especially for this event.

She glances at mine. "You look very attractive," she says. "I'm happy you came. I promise you'll enjoy yourself." She grasps my arm and guides me to a group of people. "You all know my friend, Marina." I recognize one face. "Please take care of her. This is her first dance party."

She hurries off to greet new arrivals. I hear her say, "You look very attractive. I'm happy you came."

I gaze at the couples on the floor. Their movements seem awkward and self-conscious, and only one pair is dancing apart from each other to "Rock around the Clock." A boy I know holds out his hand to me. I take it but before he can get an arm around me, I'm shaking and rolling, and after a few minutes he's also caught up in the momentum of this dance. Everyone seems to be watching us as if this were a competition and we were the best ones. Other dancers follow our lead, and soon the floor is filled with people wiggling and shaking and jumping and laughing at the discovery of the way they feel when they dance like this. I never lack for a partner, dancing without respite, and others follow as I set the pace and style.

Most of my partners want to dance, but one, a full-of-himself boy, his slicked-back hair tracked with comb lines from his pomade, asks for the next one, which is slow and romantic. I answer his questions in monosyllables; I'm not interested in him. The music switches to a ballad, "Blue Moon," and he pulls me as close as I let him. He thrusts his pelvis forward so that I feel his hard thing sticking into me.

I choke back a scream and draw in a gasp like the sound a very old person makes. Revulsion clogs my throat even as a shudder of pleasure runs through me and a tingling below makes me want him to stick it into me even though I don't want him at all.

I swallow and, barely able to breathe, like a claustrophobic in an enclosed space, pull away from him. I rush into Adriana's bedroom, close the door, and try to calm myself, gritting my teeth and knotting my legs, resisting the urge to rub myself down there. Not here, where someone might come in and catch me. Why do I have that effect on boys? What did I do to make him react? And why did his arousal arouse me?

Eventually, I stumble out of the bedroom. My distress must be obvious. When I tell Adriana I'm leaving, she says, "You don't look too good." Before, she would have shown concern or begged me not to go, but she's busy organizing a conga line.

What does Freud say about being aroused against your will? I search through his books but find no explanation. Whom can I ask? Not Mami or my aunts. At fourteen, I have all these questions about sex, my feelings and reactions to it, but no one to confide in. Not even Adriana. Anyway, she'd be too shocked.

*

My romance with the dance began when I was ten and newly arrived in Mexico City. Mami arranged for me to take dance classes twice a week. I was so enthusiastic about ballet that I'd practice for hours at home.

The school arranges shows in Bellas Artes*, the grand concert hall where the world's primary ballerinas, such as Margot Fonteyn*, have performed. I get my first taste of being onstage when I dance a solo to Johann Strauss's "The Merry Widow"* *en pointe*, and from then on I have a solo in all the shows. My mother supports my dancing in every way she can; she buys a bunch of tickets to give or sell to friends and family and tells them, "My daughter is a great dancer." There's always a large group to applaud me. I choreograph a performance for a school concert using a popular song, "Las Clases del Cha Cha Cha,"* a dance that has become the sensation in Mexico, and it becomes the most memorable performance ever. I'm driven to excel in my dancing, my studies, and in sports, as if to compensate for my shyness in social scenes.

The summer I'm fourteen, Mami decides to show off my dancing skills to the family in Mazatlán. She arranges for me to give a performance in front of hundreds of people at the Casino, an exclusive events hall. I dance the Mexican Hat Dance" *en pointe*, the way that Tamara Toumanova,* the famous Russian ballerina, did on the stage in Mexico City. I rise above myself, above this world, throw out my heart for all to see and share the glory of my limbs moving to the music. When it ends, I'm filled with both ecstasy and a sense of loss. The applause is so loud and enthusiastic that tears fill my eyes. I adore the attention, the acclaim, the recognition. This is right for me. I want to hear people clapping for me again and again.

I dream about people recognizing me on the street and honoring me as if I were a queen, the way they behave when they see Alicia, a famous movie actress who's become Mami's close friend. She's also a widow; her husband, also a movie star, recently died of a heart attack, and she lives with her two small children and her mother. Alicia is like a favorite aunt, taking me to so many performances that the glitter and glamour of them clings to me. She introduces me to famous actors, entertainers, and politicians, and I talk to them as if we were old friends. Some tell me I should become an actress.

She invites me to the set of her latest film on location near the Popocatepetl volcano. A well-known movie director and producer approaches me. Would I film a screen test for him? Yes, of course, but since I'm underage, I need my mother's permission.

"Please," I tell Mami, "it's a golden opportunity to fulfill my dream."

"I can't allow it," she says. "Only lower-class women go into show business."

"What about Alicia?" I ask. "Or Dolores del Rio?* They're actresses from good backgrounds."

"Who knows why their families agreed? If you become an actress, your father's family will turn their backs on you and close their doors to you. Is it worth sacrificing your reputation and your family?"

I hesitate. Except for Nona, who would never reject me, I'm willing to make this sacrifice. Before I can reply, Mami says, "Anyway, I'm not giving you permission, and that's the end of this matter."

I have no choice. Her word is law.

*

The year I'm sixteen, my brothers and I spend part of our holiday with our three middle-age maiden aunts in my father's hometown. Long ago my aunts decided to wear only black because they were constantly mourning some relative or another—and we have many, many of them. They were tired of putting on mourning clothes for a year and taking them off only to have to put them on again, so it was easier to wear black every day.

We like to speculate about why they never got married. They must have had suitors, since they are very wealthy. Maybe they thought every man was beneath them. Or, Mami says they might have made a pact to stay together and dedicate their lives to God, a common choice for young ladies who grew up during the religious persecution in Mexico. The only men in their lives are their old bachelor brother and my younger brother, who has lived with them since he was a toddler. It was supposed to be a temporary arrangement, but the aunts kept telling Mami that one or the other would surely die if she took him away, and to please leave him a while longer. After a couple of years it would have been too painful for them to part with him. He became the little prince of their household.

We see him only when we visit. He's more like a cousin and not much fun to play with, as he's very possessive of his toys. Since he's the only child in the household, he's not happy when we're there.

The aunts' colonial-style house is over a hundred years old and filled with the faded luxury of former days. The large living room has imported French Louis XV red-velvet furniture and an enormous cut-crystal chandelier. Portraits of hard-faced ancestors remind us that once they ruled all the land and people in this area. The rooms surround a big stone courtyard with a fountain in the middle, brightened by a cascade of purple bougainvillea. The house isn't at all modern, or comfortable, because we have to cross the courtyard to get to the only bathroom. I wouldn't dare go to the toilet at night, and I wonder how the old ladies manage. Until I find out they all have porcelain chamber pots decorated with roses under their beds.

Another aunt and her daughter, a cousin my age, come to invite me to a young people's dance in the famous Casino. Afterwards, I can spend the night with them.

The brightly lit Casino is full of people of all ages. The women, wearing heavy necklaces and earrings of precious stones, sparkle like Christmas trees. I think they're competing with each other as to which one has the most impressive jewelry. My aunt's necklace has twelve emeralds the size of my thumbnail and a centerpiece shaped like a pear. The older people sit at tables surrounding the dance floor, where about a hundred boys and girls are dancing to music from the eighteen-man orchestra.

Tonight I know I'm attractive. My cousin helped fix my hair, and she showed me how to put on eyeliner—a black stroke on the lid and underneath it—so my eyes appear bigger and darker. I'm wearing an olive-green dress, cinched in tightly around my waist and defining my breasts, with a flowing skirt that makes me glide when I move.

Before long a young man comes to our table to ask me to dance. He's so handsome, with curly black hair and dark blue eyes, that I say, "Yes," at once. Out of the corner of my eye, I see my aunt frown in disapproval. I forgot that here it's customary for boys to ask her permission first.

The dance is a slow ballad, "*Como Antes*" from an Italian song. This gives us a chance to exchange information about each other: names, ages, and what we do—he's Oscar, nineteen, going to the university.

"You're from Mexico City?" he says. "I hadn't seen you around."

"Do you know every person here?"

"Most of them," he says. "That's why I enjoy meeting someone new."

Next is a cha-cha-cha that the older generation frowns on because we dance it separately, with both of us trying to keep up with each other and with the rhythm. Many of the adults seem concerned, and several couples leave the dance floor. I pretend not to see my aunt gesture at me to go back to the table. "I'm surprised they allow them to play it here," I say.

"Someone must have paid the musicians," he says. "I bet they will have to stop." He's right. Precisely when we're stomping along with the music, the orchestra makes an abrupt switch to "Love Is a Many-Splendored Thing.*"

We dance that one. Oscar says, "Marina," and his blue eyes gaze right into mine. "I like you very much and I don't want to let you go. May I have the next dance?" I know what that means. Usually, you dance once or twice with the same person; three dances means you are partners for the evening.

"I like you too, Oscar, so let's dance another." I also like the way he draws me close to him, so close that I can feel his warmth, and even through the crinolines, his hard thing pressing against my body. The evening is full of sensual delight. I can smell his desire, barely hidden behind his cologne, and my body opens to his. Every nerve is quivering, and down below I'm buzzing with sensation. I don't want to run away. I want this dance to go on and on.

"Marina, I'm very attracted to you," he says, his voice husky with emotion. "I never expected to find someone like you here. May I see you again? Tomorrow?"

A swift image darts through my mind of us strolling in the plaza the same way that other couples do. "I want to see you."

"What's your number?"

I give him my aunt's number and he repeats it. "I'll call you first thing."

We dance until the music ends. I'm dizzy from the intoxicating evening and wanting him to keep on holding me as tightly as he can. Heat is burning a pathway through my body, and I'm so wet my panties are soaked. My crinolines will protect my dress from staining.

It is very late when we get back to my cousin's home. This is the best evening I've spent. I'd easily sing, "I could have danced all night," but that would wake up the household.

My aunt turns to me, her face hard and her voice stern. "Marina, tonight you made a spectacle of yourself. Do you want everyone to think you're an easy girl?"

"What ... d-did ... I ... d-do?"

"You don't even know that boy, the one you were dancing with. You met him this evening, and yet you allowed him to take liberties with you, ones that no decent girl should permit."

"Liberties?"

"Yes, the way you two were dancing so close it was scandalous. Hasn't your mother told you how to behave with young men? Only couples who are formally *novios*, or engaged, dance cheek-to-cheek, and even they keep a little distance between their bodies."

"I didn't know," I say. How would I?

"It's a matter of decency, something you should know without being told. You do not press your body against a young man's, especially not one you just met, unless you're trying to tempt him to do indecent acts with you. You had better go to confession tomorrow."

I hang my head and nod. It seems like sinning is second nature to me.

I lie in bed unable to sleep, going over what my aunt said, and all the details of our dances. The way his hard thing was sticking against me, and how I reacted to it. I didn't run away in repulsion. I have a sudden vision of Miguel and his thing, the one he tried to stick into me years ago. Surely Oscar's is not as ugly or as scary, but I don't want to know.

Why do I get aroused so easily? To be panting over some young man I barely know. My aunt is right. He must think I'm a loose woman, the kind who gets aroused whenever a man touches her. Why did I behave that way? Pushing my body against him.

The next morning when he calls, I tell my cousin to say that I'm not there.

"But why? I thought you liked him." I can see she's puzzled and a little annoyed. "Oscar is a nice, decent boy, and lots of girls want to go out with him."

"Who cares? I don't want to see him again."

I pull a pillow over my face to block out her remonstrations, but not before I hear, "He really likes you."

I'm having the same reaction I always have. The difference is I liked him. But the way I behaved with Oscar on the dance floor was dirty. If my aunt hadn't said anything to me, would I have realized? Whenever I feel sexual pleasure I also feel dirty. Even thinking about it. By now I should know that feeling pleasure in my body is wrong.

I'll never let a boy get close to me again.

The Wrong Prince Charming

Mexico City
1958

On a rainy Sunday afternoon, I'm sitting in my cubicle in the reservations office of Aeronaves de México*, waiting for the phone to ring. The usually bustling room is so silent and empty that I jump when the janitor comes in.

I applied for this job after I finished high school and saw an ad in the paper. I expected it to be exciting, international, and I'd meet interesting people. The truth is that all I do is take phone calls from customers and help book their flights.

The job has its upside. I finger the silky wool of my new suit from the Palacio de Hierro store and my Italian shoes with their pointed toes and high heels. My umbrella is imported from England. It's good to earn my own money, buy what I like, and be able to help out Mami as well.

For the umpteenth time I glance around the room and sigh, missing the buzz of many voices, the cheerful camaraderie, and even the phone's constant ring. I like my co-workers, and I've found a friend in Romina, my boss.

She makes all the difference between a boring and a challenging job. Only twenty-four, she's so competent that she holds a supervisory position. With her short, curly hair, vivacious face and attitude, she's pretty and smart—in both senses of the word, as she dresses elegantly—and she's an interesting person to talk with.

Since I started working here, she's made it a habit to drop by my cubicle. At first, to help me learn the reservations process, but now that I've caught on, it's more like a quick chat between phone calls. We go out to lunch often, which I take as a big compliment coming from her, my boss, since I'm only eighteen, and this is my first job.

The first occasion when we went out she said, "We'll have a good talk," and talk she did, all the way to the restaurant and through the first course. How she aspired to have a career rather than get married like other women her age, and about her family of writers and politicians, and how her brother, a pilot with Mexicana de Aviación*, was also a film actor.

"Now that I've told you about me," she said, "why don't you tell me about yourself? What do you enjoy doing?"

I told her we came to Mexico City after my father died and that my greatest delight was reading, and I didn't have a boyfriend.

"I suspected you liked to read," she said. "Everyone in my family is a bookworm, and I've found that I prefer people who also like books. I don't have a boyfriend either because I don't want to be distracted from my plans to get ahead. What about you?"

I shifted in my seat, uncomfortable with her question. It was a perfectly normal one coming from another young woman, but what could I answer? I was afraid to be near men? How my reaction to them was so intense, it bordered on embarrassing. "I haven't found anyone who interests me enough."

"I know what you mean," she said. "Young men can be so full of themselves. Most have nothing up here." She touched the side of her forehead. "You should meet my brother. He's different."

On this slow Sunday I wish Romina was here. No one to talk to, and it's boring, boring, boring. The two other people in reservations finish their shift and leave, and their replacements haven't arrived. The weekend supervisor never came back from lunch. I'm not supposed to read while working, but who's around to catch me?

I'm reading a Corín Tellado* novel when the phone rings. At last. I pick up.

"I called to check on you," Romina says in her serious boss's voice.

"Almost no calls today," I say.

"Has the afternoon shift arrived?"

I see someone entering the room. "One person."

"Then I want you to take a break," she says.

"Er ... yes."

"And join me and my mother and brother for coffee at Sanborns."

It's a surprise, but a good one. Get me out of here and meet her brother. When she told me he had the leading role in the film *Un Mundo Maravilloso,* * I went to see it. There he was, a gorgeous man in a bathing suit, scuba diving in Cozumel. After all I'd heard about him I felt like I knew him personally.

Now is my chance to meet him. Even if the rain is coming down in torrents and I have to wade through floods, I'm on my way. I stop off in the restroom to check out my appearance. What good angel stood at my side this morning and helped me decide to put on my green silk blouse, a color that suits me?

Outside, I duck under my umbrella and walk as fast as I can, given the limitations of my tight skirt and high heels, skipping around puddles to try not to ruin my new shoes with points, as fragile as they are wicked. The wind blows rain my way, and a car goes by and splashes water, but I duck back. I'm going to meet this handsome man, the pilot and actor. Will he like me?

I reach Sanborns* in La Casa de los Azulejos*, the House of Blue Tiles, a colonial building, and enter the grand dining room with its high glass ceiling at the center. I search the crowd and spy Romina waving at me. She's over at the side next to the wall with a mural of a garden with peacocks in it.

Her mother is an older, white-haired version of Romina. As we shake hands, I sense that behind her smile, she's sizing me up, from my wet shoes and stockings to my silk blouse. Romina's brother, Carlos, is everything I expected—tall, hazel eyes, and dashing appearance. His voice is deep and reassuring, as I'd expect of a pilot or an actor. He's dressed casually, white shirt open at the collar and jacket draped over the back of his chair.

What will I order? "Coffee," I say because they are all drinking it.

Carlos says, "Are you sure?" and lifts his cup of Sanborns' signature coffee.

"An *Americano*," I say, meaning the toned-down brew.

Romina's mother asks about my parents, and I tell her about my father, what he did, and how he died. Her expression is sympathetic when she hears about my mother being left a widow with five children and having to support us.

"She sounds like an admirable woman," Romina's mother says. "Strangely enough, my story is similar. I was also left a widow, but with ten children. Unfortunately, my husband lost all his money on bad investments, so I had to go work as a teacher. Then I became a book reviewer and a writer for *Jueves de Excelsior.**"

I know this is a political magazine, which means she must write about her opinions. The fact she's also a working woman makes me like her even more. I ask about her work, and she tells me which books she'd recommend and which to avoid.

Carlos has been listening and sipping his coffee; he finishes one and orders another. He doesn't seem as outgoing as his sister and mother, more like serious to the point of withdrawn. Or else I don't appeal to him.

"Now Carlos," Romina says, "why don't you tell Marina about yourself?"

He lifts his hands, palms up, in a "why bother" gesture. "What's to tell?" he asks. "I assume my little sister has told you all about me. I'm her pride and joy, of course." He gives her a loving glance. "And her reason for despair."

"That's not true," Romina says, in a teasing voice.

"Aha, but you talk about me to everyone." He turns to me. "She told you I'm a pilot?"

"Yes. And a film actor. I saw you in *Un Mundo Maravilloso*." I hadn't meant to say that, or sound like a star-struck teen. Hundreds of people must have told him that same thing.

"Oh yes, the film," he says, as if it were of little importance. "I only got that part due to a very sad circumstance." He glances at Romina. "Did you tell her why?"

She shakes her head.

"What happened," he says with resignation, "I was accompanying a friend, who had the leading role, to the filming in Cozumel, but more because it was an opportunity to go scuba diving. One morning, he got up and had a fatal heart attack. Right there in the middle of filming. The producers were desperate. They had to find an actor to replace him who could do underwater scenes. Someone told them I was a scuba diver, and they persuaded me to take a screen test. They must have liked what they saw because they asked me to take my friend's role. That's all."

"Didn't you want to follow a career as a movie actor?" I ask.

"That was never my intention," he says. "It was one of those jobs that fell into my lap. My producer started making plans for a future in the movies. I said no, I preferred being a pilot."

He sits back, explanation given, and case closed. A brief, impersonal account of how he got the role. Everyone must ask him the same thing, and he's probably fed up telling this story. I'd better be quiet and not ask him more. The three of them converse fast, making witty statements about subjects I know little or nothing about, such as politics and politicians on the rise. Their mother leads the conversation with Romina making eager contributions to it. Carlos breaks in every now and then, making a point of what they are saying or expressing an opinion that has his mother alternately nodding and glaring. I'm not as conversant in current affairs and politics, so all I can do is listen.

Romina keeps glancing at both Carlos and me as if to assess how we are getting along. Later, she tells me that since I first came to work in her department, she decided I might be a good prospect for her bachelor brother.

"Why me?" I ask.

"Because you're smart, pretty, and from a good family, and you both read. A man of thirty like him should have a girlfriend and be thinking about settling down." Neither Romina nor I have a clue that a pilot has a similar appeal to women as a film star.

"Boss, I have to get back to work," I say. Romina's mother gives me a kiss and hopes she'll see me again. Carlos offers to accompany me to my office and grasps my arm with a confident manner. As we walk out together, a warm glow runs through me. I'm safe and comfortable with this man at my side.

A few days later he calls to ask me out. I can't believe a handsome, mature man like him would be interested in me.

We go to dinner at a French restaurant, and I try *escargots*—snails in garlic and parsley sauce, accompanied by a Chateau something-or-other that Carlos orders after studying the extensive wine list. "In France, I toured both the Burgundy and Bordeaux wine-growing areas," he says.

"Do you get to Paris often?" It isn't one of Mexicana's routes, but a pilot can travel on other airlines. He says yes, and I quiz him about what he's seen and done there.

We share a love for books, though when he asks what I read, heat rises in my face at the thought of romance novels. "Almost everything," I say, "especially psychology."

He lifts an eyebrow and mentions a mild, but superficial, interest in Freud. I know I'm safe. His interests lie more in other areas, such as sports and places of interest.

"Being a pilot must be exciting."

"Flying is mainly routine. The occasional weather storm. A man who had a heart attack. A few difficult landings."

"Romina told me to ask about when you crash-landed."

He lets out a huge sigh as if he'd rather not. "Oh, that little sister of mine—she talks too much. Once, years ago, before I took up commercial flying, I was alone in a small plane on a solo flight from the border to Mexico City. I had to make an emergency landing in the Sonoran Desert."

"Were you hurt?"

"No, except for cuts and bruises, but the plane was badly damaged. I didn't know whether to stay there in the boiling heat miles from anywhere or go for help."

"What a choice."

He nods. "I remained with the plane. It gave me some shelter and was more visible to rescue planes. I had no food, so I caught lizards to eat."

"Live lizards?"

He smiles. "I killed them first. You do what you can to survive."

I can't help gazing at him the same way as a besotted film fan. He's twelve years older, and he's lived and seen so much. How can he find me interesting?

All evening I think about what may happen when he takes me home. Will he kiss me? A man like him will expect me to respond, but I don't know if I can. As we draw up outside my building, I shiver at the thought of what's coming. He smiles at me and says, "I enjoyed talking to you." He gets out, opens my door, helps me out, and shakes my hand. "Thank you for a wonderful evening. I hope there will be another soon."

I ask myself why he's going out with me. I can't say anything to Romina—she's delighted we hit it off—or to my mother, who disapproves of him because he's much older. Our next date, he holds my hand when we enter and leave the restaurant and gives me a goodnight kiss on the cheek. Progress? A month goes by and he hasn't even tried to kiss me. Perhaps he doesn't find me attractive that way.

Then he takes me to dinner at El Mirador restaurant, which has a panoramic view of the city. Afterwards, we go outside and gaze at the stars and the full moon. He puts his arms around me and kisses me.

My body tightens as his lips press mine, and his tongue moves in my mouth. My first kiss as a woman, and I don't know how to respond. All those years of refusals and guilt led to this.

"Relax," he says, breaking away. "You can breathe now."

I was holding my breath as if I were underwater. "I don't do this often," I say.

"It doesn't matter," he says. "I don't want a girl who goes around kissing everyone. And your innocence makes you all the more desirable."

I get better, though our kisses are never the flaming, breathless ones that leave Corin Tellado's heroines dizzy and reeling.

For three months we go out a couple of times a week when he isn't away on a flight. Everything about Carlos is perfect except for one thing—he's unreliable. I imagine it's because he's a pilot and flying here, there, and everywhere. But he says he'll call and doesn't. Or promises to pick me up and stands me up instead. I may be angry or offended, but it doesn't appear to affect him, not even when he leaves me all dressed up in a new outfit I bought especially for this occasion. He always has an excuse, usually work-related. At first, I believe him, but it becomes so frequent that I finally ask what's going on.

"It was a last-minute call. I had to fill in for another pilot."

"Why didn't you phone to cancel?"

"I didn't know earlier," he says, in an annoyed tone. "It was an emergency. They needed someone right away. I didn't have time to phone you."

Every time he gives me that same excuse.

"Why does he have to cover for other pilots so often?" I ask Romina.

"A pilot's life is like a doctor's," she says. "Carlos never knows what's coming. You'd better get used to it."

Perhaps I'm too innocent or I expect too much. I'll do as she says. Anyway, my nineteenth birthday is coming up, and I'm sure to see him on that day. We haven't made any plans, but we'll do something special. After all, he is my boyfriend.

Instead, I receive a letter.

I scan the lines and howl like a madwoman, "No, no, no!" He can't have written this. It's not true. I can't believe it, refuse to believe it. My howls turn into whimpers. A haze of tears clouds my vision, and the words swim before my eyes. I have to read the letter again, make sure there's no mistake as to his intention.

Dear Marina, You are wonderful, and virtuous. Your behavior is impeccable. I find you highly intelligent, well-read, and a good companion, but for these reasons especially, as well as others, I hesitate to continue our relationship. My biggest concern is you might believe it will lead to marriage, which I do not think would be right for either of us.

I thought we were a couple and he cared for me. His casual cruelty hurts most, knowing this letter would reach me today, on my birthday. Couldn't he have waited or told me himself?

Maybe it's my fault because I can't respond passionately to his kisses.

Trembling like a sick person, I stumble to my room, close my door, and weep until my eyes ache and sting, and still tears keep falling. The very thought of Carlos and my lost illusions brings on a new flow, tears as heavy as the rain on that Sunday afternoon when I met him.

I found my Prince Charming, but he doesn't love me. No happy ending for us.

Infatuation with a Woman

MAZATLÁN AND MEXICO CITY
1959

The flight attendant asks if I want something to drink, and I shake my head. Leave me alone. That's why I chose a seat at the back of the plane.

For four days I've been beating myself up mentally for being so naïve, certain that I'd found the kind of fairy tale romance that I read about in novels. I should have listened to Mami's warnings about Carlos being too old and worldly for an eighteen-year-old like me.

She has the same response to his good-bye note. "I'm glad it's over with him. He's just a jaded, philandering airline pilot."

"Why did he want to go out with me?"

"Probably to please his sister and his mother. It helped that you're young and pretty and intelligent."

The very thought brings on more tears. Crying has become an affliction. When I'm alone, I give in easily, eager to find release. But not here on the plane. A few dribble down my cheeks, and I wipe them off with my hand. I must keep my composure in public.

"Do you want something to drink?" I shake my head and pull out a book on psychology. I'll never read another Corin Tellado novel. Everything in those books is lies.

Yet again the flight attendant asks if I want anything, and when I say, "No thanks," instead of leaving, she sits on the aisle seat next to me.

"My name is Laura," she says. "What's yours?"

"Marina," I mumble.

"Marina, may I ask why you're going to Mazatlán?"

I'm on the verge of giving her a curt answer, but she has a kind face. "To see my grandmother, who's sick in the hospital." Nona had moved back to her hometown.

"I'm sorry to hear that. You must care for her very much."

"I do." Tears gush out again. "It's so sudden. I never thought…"

"It's always a shock," she says, "to lose someone you love."

The words explode from my mouth. "My boyfriend dumped me—on my nineteenth birthday."

"Oh, I see." She seems thoughtful as if considering what to say. She offers me a smile full of warmth. "If you want to talk about it, I have a few minutes." She leans toward me. "Some things are easier to talk about with a stranger than with your own mother."

Perhaps because she *is* a stranger and seems interested, I open up to her about Carlos. "My mother is tired of seeing me moping around, so she's sending me to my family in Mazatlán."

"The change may help you get over him."

"If I can talk to my grandmother, Nona, she'll understand, but she's in the hospital."

"What about your mother?"

"She doesn't ... didn't like my boyfriend because he's twelve years older and an airline pilot, and she said I'm too naïve for him. He told me I was too innocent and virtuous."

She raises an eyebrow. "Virtuous? If that's how he thinks, you're lucky to be rid of him. Most pilots are notorious womanizers; they think they're God's gift to women. It makes me sick to see all the girls throwing themselves at them."

She doesn't sound like one of those men-chasers. I'm sure she has both pilots and passengers asking her to go out with them. A beauty with curly black hair, and long-lashed eyes that sparkle when she smiles.

"I'm also nineteen," she says. This smart, sophisticated woman in her navy blue uniform? Compared to her, I'm a schoolgirl. She's been working since she was sixteen and became a flight attendant at eighteen. Since then she's traveled and dealt with all kinds of people.

She glances around. "I have to get back to work," she says. "We should keep in touch." She pulls out a little pad and scribbles on it. "Here's my address. Let's write to each other." I watch as she walks away. With her face and figure she could be a Miss Mexico contender.

We correspond for three months. Her letters strike me as being very affectionate, perhaps too much so for a woman I hardly know. "Dear Marina," turns into "Dearest Marina," and then "My Dearest," and "My beloved Marina." She writes how she's longing to see me again and wants to embrace me, and when we meet she hugs me like an old friend. That first meeting is sudden, unexpected, and hurried. Her plane is grounded after a tire blows out, and she has a two-hour layover, which means we have more like an hour to catch up.

I tell her about Nona, who took a turn for the worse, and how I was able to confide in her before she got worse, and about my job at Aeronaves de México. I've recovered from the loss of Carlos and found another boyfriend. I leave out that when this boyfriend kisses me I'm much more physically turned on than with Carlos, who didn't do anything to me.

Laura keeps on letting me know when she will stop in Mazatlán, and I go to the airport to see her during her layovers. I take special care to dress up for our meetings because she's so smart, as if she has fixed herself up. One afternoon I turn up dressed all in black, and she asks, "Your grandmother?"

I try to speak but choke on the words. I nod.

Laura takes my hand. "At least you got to see her and talk to her."

"I'm glad… " I find my voice, though it's breaking up. "I'm glad … I was there … to close … her eyes."

She puts a consoling arm around me. "Now that your grandmother is gone, what keeps you in this town? Why don't you come back to Mexico City? We could spend the night in Guadalajara and fly there the next day."

"Let me think about it."

What am I doing here? Carlos was wrong about me—I'm uninhibited and free. I make out with my boyfriend, let his hands explore my body, and use his fingers to make me come. He wants to go all the way, but I'm not losing my virginity in the back of a car.

That evening, when I go out with him, I ask myself if all I want is a boy-girl chat over a soda and making out in a car. Laura, with her knowledgeable talk and experience, is opening up the world for me. I'll miss his kisses but not his shallow conversation. After three months in Mazatlán, I'm ready to return to Mexico City with Laura.

She and I stay up late at night, talking without the usual limitations of time and her work. When, reluctantly, we go to sleep, we share a bed and lie, spoon-like, her arms around me. She drops off almost at once, but, despite my fatigue, her closeness keeps me awake. Feelings run through my body like electric circuits and clash into each other. Too many conflicting thoughts crowd my mind. Is what we have a good friendship or something else?

The next day she hands me a note with the name of a book, *The Well of Loneliness*, on it and tells me to try and read it.

My mother is waiting for me at the airport, and I introduce Laura to her. My mother says, "How do you do?" in a tone that communicates to me she doesn't think much of my friend.

Laura turns, gives me a quick kiss on the cheek, and says, "Pick you up tomorrow at two."

As we drive away, I tell my mother, "I'm going to have lunch with her family."

"Where do they live?" The all-important question that establishes social status, income, and whether or not Laura is the right friend for me.

"Near the airport, I think," I say airily. "Laura's coming by for me."

I've never been to the neighborhood where her parents live, and if not for her, I'd get lost in the maze of back streets without name signs. It's a mixture of cheap, new, brightly colored houses and crumbling old places. Most houses don't have numbers, and the ones that do are not in any visible order, with 1000 next to 27. We get to her home, one of the newer buildings, and a group of kids runs out to greet us—Laura's younger brother and two sisters. Her parents have an apartment on the third floor. It's a walk-up, as the elevator, she tells me, is permanently out of order. At the table, everyone talks at the same time, interrupting each other constantly, asking me what music I like, where I live, which movie stars I like, and why, why, why?

Laura's mother has outdone herself with a four-course meal of chicken consommé, pasta in tomato and cheese sauce, stuffed chilies, salad, and crème caramel. In my honor.

After lunch Laura announces that we're going to visit her boyfriend, Rolando. I can't understand why she's never mentioned him to me. "Is he new?" I ask as we get into her car.

"You'll see when we get there," she says.

I've never visited a man in his apartment; my mother would have a fit if she knew. But as soon as I meet Rolando, I understand. He's wearing one of those frilly, pale blue shirts fashionable among a certain type of men, and very tight jeans. His shrug and his hand gestures are a dead giveaway, even to me.

"Rolando is my best friend," Laura says. "He knows everything about me."

She guides me into a room that has a big TV and stereo in it, and a sofa, which we sit on. She kisses me. Her lips are soft and full of sweetness. Her kiss touches my emotions and plays on me like a soft piano sonata.

"I'm in love with you," she tells me.

I stare at her, not knowing what to say or do. A woman has kissed me, and she's telling me she loves me in the same way as a man. Yet I'm not surprised. Subconsciously, I sensed and encouraged it.

"Will you see me again?" she asks, and her meaning is clear.

"Yes." I want to see her and find out if this could be more than a friendship. I don't know what our connection is, but it has an emotional quality that draws me to her.

As soon as I open the front door, my mother pounces on me. She took advantage of my absence to search my personal belongings and discovered the letters from Laura, carelessly hidden in my bedside table drawer. She also saw the note with the *The Well of Loneliness* on it.

"I don't know what it's about," I say.

"Don't tell me you don't know it's about unnatural relations between two women." Until this afternoon I didn't know a woman can love another woman. "What are you doing going out with a lesbian?" she shouts. "Do you want to become one of those men-women like her?"

"She's my friend," I try to convince her, but it's hard to hide the truth. She can see through my feeble arguments.

"I forbid you to see that woman again," she says, "or to have any future contact with her."

I want to call Laura to warn her, but my mother catches me in the act of dialing and rips out the phone cord. Then she locks me in our room so I have no way to escape her tongue-lashing.

For two days, my mother hammers into my head that my friendship with Laura is wrong, how society and our family will turn their backs on me, and I'll become a pariah. She is joined by her friend Alicia's mother, an old witch with a cigarette-hoarsened voice, who goes on and on at me about how I should watch out for degenerates who try to force me to become like them.

What can be wrong with two women caring for each other? My mother and her friend tell me this kind of love is forbidden by God and the laws of nature.

"It's a bad thing, evil, to have those feelings for another woman," the old girl says. "They come straight from Satan." But mine for Laura are pure. Why should I pay for having them?

Between the two, they tell me over and over, "Something is wrong with you," and though I never admit to the forbidden kiss, I accept they are right and my friendship with Laura is wrong. Numb and unable to stand up for myself against them, my mind is empty. I'm like an American soldier brainwashed in Korea.

When Laura comes by for me the next day, my mother is waiting for her along with the old witch who pretends to be my grandmother. Laura seems taken aback, with a question in her eyes when I don't come forward to greet her. Despite this, she lets them take her inside and to the bedroom. I trail behind like a scolded child. "Marina, what is going on?" she asks.

My mother answers for me. "You'll see," she says.

They tell Laura to sit on the bed, and the old witch makes herself comfortable in the armchair. My mother takes out the bunch of Laura's letters to me and waves them in her face. "You perverted degenerate, trying to seduce my daughter."

Laura's head snaps back, and she flinches as if my mother had hit her. The old witch is even fiercer with her insults, accusing her of vile acts I'd never heard of.

"I haven't done anything wrong with your daughter," Laura keeps insisting, and still, like inquisitors forcing a confession, they won't let up on her, not even when she bursts into tears and swears by the Holy Virgin of Guadalupe that she's innocent.

I watch from behind, helpless to do anything, or defend Laura against my mother's rage and the old witch's insults. What she did to me was wrong and her intentions were wrong, and now we're both being punished. I don't care anymore; just want it to finish, to go away.

The old witch joins my mother. They form a barrier, standing over Laura imprisoned on the bed. Laura looks beyond them and speaks to me with her eyes. *I love you. Why are you betraying me?* Her proud body droops from this verbal flogging. She lowers her head, and when she says, "*Si, Señora,*" she sounds like a reprimanded schoolgirl.

Once they are satisfied they have crushed any desire in her to see me again, my mother escorts her out of the house. The old witch blocks my access to her with her body and her anger. Two hundred years ago she would have led the charge against Laura.

She fastens her gimlet eyes on me and speaks with the grating, tar-covered smoker voice that drills holes in my mind.

"It is better to be a whore than to be a lesbian," she says.

*

The old witch's words shock me. Its interpretation is almost too cruel to consider. A whore sleeps with many men for money, while a lesbian, as far as I can tell, has a relationship, and doesn't charge. Yet being a lesbian is considered the lowest form of sexuality, while the whore is mainly accepted as a necessary sexual outlet for men.

Perhaps Laura's understanding at a vulnerable moment is what drew me to her. Not because she's a lesbian. If my mother is right, it is a perversion to love another woman that way. Yet when I sensed Laura's interest, it didn't deter me. Rather, it spurred me on. I let her kiss me. I chose to be with her instead of my boyfriend. Does that make me a lesbian?

My mother keeps telling me that both the Church and society consider being physically attracted to a member of your own sex a mortal sin. "If you continue on this path, you will become a social pariah in this life and condemned to Hell in the next," she says. She goes on and on, doesn't stop even when I tell her that, yes, I got the message. Basically, I'm scared at what might be the consequences of such a dangerous friendship.

"I have to drive it into you so that you will never forget," she says. She's scared also, I can see, that I may go down a path that will lead to my, and possibly her, condemnation by the very society that she values so highly.

Catholic Guilt

Mexico
1959

"Wake up."

A soft voice, and a light hand nudges my shoulder. I half-open my eyes. The room is dark except for a silver-gray light that enters through the narrow window.

"It's five-thirty, and Mass is at six a.m.," the nun says.

"No, thank you." I turn over and go back to sleep to dream that Laura is lying next to me, yet I'm rigid, unable to reach out my hand to touch her, or caress her luscious black hair, or talk to her and explore the secrets of her mind.

Much later, wakefulness—and bells ringing—drags me out of sleep and into the day. I don't get up. I'm being punished for my affection for a woman when, in fact, my only sin was the kiss Laura gave me. Would I let her kiss me again? Probably, and that sin I haven't committed makes me a sinner. I can't take Communion in this state, not when I'm having impure desires.

No one disturbs me, though occasionally a nun pokes in her head. I have my own starkly furnished room, one of several guest rooms with bathrooms for people who come on retreat; it contains five pieces of battered furniture—the bed, a nightstand, a chair, a table, and a wardrobe. The only decoration is a picture of the Sacred Heart.

My world has gone dark. That verbal flogging of Laura crushed any spirit in me and left me empty of hope. At home, I lay on my bed and studied the white plaster ceiling for hours. I refused the food that my mother or the maid brought me. After three days my mother forced me to drink a cup of chicken broth. It took two hours to get it down, with my mother standing over me and pushing the cup at me, treating me like a willful child.

"Something is wrong with you," she told me. "If you spend some time in a convent, you will understand why I can't allow you to follow your unnatural inclinations."

The second night in the convent I have the same tortuous dream about Laura. The third night, I fall into a deep slumber. In the morning I get up and go to early Mass and then join the nuns in a breakfast of coffee with frothy milk on top and wheat-flour *pan dulce*, sweet rolls puffy with sugar and cinnamon. The nun seated next to me says, "We bake our own bread. Would you like to learn how?" She's young—late twenties—and she has a pretty face and a sweet smile.

"Oh yes, my favorite food is bread."

"Here in the convent, you can eat all you want," she says, "except on fast days," and she passes me the bread basket.

All my mother told me was to pack light clothes because I was going to a convent in Cuernavaca, "the city of eternal spring," where it's usually hot. As I walk around, I notice how this large, colonial house has thick walls that keep it cool indoors during the day. A tall, heavy door guards the entrance and the exit. The walls are ablaze with crimson and scarlet bougainvillea, and the garden has orange and avocado and fern trees. Terra-cotta pots filled with multicolored flowers adorn the hallways.

The serene atmosphere fills my spirit with tranquility. God is forgiving, but I must still make amends for my impure thoughts. I pray for hours, on my knees until calluses form, to the Virgin, to Jesus, to the saints, and to God, to help me find a way out of this confusion. Little by little, I sense a response building up. I came here in a state of confusion and found peace within these walls. This is a way of telling me that I have a vocation, and I'm being called to service as a bride of Christ.

Every day now I get up at five, take a cold shower, and go to Mass and Holy Communion. I am pure and whole again. Then I work in the convent bakery, where I learn how to prepare the buns and sugary breads for both our own consumption and to sell to restaurants. Every weekend we also send a batch to an orphanage.

I play softball with the nuns. Since I'm good at sports, they make me leader of a team, and my team wins more often than the other. When we play, I find the only difference between these and other women is that nuns live in a convent. They seem so friendly and carefree, with none of the problems facing women in the outside world. Even the older nuns appear to be content to have dedicated their lives to God.

I make friends with Sister Rosenda, the young nun who introduced me to the bakery. She wears a black habit, so all I can see is her face under her veil. We fall into a pattern whereby we seek each other out for a little talk, or a walk in the garden, and when we're baking bread.

"In the months you've been with us," she tells me, "I've seen a big change in you."

"I'm happy here," I say. "This is a tranquil, undemanding life."

"Have you thought about... " She covers her mouth with her hand as if unable to go on.

"Entering the convent?" I ask, and she nods. "Yes. I think so."

"You think you're hearing the call? Like a voice in your head?"

"So that's what it is." What I thought of as a response. "Yes, I believe I've heard it. And yes, I want to become a bride of Christ like you."

When my mother comes to pick me up, I tell her that I want to enter the convent and become a nun.

"A nun? Are you crazy?" Her voice is clogged with horror. "You have no idea what you want. I'm taking you out of here."

"Mami, I'm not changing my mind." Or letting her do it for me. Not now that I've discovered my true vocation. "I already spoke to Mother Superior, and she gave me a list of things I need to buy to come here."

"I can't believe it. I won't allow it!" Her voice rises. "They've brainwashed you."

I keep my voice steady. "I heard the call."

"What call?" Her tone is edged with suspicion. "Is this your way of getting back at me?"

"It's what I want to do." This is almost the worst thing I can tell her—that I want something she doesn't want for me.

Her face twists as if I'd struck her. "I think I should have a word with Mother Superior," she says.

As soon as Mother Superior comes in, my mother says, "I asked you to take care of my daughter, not to take her away from me."

"Whatever she decides must be of her own free will," Mother Superior tells her.

My mother starts crying and arguing with me about this decision.

"Calm yourself," Mother Superior tells her. "We won't take your daughter until she's had time to consider her decision to become a nun." She turns to me. "Go home with your mother. In a few months, if you still have a vocation, we will welcome you back."

My mother has won again, but only for a while. As soon as I can, I'll return for good.

*

I keep going to Mass and Communion every day. I don't wear makeup, and I dress as plainly as I can in long, dark skirts and simple white blouses. Nothing will change my mind. God has called me, and I will follow Him.

My mother calls the son of an old friend and asks him to take me out. I imagine she's told him I want to become a nun and need to be dissuaded.

Tito is twenty-one, charming and friendly, and he makes a big effort to give me a good time. I know my mother asked him to try to make me forget what everyone calls a crazy notion.

"Come on, Marina," he says, "have some fun. There are many great things to do and see." He takes me to the movies and afterwards for a meal at Sanborns on Reforma, where young people meet in the evening. He invites me to the theater to see a musical starring actress Silvia Pinal, and then to the elegant Normandie for dinner. We're both bookworms, though he's more into mystery and adventure novels. But rather than sway my decision to become a nun, my dates with him only affirm it more.

No amount of pressure or type of persuasion works on me.

After four months my mother reluctantly and, as she puts it, "with grave misgivings," gives in, and she takes me shopping for the clothes I will need in the convent. When the salesgirl brings out the underwear, I stare at it in horror. I never expected nuns to wear different underwear—rough, woolly vests and pink, thigh-length bloomers. How can I stand them—how can the nuns?—in semitropical Cuernavaca, where the temperature often reaches a hundred degrees?

"I'm not wearing those things!" I shout.

So their undergarments must be what Sister Rosenda once mentioned as, "The cross we all wear."

*

For the first time in months, I study myself in the mirror. I see my face, shiny and devoid of makeup, and the frumpy clothes I wear. Who is that person? A bit of lipstick wouldn't hurt, and some base to cover spots on my skin, and since I'm at it, how about some eyeliner? That's more like the "me" I remember. But I should change my blouse.

*

I call Mexicana Airlines to check on Laura's schedule. When she arrives, I'm waiting for her at the bottom of the electric stairs. She flinches when she sees me and glances around as if seeking escape, but I block her way. "Laura, please, hear me out. I want to explain."

Her eyes narrow in disbelief. "You don't owe me an explanation. That was months ago. Forget it." She tries to get by me, and I grab her sleeve.

"Please, let's have coffee upstairs."

"Promise me this isn't another setup." She glances over her shoulder as if expecting my mother to be waiting to confront her again.

I tell her everything. How my mother and the old witch gave me such a hard time that by the time she arrived, I was so brain-dead that I did nothing to stop them from attacking her. Then my mother sent me to the convent, and I decided to become a nun. "It didn't work out, but I'm more secure and calmer than before."

"Think you had a hard time? You have no idea of how much pain I was in after that day. Your mother and your grandmother humiliated me and made me feel sick and dirty, an aberration, as they called me."

"I'm sorry," I mumble.

"You should be. I cared deeply for you, and you betrayed me."

"That's not true. It was their doing."

"You were silent, never said a word in my defense. That's betrayal. I stopped eating, lost weight, couldn't work. I went into a depression." Her misery shows in the dark shadows under her eyes, her gaunt face, and hollowed cheeks.

"The last thing I wanted was to hurt you."

"You didn't just hurt me, you turned your back on me with your silence."

48

"Please forgive me, Laura. I wanted to warn you, but my mother wouldn't let me use the phone or leave the house. She and that old witch controlled my every move."

She offers me a small smile. "After seeing them in action I can understand. Anyway, I'm fine now. I have a girlfriend who's also a flight attendant."

"Can we be friends again?"

"We never stopped," she says. "You were an innocent caught in the grasp of two controlling women. They want you under their thumb and make you do what they say."

"Yes," I say slowly, "but I don't know how to get away from my mother."

She seems pensive. "It seems like the convent helped you escape from her, and you also found a group of women that you enjoyed being with. Let's see." She drums her fingers on the tabletop. "What if I introduce you to a few of my friends? They may help you understand yourself and what you're going through."

"Other women?"

"Yes, women like me. You need to find out what you really want in life."

BARRIER ELEVEN
Loving a Woman

At first glance the group of women appears the same as any other women's gathering. Then I see a couple holding hands, and two others with short haircuts and masculine clothing who resemble men. For someone in the early 60's, with limited worldly experience, it's fascinating to enter this socially unacceptable lesbian world.

As Laura explained to me, most homosexuals and lesbians stay in the closet and pretend to lead normal lives. Some are married women who are attracted to other women as well as to men. I find out this attraction to both genders is not as unusual as it sounds, which makes me wonder about my own inclinations. Women meet in homes where there is no husband or family to deal with, at reunions that to all outside appearances are just normal get-togethers.

I seat myself at the edge of the group surrounding an attractive young woman and listen to her funny, quick-witted comments about a recent political scandal. I see how everyone is vying for her attention and trying to get closer to her. I also want to share her aura, or her shadow.

Manón takes a cigarette and lights it, and her sensual lips caress the cigarette that she holds between two fingers. She leans back as if surveying the room, and her honey-colored eyes meet mine with such intensity that I'm compelled to look back at her. "*Muchachita*, is this your first party with women?" she asks me.

"Yes," I say, blushing. "Laura brought me so that I can meet new friends." The other women turn and stare at me, the newcomer who is receiving Manón's attention.

"Come, sit here and tell me about yourself," she says and pats the place next to her. "We'll resume our conversation in a while," she tells her friends. "I want to get to know this young lady." Most of them move away and form a group of their own; a couple dawdle as if hoping she will include them. Then seeing it won't happen, they go to join the others.

"I'm Manón," she says. "I'm a *Cubana*. Now, what about you?"

It's easy to open up to her, talk about my problems with my mother, and how at twenty, I've never had a real sexual experience and seldom dated men—except for Carlos.

"Men can be so cruel," she says. "That's one reason why I prefer women. We understand each other." She tells me she's twenty-seven, and when Castro took over in 1959, she fled Cuba and came to Mexico. Her family remained in Cuba.

Her face becomes serious; her expression sad. "After the Communist government decreed that no one could own property, they confiscated the family home and land and forced my parents to work for almost nothing. They got out of Cuba and went to Florida, but they still hope to return someday. As do I when Castro is overthrown. Cuba used to be a country of happiness and music, but now the people have no reason to celebrate. That's why I love Mexico City; it's so alive."

"Is it like Cuba?"

"There are many similarities, and I like this country and its culture." She flicks back her hair, and it gleams like deep burnished copper. I long to touch it, run my fingers through it, fold it in my hands. She's a golden woman. Her eyes sparkle, her skin glows, her hair reflects golden highlights. "New friends," she says, and laughs, a spontaneous, abandoned laughter, opening her mouth wide. "I like you, Marina. You are very young and pretty. If you want, I can teach you many things."

To be chosen by this charismatic woman is flattering and a little scary. "I want to know you better, Manón, but I don't have any experience with this kind of … friendship."

She lets out a laugh, throwing back her head so that her hair spills all around her. "I realize that, *muchachita*. You don't have to worry."

She is my first sexual experience. At first, we kiss gently. Her approach is tender, and she goes slowly with me. Soft, touching sex. My sexuality blossoms. My first thought in the morning is of her. My last thought at night is of her. I need, with an all-absorbing passion, to see her every day, and when I'm with her, we exist in our glorious cocoon.

We need a cover-up to stop my mother from finding out about us. It comes in the form of Raul, a young man from my hometown, Mazatlán, and a friend of Manón's. He's tall, attractive, masculine—and homosexual. The three of us scheme to pretend he's my boyfriend and introduce him to my mother.

"When I'm going to be with Manón, I'll tell my mother that I'm with you."

"And when my family comes to Mexico City, you'll be my girlfriend," he answers.

I introduce Raul to my mother, and she beams with approval. Not only do I have a new boyfriend, but he's also from Mazatlán.

Raul invites Manón and me to a party at his house. I've never seen men as couples. At first, I can't get over watching them being intimate with each other, or dancing closely, kissing and rubbing their bodies against their partner's. In public men wouldn't dare show this kind of affection for each other.

"Welcome to our gay world," Manón tells me. The first time I've heard the word "gay."

*

We meet at Manón's apartment, not far from my house. I keep this secret from all my friends; I don't want my mother to find out and interfere again. Also, I go to work for Manón. She heads a company that sells magazine subscriptions. Many of my mother's friends and contacts buy subscriptions from me; I become the company's star salesperson.

With Manón I step into an exhilarating world of high living. Under the guise of work, we travel together all over Mexico. I'm enjoying my work, making good money, and being with her.

One evening I get home after being with Manón, and my mother says, "Today I went to the jewelry store," where she and I have an account. "I saw you bought a ring. Why don't you show it to me?"

"I don't remember where I put it," I answer quickly, too quickly.

She peers as me. "You can't remember where your new ring is?"

"No. I'll have to search for it."

"You don't know where you put it?" Her voice is heavy with suspicion.

"I'm too tired. I'll find it tomorrow."

Each time she asks I make an excuse, and each time it's harder to find another reason why I can't show it to her. I might as well admit part of the truth to her. "Actually, I bought it as a gift for a friend on her birthday."

"What friend?"

"You don't know her." I shift my eyes from her gaze. I don't have to put up with her interrogation. "Why do you have to know? I paid for it with money I earned."

Maybe it's my defensive tone, but she has a knowing look, as if she understands this is no ordinary gift. "What ... is ... going ... on ... Marina?" she demands, in a voice that makes me cringe and want to scuttle away to a place where she can't find me.

"Nothing," I say. "It was a gift for a friend."

"An expensive gift indeed." She shakes her head. "I know when you're hiding something, Marina," and she goes at me in her own inimitable way, set on breaking down my defenses and my search for some private corner untouched by her.

It takes another day, but she won't let me be until she gets an answer.

Is it really that important to hold out on her? Yes, I want to keep Manón to myself. Our involvement is a treasure I can't share with my mother. Yet she won't give up until she finds her way to it.

Today, Saturday, I should be with Manón instead of sitting on my bed and facing yet another round of questions and recriminations. I can't take this anymore. I have to break free from her. Telling her the truth is my only way out.

I give her a cold stare. "If it's that important for you to know, I bought that ring for the woman I love."

Her face changes hue, from pale to purple-red, and she retches as if she's going to throw up. She flings herself on top of me, her hands out like grasps ready to choke me.

I grab her wrists and yell, "Leave me alone! Don't touch me!"

My cry helps make her come to her senses. Shaking, she backs off and falls into a chair. I can see she's trying to compose herself. She wipes her mouth on the back of her hand as if to show disgust. "What about your boyfriend, Raul? Or is he another lie?"

"He is my boyfriend," I say, "but he's queer."

Her hand goes to her throat to stifle a gasp. Disappointment rushes across her face. The way she must see it, the perfect partner for her daughter has turned into a sordid incident. "So, who is this woman? What have you been hiding from me?"

I sit up and speak in an even tone. "Why don't you calm down, Mami, and we can talk about it?"

As much as I explain to her how I feel about Manón she refuses to try to understand. She crosses her arms and sets her jaw against all my explanations and pleas. "You are still a minor, which means you have to do what I say until you're twenty-one. I will not allow this affair to go on—not as long as you live under my roof and aren't yet of age."

"Mami, you don't care about my feelings."

She scoffs. "Your feelings? I thought we'd already dealt with this devious inclination of yours. What does it take for you to realize that an affair with a woman isn't acceptable in our society?"

"What's wrong with loving someone of my own sex?"

She balls her hand into a fist and hits her forehead to show frustration. "I've told you, it's against the laws of nature, of God, of society." Her voice goes up; she, who's so careful to be discreet, is shouting. "Do you want to be an outcast, someone no decent person will associate with?"

My defiance comes back. She's set on ruining my life. "I don't care. I want to be with Manón."

"This is final: I will not allow my daughter to be a lesbian." She pronounces the word with distaste, wrinkling her nose as if at a bad smell.

I sink back on the bed and grab one of my pillows for comfort—or protection against her wrath. "So what do you plan to do? Send me back to the convent?"

She sits and folds her hands, moving her fingers back and forth, as she thinks about it. "No," she says, "what you need is a change. This all started after that Carlos broke up with you. You need to get away, go someplace that's different."

"Mazatlán again?"

"No, Los Angeles. I'll call your Aunt Ceci and ask if you can go to them. What's more," she sounds pleased, "I'll talk to one of your father's friends and get you a job in the tourism office there. And you can go to school, brush up on your English."

"What if I don't want to go?" I ask. "You can't force me."

"Oh yes, I can. You're still a minor. You don't have a say in the matter until you're twenty-one."

"That's only four months away. If I have to, I'll lie in bed and refuse to budge."

"I don't care if we have to carry you out of here. I'm offering you a golden opportunity, and you'd be an idiot not to take it."

No use crying, or begging, or trying to make her understand. She cares only about what other people might think and not at all about me. Once again she's separating me from a woman. But it's worse than before. Manón means everything to me.

My mother can't stop me from going to work. Monday, I burst into the office, which Manón and I share, and tell her what happened.

"Calm down," she tells me and leads me to a chair, where I sit, trembling with renewed anger at what my mother is doing to separate us. "Don't worry, *muchachita*," she says in a soothing voice, "you hold the winning card. In four months, you'll be twenty-one and you can do as you please." She strokes my head. "But for now, you have to pretend to agree with her and go along with her plans."

"But I won't be able to see you again."

"Of course you can." She strokes my head. "You'll return and come live with me."

"How can you say that? I can't bear not to see you." Not to be near her. I'm used to being at her side—and touching her—every day.

"I'll visit you there, and it will be a good experience for you to spend some time in Los Angeles." She pulls me to my feet and puts her arms around me, facing me so that we're looking into each other's eyes. "Also, if you refuse to do what your mother wants, she may come after me. As a foreigner, I can't take that risk."

Reason enough to comply with my mother's wishes. How can I be separated from Manón when I live to see her every day?

*

At 5 p.m. I leave work at the Mexican Tourism Office in Beverly Hills and walk the six blocks to Loretta Young's School for Models. I've learned about cosmetics and how to apply them, to others and to myself. Each girl experiments on the other girls and, eventually, on people who come in for a low-cost makeover. I've started to wear eye makeup—eye shadow and liner—though I don't need false eyelashes, as mine are long enough. I'm good at modeling—being a dancer helps—and with practice I might consider becoming a model. My mother would never approve, but who cares? She isn't here to stop me.

Or I can follow another path and fulfill an old dream. I've been studying psychology at a community college, and I'd like to finish and get my degree.

Forty minutes until the lesson starts. I go into the cafeteria, where three girls from my modeling class wave at me to join them at their table.

"We saw you on TV, at the Rose Bowl Parade," one says.

"My boss asked me to represent Mexico," I tell them.

"We want to hear all about it. Where did you get that gorgeous costume?"

"I rented it. It's from the state of Chiapas in the south of Mexico." My long white dress was embroidered with different color flowers. "I got the braids at Max Factor."

"That may be your lucky break."

"It has led to radio and TV interviews," I say. "Let's see what happens."

They talk about their lives, the places they go to, and their dates. If only I could be like them and live my life.

"Do you plan to go back to Mexico?"

"Yes, but not for a while." I need to be far away from my mother, or she'll try to control me again. Even here, I sense her long reach. Aunt Ceci constantly asks me whom I was with and where I went, and restricts my movements because of whatever my mother told her. My uncle drops me off at work and picks me up after class except for when I come here.

"Why don't you move in with us?" one of them asks, and the other two echo her.

I blink. Did I hear right? "Move in with you?"

"Yes, why not?" The other girls nod their agreement.

Just when I'm thinking how I want to be free like them. "Yes, but I can't for three months." When I turn twenty-one and can do whatever I like.

"No problem," she says. "We can wait."

This prospect of freedom is so exciting that all I can think of is how to pull it off—until halfway through my class. What will I do about Manón? After two months, I miss her a lot, but it's not the sharp pain of before. I have to phone her and tell her I'm not going back to Mexico.

As I'm not supposed to contact her, I can't call her from the house. I use a public phone. We can't talk for long, since I keep on having to feed coins into the phone or another person wants to use it. Somehow our conversations seem a bit sordid, like in an adulterous romance, or I'm guilty of doing something I shouldn't.

I tell her my plans and she says, "*Muchachita*, I'm coming to see you."

We have one afternoon together—all I can manage without arousing Aunt Ceci's suspicions. We see each other at a friend's home. We embrace and she gives me a long kiss full of emotion. Right there I would take off my clothes and let her make love to me, except that she pulls away and says, "We can't do anything. My friend might return at any moment."

Reluctantly, I sit on the sofa. "I suppose that means we must behave ourselves."

"We'll have time later on, *muchachita*," she says. "You've changed your makeup, and you have a new hairdo." My hair is cut to above my shoulders, defining the angles of my face and highlighting my eyes. "You seem happy and relaxed. Los Angeles is good for you."

"It's been good for me to get away from my mother," I say. "It's like she put an iron collar around my neck, and it's finally been loosened."

"Does that mean you've changed your mind about coming back to Mexico?" Her compelling eyes look straight at me and seem to see what is in my mind.

"No," I say. Then, "Well, yes, but not to my mother's house. I don't want to see her again, at least not for a while. I can't let her interfere anymore."

"Do you still want to come live with me?"

Visions of my new friends and their apartment flash through my head. I hesitate.

"It's all right, *muchachita*," she says. "I understand. You prefer to live here. Only consider if this is what you truly want or if it's because you want to get away from your mother."

I see her desire, and she embraces me. Again I am lost to her.

After a while we make plans for me to return to Mexico City in a couple of months, when I turn twenty-one. "Your mother can't know," she says.

"She'll find out soon enough."

"I'm sure she will, but once you're installed in my place, you can refuse to leave, and there's nothing she can do to force you out."

"Don't be so sure of that."

"*Muchachita*, your mother can't rule your life forever. She'll have to give in." Not my mother. When it comes to me, her manipulation has no bounds.

I plan my departure in secret, for right after my twenty-first birthday. I confide in a neighbor, and she agrees to help. After buying a new suitcase, I take my clothes in small bundles over to her house. I get my plane ticket.

The day of my departure my uncle drops me off at the office the same as he does every day. I watch until he's out of sight, walk to the corner, and use a public phone to call in sick.

A friend is waiting for me in her car, and we go to pick up my suitcase, and she takes me to the airport. It's a matter of hours before I'll be with Manón for good. My heart is churning with anticipation, and I count the hours, minutes, before I can embrace her again.

When I arrive in Mexico City I catch sight of Manón waiting for me at the passenger exit. I want to rush straight into her arms, but people are blocking my way. That's when I see my mother and my younger brother, Roberto, and my heart dives into the pit of my stomach.

Why are they here? I draw back, trying to work out what to do, combing my mind for excuses, explanations. But why? I'm of age and she can't stop me from doing what I want.

I didn't come back to be with my mother. I walk right past them, pretending not to see them or hear my brother calling out my name, go up to Manón, and tell her, "We have to move fast. My mother's here."

"Did you tell her you were coming?"

"No. I don't know how she found out."

Too late. My mother, taking strides that would make an Olympian proud, joins us, or rather me, as she ignores Manón. Her face oozes fury. "Marina, you're coming home with me."

"No, I'm not, Mami. I'm going with Manón." I try to make my voice strong and decisive, to show her I'm now my own person and she cannot order me around.

Her arms flail the air as she yells, "No, you're coming with me."

Behind her, my brother raises his hands to indicate it's futile to argue with her.

I persist. "Sorry, Mami, but now that I'm twenty-one, I can do whatever I want."

"No, you can't." Her voice is so loud that people turn to look at us. "You're my daughter and you will do what I say, no matter how old you are."

Again, I refuse, but a nervous tic starts over my eye.

"I won't let you throw away your life." My mother's voice trembles as if on the edge of hysteria. "You can't go with 'this kind' of woman." She does not glance at Manón. She's playing a role that she knows very well, the upset mother trying to control her wayward daughter.

People are staring at us and a few stop to watch. I should try and soothe my mother, but the only way is to give in to her, and that's not going to happen.

"How can you prefer to be with this woman?" she asks, and gestures at Manón. Her tone changes to wheedling, but it's the one I can't stand. "Please, come home and we can talk it over."

Manón glances at the people watching us. With a sigh she puts her hand on my arm. "Marina, better go with your mother. See you tomorrow."

I gaze at her in disbelief. She nods, gives my mother a cold stare, and with a good-bye hand gesture, turns and walks away. I can't believe it. Strong Manón, my bulwark against interference, has given in to my mother's manipulating. Or so it seems.

My brother jerks his finger to indicate we should get going.

"If I go with you," I tell my mother, "it's only because Manón told me to."

"You had no right doing this to me," she says.

"It's you who have no right *doing this to me*," I answer, but if I don't go with her, she's capable of taking it out on Manón. "Okay, I'll go with you for now."

Once we are in the car, I ask, "How did you know I was coming?"

"Your Aunt Ceci told me," she says.

"How did she find out?"

"Coincidence." She recounts the string of events that led to my being caught *in fragrante* in the Mexico City airport. My former boss, Romina, now a manager at Western Airlines, saw my name on the passenger list. She called my mother to say that since I was coming back to Mexico, she'd like to see me. My mother told her I was living in Los Angeles and wouldn't be back for a while. Romina said she must have made a mistake, but her innocent request was enough to tip off my mother. She phoned Aunt Ceci, who told her I'd gone to work this morning, but she checked and was informed I'd called in sick.

The way my mother sees it, my behavior is unforgivable. I embarrassed poor Aunt Ceci, jeopardized my chances, probably lost my job—the one she wangled for me—and all because I want to see "that woman."

I hear her out in silence. I still can't believe she's overturned all of my plans to be with Manón. A little over an hour ago I was counting the minutes until I embraced her again.

I go home with my mother, but I make it clear that, being of age, I have a right to make my own decisions. If she wants me to remain with her, then she can't get in the way of my seeing whomever I want.

"Why did you tell me to go with my mother and not with you?" I ask Manón as soon as I enter her apartment. "I spent the whole night wondering why you gave in so easily."

"I was afraid," she says. "Your mother was making a scene, and people were stopping. I saw she was capable of doing anything to get her way, like asking the airport authorities to intervene, and I wanted to avoid a problem at all cost."

"We could have walked away," I say.

"Don't be so *inocente*. Your mother was out for blood—my blood—and she might have accused me of terrible things. I'm here on a visa, and I don't want any trouble. That's why I asked you to go with her, even though I hated doing so."

For a month, Manón and I spend all our free time together, except for the nights when I go home to sleep. With my mother, I'm polite but distant. She has to let me do as I want. She won the battle and is smug about it. Maybe I'll get over this "infatuation," as she calls it.

Through my haze of happiness, I notice traits about Manón I hadn't before. She likes to flirt; from the start, I saw how she drew other women to her. A charismatic personality like hers demands attention and flattery. We're rarely alone, as she constantly has people around her or dropping by. Like her neighbor, Lucero, a former girlfriend who I believe is trying to get back with her. Since Lucero lives in the same building as Manón, she comes by on several occasions when I'm there in the evening, and they flirt with each other. Lucero acts as if they were still a couple and I'm a temporary conquest.

I can't quell my suspicions. I was gone four months, and Manón doesn't like to be alone. Lucero makes no bones about having been intimate with her. Maybe they still are. No, that's my insecurity poking at me, but I ask Manón.

She laughs. "Why, *muchachita*, I think you're a little jealous. If you had any idea of what a difficult person Lucero is, you wouldn't be concerned."

Late one night, after I've left, Manón and Lucero get into a fight. A real fight. They yell and go at each other physically in the passage outside Manón's apartment, where anyone can see them. They make such a racket the whole building hears them, and an irate neighbor calls the police.

The next day, when I go to visit Manón, her face is bruised, her lip torn, and she has yellow-blue marks on her neck and arms.

"What's going on between you two?" I ask.

"Nothing, *muchachita*. We broke up before I met you."

"Then why tolerate her here?"

"She's my neighbor, and she's lonely." She hesitates. "The fight was because of you. She's very jealous of us and what we share."

"She wanted to get back with you?"

"Yes, but I didn't. That's why she was so angry. I promise never to speak to her again, not even if I meet her in the hallway."

Can I believe this? How can they avoid each other in the same building? Will Manón say hello to her, or flirt with her? Manón has a way of making each one of her friends feel like she's the only one who matters to her. Surely I mean more than Lucero.

A week later I arrive at Manón's apartment to find her ashen-faced and shaking. "Here's what I got today," she says. An official letter from the Secretary of the Interior giving her two weeks to leave the country. "That fight and the police coming got their attention."

My hands shake like hers as I take the letter from her and read it. "A deportation notice?"

"It seems the police reported the fight with Lucero to the Secretary of the Interior."

The letter mentions disorderly conduct, disturbing the peace, and unacceptable behavior. "As if Mexicans never get into fights," I say with disgust. "I'm sure you can argue against this."

Then I see the signature at the bottom. She won't be able to do anything. I know the man who signed this letter. My father's old friend. I see my mother's hand in this order.

All this time that she seemed to accept my relationship with Manón, she has been conspiring to get rid of her. She met with my father's friend, a high-placed official in the Secretariat of the Interior, and told him how this Cuban older woman, a lesbian and a degenerate, seduced her daughter, and asked his help to get rid of her. He checked up on Manón, her background, her years in Mexico, her contacts, and anything that might be a reason for deportation. The fight with Lucero provided that.

"You'll be sorry you did this to Manón," I tell my mother. "I'm going with her."

She has a fit of histrionics and accuses me of being the cause of her premature death. "You will return to find me buried, with four white candles on my grave."

"Buried or not, I don't care." I'll go with Manón and get away from my mother for good.

But I can't find my passport where I had put it with the rest of my papers when I came back from Los Angeles. I grab my mother and demand she give it back to me.

She surveys me coldly. "I burnt it."

"How could you?" I shriek, and it takes all of my control to stop from slapping that smug smile off her face.

"I'm only protecting my daughter from that woman."

"I'll get another passport." I don't need her consent or signature anymore.

"I'm afraid not." She's in command here. "I have influence in high places. I arranged for your degenerate friend to be kicked out of the country, and I can arrange for you not to be allowed to leave."

"You can't."

"I can and I will. And don't think you can slip away. My friend had her daughter taken off a plane when it was already on the runway."

"You can't stop me from moving out."

We glare at each other. "If you leave here, Marina, you have nowhere to go," she says. "You don't have a job or money of your own, and you can't expect anyone in our family to take you in, not after the way you left your Aunt Ceci's home."

I sink into a chair, defeated.

My mother wins again.

PART II
CARLOS AND CLAUDETTE

Marriage as a Solution

MEXICO CITY
1962-71

My dress is tight, very tight, and so low-cut that the crack between my breasts is visible; cinched in at the waist, it shows off my figure and rounded hips.

"You're stunning," Alicia tells me. "And your makeup is perfect." She tilts her head.

"I learned how at modeling school in LA."

"Are you going somewhere special?"

"My friend, Romina, invited me to a family birthday lunch." I don't mention that my former boyfriend, Carlos, will be there.

Two years have gone by since Carlos broke up with me, leaving me bewildered and in tears. I haven't seen him again. Nor have I wanted to. But today he's going to see the new me. I'm not the naïve young girl whom he played around with and then dumped with a note on my nineteenth birthday. I still get angry over the cowardly way he did it. In the last two years, I've grown up, fallen in love—with a woman. I've had sex—with a woman. I know the difference between his formal kisses that left me unmoved and passionate embraces. I've tired of crying over loss of love. Most important, I've learned I can move forward with a defiant optimism to face the future.

"You've changed, Marina," Carlos says as we shake hands, and his eyes travel up and down my figure, linger on my bosom, and come to rest on my face. "More beautiful than ever, and sophisticated."

"What did you expect? That I'd still be that dumb little girl you knew?"

"I never thought you were dumb."

I lift my chin. "You could have fooled me. Anyway, why should it matter now what you thought then?" Challenge a man like Carlos and he's bound to respond. "Well, it's nice seeing you again," I say. "Now, if you will excuse me, I'd like to talk to your mother."

"We'll talk later," he says. "I want to hear all about what you've been doing." I stifle an inner chuckle at the thought. How would he react if I told him the truth?

Throughout the party, Carlos finds ways to be with me. I'm certain that Romina and her mother have a hand in this, especially when he and I are seated next to each other at the table. I find him attractive and manly, and his conversation as stimulating as before. I'm not falling for him, not again, but I enjoy talking to him. When he asks me out to dinner, I accept.

Watch out, Carlos, because I'm going to make you pay for what you did to me.

We're dating, but this time I behave like he used to—turn up late or leave him waiting, then give him some weak or transparent excuse. For a short while. I can't keep it up. I understand how mismatched we were before. I was too young and innocent to keep his attention, too much in awe of his being a pilot and twelve years older. Neither of these matters anymore. What does is that we share the same interests and going to the same events. I like being with him and walking on his arm. People treat me differently, regard me with respect. As if a man at my side makes me more important.

Carlos seems more interested in me than I am in him. Perhaps he senses I won't put up with being sidelined again. When he kisses me, I know how to respond. His hard, passionate kisses are nothing like his gentlemanly ones two years ago. The real thing. More arousing. I try not to remember Manón's tender ones.

After a month Carlos and I have a friendship, though we're not what I'd consider close. All the more surprising when, over dinner at La Mansión, without any notice or lead-up, he says, "Marina, there's something I want to ask you." I glance up but go on eating. "I'm a mature man," he says. "I make a good living, and it's time for me to settle down. We should get married."

I stare at him, unable to hide my shock. Whatever I'm chewing sticks in my throat and I have to cough. He comes around the table and thumps me on the back, which helps dislodge it. He waits until I finish gulping and goes on. "I believe you have everything I'm looking for to be my wife and the mother of my children." He takes my hand almost as an afterthought. "I want to spend my life with a woman like you."

This is nothing like the romantic marriage proposal I dreamed of when I was younger. He hasn't told me that he loves me, and his proposal is all about him. I search his face for some sign, but it's as earnest as if he were proposing a business deal.

"So you think I'd make a good wife and that's why you want to marry me?" I say, my voice tight and slightly mocking.

"Yes, Marina." He's absolutely serious, set on convincing me of his good intentions. "I'd be fortunate to have you as my wife. You're gorgeous and intelligent, and I enjoy your company, your conversation. I'm sure we would have a good life together." His words should make me glow, but one basic element is missing—emotion. "However," he goes on, "there is one condition." He stops, and this pause is more eloquent than anything he's said. "I want to have sexual relations with you. But only if you accept my marriage proposal. I'm sure you can understand I have sexual needs, but my intention is to be faithful."

All I can reply to this blunt proposal is "I don't know, Carlos. Let me think it over."

I go home and ponder whether to end it with him. Send him a letter and turn him down. It seems like what he wants is sex, and he's offering a marriage guarantee as persuasion. I'm not in love with him. I can never care for him that way again.

I tell my mother about his proposal with the condition that we have sexual relations. She consults with Alicia, as, in her mind, an actress is worldly and able to assess the situation objectively. They sit down with me and talk about the advantages of marrying him.

"Carlos is a good catch," my mother says. "Since you never go out, where will you find a man like him?" And the unspoken. *He's not another woman.*

"Don't you remember what he did to me?"

"Let bygones be bygones. You were too young for him."

"You didn't like him before. Why now? Because he's a man?"

She hesitates, giving credence to that question. "He comes from a good family. He has a good position and will be a good provider." What she doesn't say is more important. If I get married, no more lesbian lovers, and I'll be a respectable woman. It's obvious she's as set on my marrying Carlos as much as she was against my being with Manón.

"I want him to show some emotion," I say, arguing against accepting his proposal while knowing my mother won't let me turn it down. "When he proposed, he didn't ask me—he said he thought I'd make a good wife for him."

"He may not be the most romantic of men, but he's honest enough to admit that he wants sex," Alicia says. "Many men have their little virgin *novias* and another girl on the side for that reason."

"You won't have any horrible surprises on your wedding night," my mother says. For a few seconds I wonder why she would mention that.

"It's better to know you're compatible in bed before you're married than have an unfortunate experience afterwards," Alicia adds. "Many unhappy marriages could be avoided if the couple knew each other physically before they walked down the aisle. Why draw it out? Couples often have sex before marriage."

"It's not unusual for a girl to walk down the aisle in a white dress with a full skirt to hide the bump in her belly," my mother says. "Make sure Carlos takes precautions. You don't want to have to rush the wedding date or for people to say you lured him into marrying you."

If he wants to go to bed with you before marriage, that's all right, they tell me. As long as he honors his commitment to marry you.

"Give it a try," my mother advises me. "You loved him before and you can again."

"I thought I did."

"He's handsome," she goes on as if she hasn't heard me "Intelligent, financially stable, has good genes, and his family likes you. You'll have healthy, beautiful children with him. What more can you ask?"

What more can I ask for, indeed. Someone more sensitive, more romantic, and less self-centered. Carlos has a big ego and thinks everything revolves around him. I'll be another moon basking in his sun. But I can see the sense in what they both tell me.

Cool-headed, I review the advantages of accepting his marriage offer. Then I study my other side—the one drawn to the forbidden, to women. I've heard and read about lesbians and how society regards them. I don't want to be labeled as one. If I'm married, I won't have that problem.

I remember reading in a book by Thomas Moore*, "The soul is a wide, spacious area in which family, society and history—personal and cultural— are major influences."

I accept Carlos's marriage proposal and his conditions. "But I don't want to get pregnant," I say, remembering my mother's warning.

"You won't," he says. "I'll take care of that."

We go to a motel, one with flashing neon lights and garages with curtains instead of doors to conceal the cars. We enter a room, impersonal in appearance but personal in the use it's been given. The many couples who have had sex there have left a little of themselves—in the air or in the ambience or on the furnishings and bedcovers, even in the walls that have heard their groans and whispers. I sense the remnants of their presence, and something raw and innocent inside me mutates, adding to the charged atmosphere in the room.

In the beginning I don't enjoy sex with Carlos. I'm a virgin, and every thrust hurts. This carnal ritual seems to have little to do with fulfilling my or his emotional needs. I try to banish memories of those softer moments with Manón when touching was more important than the act itself. After he comes with a gasped shout, he sinks down on me, panting as if he's made a big effort. We remain like this for five minutes, his sweaty body on mine, until he lifts himself and, glancing at the blood stains on the sheets with an air of pride, asks, "Did you like it, my little *virgencita?*" My insides are throbbing; the act was painful and nothing like the romantic binding of two beings as portrayed in books and movies. Sex with a man is a basic act where the man is master. I force a smile and say, "Yes, it was good."

"I didn't hurt you?"

"A little."

He lies back and puts his arm around me, and we stay in that position for a while, content, a couple, and a warm feeling of security fills me. This is the part I like, this closeness after sex when I feel loved and protected by this strong man who will be my husband.

I go to the bathroom to clean myself and prepare mentally for more. Will I ever enjoy this act with a man after loving, delicate sex with Manón? This second time, before he enters me, he inserts a vaginal suppository so I won't get pregnant.

Over time I learn to enjoy making love with Carlos and taking my own pleasure rather than expect him to give it to me.

I never warm to his kisses. Instead, I turn my head to avoid them.

*

I go through my wedding ceremony numbed, doing and saying what I have to. I know I have to act a certain way and pretend this is the happiest day of my life. In my pearl-embroidered gown with its swirling skirt and long train, I'm the star. To everyone, I must appear to be a joyful bride; I give as good a performance as a seasoned actress. I'm marrying Carlos with my head and not with my heart, promising to spend the rest of my days with him. I'll try to forget the turmoil of the last two years, and loving a woman, and start anew.

I'll be free of my mother, out of her control forever.

Perhaps at the reception, for a splinter of a minute, I ask myself why I'm going through with this. To please my mother? Or to get away from her and make my own way?

Or because loving another woman is forbidden.

*

We spend a month in Europe on our honeymoon, visiting the great museums and historical sites. Carlos acts as my personal guide and mentor, making history and culture come alive for me, and for others. In El Prado Museum* in Madrid, he's giving me the background on Goya's *Black Paintings**, and people, drawn by Carlos's sonorous voice and what he's saying, come over to listen, and he ends up lecturing a group. This happens on several occasions. I'm so proud this erudite man is my husband.

On our return to Mexico City, I'm pregnant with my first child. I focus on my pregnancy, establishing a home, and being a good housewife. When my first son, Armando, is born, he becomes the center of my existence. I spend hours contemplating him, smelling his skin, kissing and holding this precious little being. Seven months later we decide to have a companion for him and plan another child. We work out when I'll be fertile, and stop using vaginal suppositories. Our second son, Jaime, is born nine months later.

We buy a house in a high-end neighborhood and employ two maids. They help take care of six-month-old Jaime and Armando, going on two. After two years of domesticity, I yearn for a creative outlet, and before long I'm taking ballet classes again. My teacher asks me to join her dance group and appear on a weekly TV program at Televicentro, the television center.

Carlos is annoyed that I'd consider such a move. "Aren't two small children enough to keep you busy?" he asks, though I suspect he dislikes the idea of my dancing in public.

"Dancing is my passion, and this is a great opportunity," I tell him.

"For what?" he asks with an imperious expression. "If you spend all day at Televicentro, you won't have time for our home and the children."

"It's only once a week when they record the program."

66

"What about rehearsals?"

"They're a couple of hours, and I'll call to make sure everything's all right."

"I'll allow it on condition that you're available to them and to me whenever we need you," he says.

His words have a razor-grating effect. My underground sentiments of frustration at his dominating me burst forth. "Dancing fulfills me," I say. "It's an important part of my life. I don't need your permission to dance."

His face reflects anger and dismay. Before I feared his reaction, but now I'm in charge of my life. Not my husband. Not my mother. Me.

Before long, I see an opportunity to turn my passion for dancing into a business. I install bars and mirrors in an empty room at home and put up a sign outside our home advertising my dance lessons. Within a week I have my first students.

Carlos comes back from a flight and seeing the sign, he kicks it down. "Why do you have to turn our home into a school?" he asks.

"It's not a big deal," I tell him. "And didn't you want me to spend more time at home? This way, I won't have to go out."

"Just take down that sign," he says. I do, after several more students have signed up. By then word has gotten out, and students from all over the neighborhood are coming to classes. Within a year, I have too many to teach at home. I find a venue a few blocks from my home and open my dance school.

Carlos no longer objects; or maybe he's grateful that I've moved the school out of our house.

*

Three years into my marriage, the phone rings early one morning. I'm on my way out, but I pick it up in the living room at the same time Carlos answers in the bedroom. It's Marcia, the secretary from the pilots' club where he's president. *"Pollito,"* she says, "what happened? Why didn't you bring me my underwear from Los Angeles?" Her voice is husky, intimate.

"Marcia, I can't talk right now. My wife's here."

"Oh, I thought she'd left for work. Will I see you today?"

"In a couple of hours."

"Okay, *pollito, mi amor*. I can't wait to see you."

A fang of fury races through me. Sounds like they're having an affair. Of course they are. Underwear, no less. Panties? Bras? I found out only because I'm here later than usual.

I march into the bedroom. Carlos's face dissolves into a mask of horror at seeing me here. "It's not what you think," he says, raising an arm as if to shield himself. "That's the way she talks to the pilots—to all of us."

"Sure, *pollito*."

"You know that everyone in the airline calls me that." His voice fills with false indignation.

"But does everyone call you *Pollito, mi amor*?"

"I tell you, Marina." He gets off the bed and confronts me as if I'm the one at fault. "That's the way she speaks to everyone. Ask el Toro."

"Your best friend? Does he also buy her underwear in LA?"

"We all do." He stares me straight in the eyes. "Marina, I can't believe a little thing like this would make you doubt me." He says this with such sincerity that I'd almost believe him. But Carlos never owns up to doing anything wrong.

"So she can't wait to see you? Because of the underwear you didn't bring her?" I tell him and walk out of the room.

My gut roils at what he's doing. Now I know he's having sex with her and probably with others. Before we were married, someone warned me that pilots had many women. "Like sailors, one in every port." I thought it was a joke, like people saying air stewardesses were all easy lays, and Carlos was above it. Until now. I shouldn't have forgotten what a philanderer he used to be.

My marriage is one big farce. My peace and contentment are superficial. Except for the children, it's worthless. Everything appeared to be going so well, and it's all crashed down. I never suspected. How can he want sex every day if he's getting it from someone else? Why did I expect a man like Carlos to change his ways?

Within a short time, because I'm on the alert, I discover Marcia is only one in a long line of women. In fact, he's been having affairs all the time we've been married.

To hell with being faithful.

Eckhart Tolle* says, "Life will give you whatever experience is more helpful for the evolution of your consciousness. How do you know this is the experience you need? Because this is the experience you are having at this moment."

*

I have a brief affair—a revenge affair—with a married doctor. Then relations with a woman. Carlos has no idea. Not as long as I stick to his rule: "When I get home from a trip, you have to be there. I'll call from the airport." With the maid's collusion, I make it back before he arrives. Until I get careless and linger too long with my girlfriend. He's angry not to find me at home. "I know you were with someone," he says. "You have that air of satisfied sex on you." He, who is so unfaithful, is furious because he suspects me of infidelity.

"I was with someone," I admit brazenly and cock my head, challenging him.

He frowns, puzzled. "A woman? I don't understand."

"I've always been attracted to women. I had affairs before I married you."

He doesn't seem to be able to grasp what I'm saying. "But you were a virgin. Innocent."

"In a way. Before you, I had an intense liaison with a woman named Manón. My mother broke us up."

He sucks in a quick breath. "You like women?"

"Yes, and I'm with someone who's important to me. I want a divorce." The words come out, though I haven't contemplated taking this step.

He shrugs as if he doesn't care. "I'm not giving you a divorce. Not so you can play around with women." His eyes shine as if he's discovered a secret. "I know you've been planning this for a while. It's why you've worked so hard to make your dance school successful. So you can be financially independent."

"Yes, I am financially independent, but it's not why I want a divorce. It's you, Carlos. I have to get away from you. We can't go on like this. You with your *movidas* and me with a woman I care about."

"If you like her that much, you can leave. I'll stay here with the children."

A shiver of fear runs through me. "You know I'll never leave my children. And as their mother, I'll get custody."

"No judge in the world will grant you custody." His face is cold, determined, the face of a man who knows he holds the winning cards. "Not if it comes out that you're a lesbian. The law won't treat you kindly. You'll lose the children."

If I were violently inclined, I'd grab a vase, a lamp, anything, and bash it across his head. Instead, I say nothing, turn and go to the bathroom, where I lock myself in. He can't do that to me. I won't let him. He can't prove anything, but can he? Why is his adultery acceptable in society while my affair with a woman could destroy me? Who will understand that I can enjoy being with both a man or a woman? Life can be so unjust. I weep until my mind is a blur, a frenzy of emotions that explode inside me—and against me. I swallow ten sleeping pills, not a serious attempt to kill myself but because of his uncaring attitude. I need to make him react, show some emotion beyond wanting sex almost every day, whatever my mood.

I remember him knocking on the door and telling me to come out, ordering me and pleading with me, and then everything goes hazy, and I'm falling onto the floor. Next I'm being carried and bundled into a car, taken to the hospital, where they give me a liquid to throw up, and sent home with him around midnight. I don't understand what he says to me, but it seems threatening. I don't have the energy to stand up to him.

I awake, confused. When he comes into the bedroom, I want to shriek at him to go away. His presence drains me, makes me feel weak and unable to function. I huddle in my bed in my darkened room, shuddering when I hear him come in and approach me. He asks how I'm feeling and I tell him to get out. I can't share the same bed or the same space with him.

What can I do? What can I do? The question is so huge, so impossible that I take refuge in a mental limbo where everything goes blank for a while. I return to face it, but it's become like a tall wall with no way to climb over or get to the other side.

He goes away on a flight for a couple of days, and I emerge from my bedroom. Battered and bruised emotionally but able to function without him around. He'll be back and my repulsion will start up again. I have to get away from him and sort out what is going on in my mind. Maybe on my own I can reassess my situation.

What about my children? I can't leave them when they need me most. I'll go somewhere nearby and come to see them every day when he isn't around.

I find an apartment three blocks away. This move isn't about sex or infidelity; it's about lack of love—it never existed in our marriage. He wanted, as he said when he proposed, a wife and a sexual partner. I craved the security of being with a man, and the companionship, but without love our marriage has fallen apart.

*

Every day, I go to see my children. "When are you coming home to live with us?" three-year-old Armando asks, and little Jaime says, "Come home, come home," and sucks on his blanket. Armando isn't doing well. He's listless, not his cheerful little self at all. He doesn't want to eat or play. At first I think it's a reaction to my leaving, though he sees me every day. He's not running a fever. After several days I know something is wrong. I call the doctor. Armando has hepatitis, a liver infection that creeps up on its victims and makes them listless, wearing them down before it's diagnosed. His skin and eyes go yellow and he's too tired to raise an arm. He needs me with him day and night. So I come home and sleep on a cot in the boys' room until he gets better.

*

While Armando is sick I reconsider my decision to live alone. It seems selfish and self-centered to put my own needs in front of my children's. I should be here to respond when they call out at night or see them when they get up in the morning. My dilemma is whether or not to return to my apartment. While I'm nursing Armando, he's my focal point and I have to be strong for him. He and his little brother need me here.

It takes a month before I'm ready to discuss our marriage with Carlos, and how we're going to handle it. For the children's sakes, I'll come back and live with him. But what about the incidents that started all this? His other women?

"What about yours?" he counters without answering my question. Always the king of denial.

"If it means being with my children, I'll give her up," I say.

His lips lift at one end in a crooked smile, and he nods slowly as if weighing my offer. "You don't have to," he says.

He must be playing with me. "I care more for my children," I tell him. "And I don't want them to lose their father."

He nods slowly as if considering my offer. "I appreciate that, Marina. And I'll let you have your lovers on one condition: as long as you're here at home for me and the children when we need you, you can fool around with women all you like."

"What made you change your mind?"

"It's important we keep up appearances for the children's sakes."

"For them?" I repeat. "Or for society? Your family?"

"You're a good wife and the children need you. So does my family. And believe me, I care for you as well. Just don't expect me to be faithful."

"You still want to have your affairs? And go to bed with me?"

"A man has his needs. You have your dance school and your women friends. I'm away a lot, and sometimes I have to seek fulfillment elsewhere."

"What does that mean? We agree that I can have my women and you can have yours?"

"As long as you're discreet and it doesn't affect our marriage. Nothing serious. I don't want to hear about divorce again. And no men."

"Why women and not men?"

"Because there's no sex act with women," he says. "With a man, there's penetration."

I scream at him, "The only thing that matters to you is the power of your prick and sticking it into a hole." What he's suggesting is a double standard. I don't know if I can accept that kind of marriage. One face for the world and another in private. But if it's the only way to keep my children, I'll try to go along with it.

*

I go to see my mother-in-law. She's concerned about our marital situation. I confide in her about Carlos and how this is affecting my health.

She lowers her head and covers her mouth with her clasped hands. If I didn't know her better, I'd say she was praying. She looks up and lets out a big sigh. "Oh my son," she says. "It's a pity that he's ruled by his carnal desires."

*

This arrangement works for two years. He has his affairs and I have mine with women. Emotionally draining. I want desperately to leave Carlos and ask him for a divorce several times; he's adamant about not giving it to me—using the children as bait to keep me in the marriage.

Again, I'm dating someone, and again, I ask Carlos for a divorce. I consult a lawyer so I know my rights. Usually, when I mention divorce, Carlos doesn't take it seriously, treating it more like a housewife's outburst that can be settled in bed. He likes to have intercourse almost every day, so I turn sex into a weapon and withhold it for several weeks. I ignore his pleas, threats, and snide remarks, and avoid him as much as I can.

One morning when I'm in the kitchen, he comes in. I'm busy making a to-do list so I don't look up when he says, "Good morning," and keep on with what I'm doing.

"I'll give you the divorce," he says.

Slowly, I lift my head and regard him. A ploy to get me back in bed? "Honestly?"

"Yes," he says. "And I'll ask for only one thing in return—that we have sexual relations."

There must be a twist somewhere for Carlos to give in after holding out so long. Can I take him at his word?

"That's all?" I ask, too stunned to turn him down. I have a nagging feeling this may not be what it seems, but he's not used to asking for sex. Maybe that's why it's hard to assimilate.

He grins like a gold medal winner. "Yes, that's all."

*

Twenty days later, I discover I'm pregnant. I could whip myself for my stupidity giving into Carlos. A suspicion forms in my mind. Why did he suddenly agree to a divorce after years of holding out? On condition that I let him have sex with me? I took it to mean that he put a price on everything. Might he have had another intention? He can be sneaky but to deliberately impregnate me would be too underhanded even for him. But it is possible. We planned Jaime after working out the dates when I'd be fertile. I'm regular every twenty-eight days. Suppose he pretended to slip the suppository into me? The more I think about it the more certain I am this happened.

I confront him and he admits to planning to get me pregnant— his way of forcing me to stay in the marriage.

"I'll get an abortion."

"Don't think you can get away with it," he says. "I'll tell my lawyer I didn't agree to it, and I don't."

"I can manage very well without you," I say, more bluster than truth. *Not if I have a new baby.*

"You can't support yourself," he says, taunting me. "You don't have the skills. You're just a spoiled little girl."

His words, intended to be insulting, have the same effect on me as when I was a teenager driven to excel in studies and sports. They challenge me. I'll show him what this "spoiled little girl" can accomplish. I throw back my head and tell him, "I'll find a way. You'll see."

I don't want this baby, and I want out of this marriage. I make an appointment to have an abortion. The night before, I go with my girlfriend to see *Doctor Zhivago*. When I come out, my heart is overflowing with love for my unborn child.

"I can't go through with the abortion," I tell her. "What if it's a girl?"

She's supportive, though I'm sure she'd prefer for me to get rid of it and start over with her. "I'll go along with whatever you decide," she says. "It won't affect us."

But it does. Having a baby leads to reconciliation with Carlos. I don't think it will last, but we can try to make a go of it.

My unwelcome pregnancy brings unexpected joy. I am blessed with a wonderful daughter, Gabriela. What started as an act of treachery has turned into a treasure. Perhaps she's the gift that will mend our marriage.

BARRIER THIRTEEN
Married, but Loving Another Woman

MEXICO CITY
1971

Her hair, black and thick as heavy silk, cascades to her shoulders, and long lashes enhance dark eyes that gaze at me and lock with mine. My chest tightens, and I force out broken little breaths. I'm as winded as if I'd run a long distance, which, in a way, is true. More like a long distance emotionally, until she caught me in her thrall.

She's belting out a country song, "*Que bonito amor*," in a strong, cowgirl's voice, but when she ends it and sings a ballad, her voice becomes rich with emotion. With this song she declares herself to me. Our eyes hold and embrace, visually making love. All I know about her is her name, Claudette. I joined this women's gathering two hours before.

She ends her song, comes over, pulls me to her, and we dance. Her hand strokes my back. We don't speak out loud; instead, we communicate with our eyes. She kisses me, a delicate first kiss, but enough to set off a light inside me. We forget who we were before we met. Only the now counts, and who we are with each other—until other people intrude. Claudette goes for a rum and coke for herself and a soft drink for me, and we sit on the couch and talk.

"I can't place your accent," I tell her. "It sounds Spanish but has a South American lilt."

"You're almost right," she says. "I lived in Argentina and Brazil as a child and spent most of my life in Spain, but I'm half-Belgian, half-Greek." A singer, she belongs to the world of cabarets. Night after night she uses her beautiful body and face to entice her audience, and her voice to seduce them, and she revels in their adulation. She has no responsibilities beyond keeping her voice, her face, and her body in shape. She has no romantic attachment. "My audience is my passion," she says.

We keep on talking, not wanting to let go of this evening, until late, when most of the women have gone and the ones still here have gathered in the kitchen.

"I'm going for more drinks," Claudette tells me and gets up. Her voice is slurred and her eyelids droop.

"I don't want another," I call after her. She's finished three rum and cokes so far plus whatever she drank before we met. I'm in a semi-daze—not from alcohol. Who knows what will happen, but of one thing I'm certain. Claudette is in my life to stay.

Screams and yells rip through the vibrant images in my mind. Ugliness fills the air.

"What's going on?" I yell.

"Claudette and her sister, Darci, are fighting each other."

I rush into the kitchen to see them hitting and pulling each other's hair, like a couple of kids. Except it's worse to see two women going at it. Someone shouts, "Stop it, stop!" Darci lands a blow to Claudette's stomach, and she doubles over and gasps in pain. A woman pulls Darci away from the melée and takes her to the bedroom. I help Claudette, who seems to be hurt, up from the floor. Her face is bruised and purple with exertion, and her hair, undone and in clumps, looks as if her sister chewed on it.

I support her as we stumble to the living room and lay her on the sofa. Her sobs turn into whimpers. "Darci is so mean. She's trying to control me. I'm tired of her doing this." The sweet smell of rum is on her breath.

"Calm down, Claudette, both of you should talk tomorrow when you're not drinking."

She holds out her hand to me. "Don't leave me."

How can I go when her eyes are filled with tears and she's frightened? She seems so fragile. My mind flies back to when my mother left me to fend for myself with no one to comfort me when things went wrong. Claudette needs someone to care for her. I'll be the one who will help her become whole again.

*

"I'm seeing a woman, and it's serious," I tell Carlos after a month with Claudette.

"What's she like?" he asks, showing no emotion beyond curiosity.

"Gorgeous," I say and try to describe her in a way that does her justice. Carlos likes to hear about the women I see. He gets a vicarious pleasure out of knowing about them. If he could pry more personal details out of me, he would. So far, he's allowed me to see women with the proviso that we stay married and don't break up our family. Because I tell him it's serious with Claudette, he wants to meet her; it's similar to giving his approval, I think, but I agree.

I take him to the nightclub where Claudette is singing. She's wearing a brilliant green, two-piece sequined dress, cut low at the back so that it shows off her curves. The skirt opens at the sides to reveal her well-toned legs. She moves gracefully across the stage, swinging her hair from side to side, as she sings the Argentinean Sandro's, "*Yo te amo*." Her smile is for me as she sings these words. A thrill of excitement runs through my body, and I clutch my throat before a moan of desire escapes it. I'm like a fine-stemmed glass filled with wine that makes me heady with emotion.

Carlos can't stop watching her. "I'm impressed by her beauty and talent," he tells me, as if he's an agent assessing her. I can see it's more than that formal observation. His expression—as if he'd like to eat her up—gives him away. He's smitten.

I don't know how to react to this. It adds an undercurrent to my association with Claudette. Up to now, it's been us two. This is like sharing what we have with him. Not physically, though I can't stifle my fear that the wolf in him may want to go after her to see if she will succumb to his wiles.

"She has a contract to go to Guatemala for a week," I tell him. "I'd like to accompany her."

"I don't have a problem with that," he says, so matter-of-factly that I ask, "How come you don't mind me being with her?"

"I told you, she's a woman." He looks straight at me. "It's not the real sex act."

That doesn't make sense. Infidelity is when you have sexual relations with another person of either gender apart from your husband or partner. I suppose that some men tend to invalidate a relationship between two women because they don't consider it the real thing unless it involves a prick.

*

After we return from Guatemala, I ask Carlos if Claudette can come home and spend the night with me. It's painful to separate again after being with her day and night for a week. I want her with me all the time.

"By all means, bring her here," he says, as casually as if I'd asked to have any friend come over. He even offers to go sleep with the boys when she's here. It seems very generous of him; he must have some trick up his sleeve. After nine years of marriage, I know he's the kind of man who can't resist the lure of another conquest, or another promise of sex. I've heard about men like him who need sex as much as food. I have to keep Claudette safe from him. I wouldn't put it past him to think that having her in our home might open the door to sex with both of us. From the way he gazes at her, he's planning to get inside her.

At first Claudette spends the night once a week, then it becomes two and three times. I hate the nights when she doesn't. He's there in the bedroom, wanting to have sex with me, and I agree, though more out of guilt because of Claudette. Throughout our marriage, there's never been a lack of it. If only this translated into affection.

This situation can't go on. I play the role of dutiful wife in public and keep my true feelings under wraps, but this act has lasted too long. I'm not comfortable with myself or with Carlos. Leading a double life goes against everything I believe in. I've had to be dishonest, lie to my children and to my friends. This arrangement isn't working. We need to resolve it.

"I want Claudette to come and live with me, and share my life with her," I tell him.

"I don't have any objection," he says.

"I'm sorry, Carlos, but I don't mean the three of us. I want a divorce."

His head pulls back as if I'd slapped him. "You want *me* to move out?" His tone is incredulous, but it hardens with anger. "I thought we settled that you could keep your lover as long as we kept the marriage intact. I've done everything to make it easy for you."

"It seemed like a good solution, but we can't have it both ways." On the exterior, I'm calm, but inside I'm asking myself if this will convince him to finally agree to a divorce.

"Why not?" he asks. "I don't see a problem with you having your female lover, so why can't we keep things the way they are?"

"Yes, in theory I can have my lover and you can have yours. All of them. And we can stay together for the sake of appearances. The same as we've been doing for the past two years. But what about our children when they realize our marriage is a sham? I can't pretend to be happily married to you while I'm with another person. I'm not being true to myself or to you or to them. I want a divorce, and I'm not backing down."

"But Marina, we had an agreement." He acts offended, as if I've turned against him. "Why are you doing this to me?"

 .   *Because I've found love,* I want to scream. *The love you aren't capable of giving me.* I restrain myself because Carlos wouldn't understand. "I'm fed up with living a lie. I'm tired of this emotional roller coaster. It's not right—not for us or for our children."

"You were fine with it before."

"I've tried to repress my feelings, but I can't go on like this. It's best for all of us if we get a divorce."

"Do you give me a choice?"

"No, it's my decision." I have to stand firm against him. "I'm not a spoiled little girl anymore. I won't ask you for alimony or any support except to pay for the children's private schools. I can support them with what I make with my dance school." At least I can do that now that my business is booming. Or, as Carlos puts it, "You created a giant." I must be making as much as he, a pilot, does, or even more.

He's obviously shaken, tumbled from his lofty perch as my lord and master, and it shows. He's like a man in the dock desperately appealing a long sentence. "Marina, I accepted this affair of yours on one condition— that we keep our family together. I'm very fond of my children, and I want to live with them, not see them on weekends. And they're still small. How will they understand?"

"Small children adapt more easily," I say. They are eight, seven, and three years old. "It would be harder if they were older."

"How can I compete with a woman?" He asks, his voice heavy with anger.

"You can't."

His face tightens; his eyes seem to fade into their sockets, and his jaw droops. His fingers curl into fists. He's struggling for control. After all the years of asking for a divorce, it's finally hit him that I won't back down.

"I never thought you'd turn out to be so cold and calculating," he says. "If you want that woman instead of me, you can have her."

He grabs suitcases, fills them with his belongings, and storms out of the house.

When the boys don't see their father, or his pilot's uniform hanging on its perch, they ask why he left without saying good-bye. Carlos always tells them where he's going and how long before he'll be back.

"Don't worry, he'll come over on Sunday to pick you up to spend the day with him." I explain that Papi won't be living with us anymore. Why not? they ask. A question hard to answer.

"Sometimes papis and mamis have problems living together," I tell them. "So it's better to be apart."

Armando says, "It happens to lots of parents."

"How do you know?" I didn't expect my eight-year-old to come up with an explanation.

"Everyone knows," he says. "Pepe's parents are divorced, and Sonia's, and Beto says it's the best thing that can happen because his papi takes him to fun places and gives him whatever he asks for."

As far as the children are concerned, the matter is settled.

*

Carlos has agreed to give me a divorce. Second thoughts niggle at me, but I don't allow them to surface. When I make up my mind, I follow through.

We agree to make it amicable. Carlos drives me to the divorce lawyer's office. On my way, the dam inside me breaks. Visions of our years as a couple flash through my mind like a movie trailer, poignant in their memory, and tears gush out.

"Are you sure you still want to go ahead with it?" Carlos asks.

"Of course," I say, wiping my eyes. Then why am I crying? He doesn't ask again, and if I told him, I doubt he'd understand. I'm not so sure that I want our nine years of marriage to end in failure. There might be some way we can remedy this. Call off the divorce and make a new start. No, I made up my mind long ago. I'm going to stick with my decision.

After the divorce, I agonize over it, reevaluating my reasons, and the repercussions. A divorce is a loss of illusions, companionship, and security. Why did our marriage end? Because of his affairs and his detachment? Or when I found someone else? A specific moment or a combination of events? Perhaps I'm as guilty as he is for the breakup. No, I'm not. It had to happen. From the moment Carlos proposed to me, it was doomed.

Divorce has thrust me, at thirty, into a single-life situation that I'm not prepared to handle.

Christmas Eve has always been a family celebration. The children open their gifts under the tree. I see their excitement, the happiness on their faces, and experience the gleam of the magic of this evening.

After the divorce I spend the first Christmas Eve in the nightclub where Claudette is singing. Alone at my table, I wait for her to finish her act. I glance around the smoke-filled, darkened room with its paltry Christmas adornments, and its air of pretended cheer, and study the people here. Are they like me? Without families on Christmas Eve? My sense of being alone deepens. I'm not like them. I have a family, but they aren't here, they've gone with their father on a ten-day holiday. Carlos will play Santa in Winter Park, Colorado.

A group of merrymakers beckons to me to join them. I shake my head, preferring to be alone than with strangers.

I never considered the aftermath of a divorce, or the loss of status and privilege that go with being married. Or spending weekends and holidays like this one without my children. I didn't expect to grieve for my broken marriage. Or feel remorse for not knowing how to handle our situation.

A heavy tear falls into my wine glass. Another. One by one, they fall, each filled with a lost illusion.

I had to be true to myself, but at what a cost.

Finding a Father for My Lover's Child

MEXICO CITY
1973-75

My son Jaime and his dog, Alex, dash into the house followed by a panting and flushed Claudette. With her hair pulled back in a ponytail and wearing a loose peasant blouse, she could pass for a teenager.

She flops into a chair. "We had lots of fun," she says. "We played ball in the park."

I love her childlike nature and her way with my children—they are best buddies. In two years, she's become part of our family. As far as the children are concerned, she's a friend who lives with us. When we're with them we're discreet in our affection for each other, confining it to nighttime when they're asleep.

Claudette has an ovary removed. The doctor recommends she should have a child before too long in case her other ovary ceases to work. When she hears this prognosis, I can see the fear in her eyes. At home, she breaks down. I hug her, trying to find words of comfort. "Why don't we have a child? It will be a symbol of our love." And give her the fulfillment she lacks.

"But how?" she asks. "I don't want to betray you with a man."

"We'll find a way," I assure her while trying to quell my misgivings that this may not be possible. It's a two-sided problem: her only option is to have sex with a man, but it will be hard for her to go through with it. She says her stepfather raped her when she was a teenager. The sex act with a man fills her with self-disgust—unless she has some hefty drinks before.

Another problem is finding the right man to act as sperm donor—have sex with Claudette only once with the sole intention of impregnating her. Not any man who's willing. We need someone exceptional, someone who we know will provide us with a fine son or daughter.

One man fits the requirements. Carlos. He has good genes—we produced three strong, beautiful, intelligent children—but I balk at asking him to have sex with Claudette, my lover. I doubt he'd have any reservations;

quite the opposite, he's lusted after her since he first saw her, and he'll probably jump at the opportunity. The idea repulses me. I don't know if I can go through with it, or how Claudette will take it.

I swallow my disgust at the thought. He's our best chance.

When it comes to telling her, the words stick in my throat. "I'm going," I croak, "to ask," I pause, "Carlos." I stop and gulp. "To be your child's father. Do you think ... you can do it? With him?"

A frightened expression scurries across her face. She shivers, moves back in her seat, as if trying to hide her body in it. She's small and vulnerable, and cornered. "I don't know. I suppose I can. Better Carlos than a stranger."

When he comes to pick up the children, we usually chat a few minutes. We're on good terms. I tell him how Claudette wants to have a child; indeed, she has to for medical reasons, and we might ask my brother to be the sperm donor. "The problem is his wife," I say. "I don't think she'd agree."

Carlos is thoughtful. He glances around the room as if seeking an answer and folds his hands and taps his fingers on his knuckles. "I understand your predicament," he says. "I don't think you should ask a stranger to father her child. How about me? I could be the sperm donor, and Claudette's child would be our children's sibling."

I act surprised and pleased, which I am. "What a great idea, Carlos. Let me ask Claudette what she thinks."

I tell Claudette about his offer. "Yes," she says, and I can see how much effort goes into her saying that one word. "But," her voice strengthens, "this child will be yours and mine, not his. We will raise him or her ourselves."

"Only if you're certain about going through with this."

"Yes, I am." She straightens up. "You know how I love your kids. I want to have one of my own."

We plan the pregnancy. We have to wait until fourteen days after Claudette's period, when she's more fertile. As the day approaches, my certainty ebbs. I question our choice. How can I let my ex-husband have sex with her? The idea is so repugnant that nausea rises in my throat. I torture myself with visions of them in the act and think of ways to stop it from taking place.

Claudette is twenty-six. We can wait a couple of years and find another donor, someone not as close to us. But who better than Carlos? He's already given me three fantastic children, and Claudette's and my child will be like them. Part of my family.

I must let this go forward, but one thing I know for certain—I can't leave Claudette alone with Carlos. No matter how difficult it is for me to witness him having sex with her, I have to help her through it.

The day arrives. Before we leave for Carlos's apartment, Claudette drinks three strong vodkas. She runs the range of feeling scared, to annoyed, to apprehensive, to wanting to back out, and, after another drink, to deciding to go ahead. When we reach his apartment, she's unsteady, but the first thing she asks for is a vodka.

Carlos throws me a questioning look; I nod, and he pours her a stiff one. She downs it like soda. She's swaying and woozy. "One more," she begs, and with that last drink, she's too drunk to stand on her own.

Carlos and I prop her up and support her as we go into the bedroom. We lay her on the bed, and I take off her skirt and panties so she's naked from the waist down. I put my arm around her for her to rest against me.

Carlos removes all his clothes and climbs on top of her. He doesn't appear concerned that she's inebriated and lying there like a limp doll. He separates her legs and lifts them.

With no preamble, he plunges into her. She winces and her *No!* comes out as a whimper. Her body stiffens, and she wriggles her legs, trying to push him off, but her efforts are feeble. He's so intent on what he's doing, he doesn't notice.

I tighten my hold on her and kiss her to reassure her, but I can feel his every thrust as if he were thrusting into me. His face has the distorted expression of a man set on one thing—his satisfaction. Has he no compunction about having sex with a woman who's almost passed out?

Tears pour down my cheeks. What he's doing hurts me as much as if he were forcing himself on her, raping her in front of me. It makes me think of all those mothers during wars who have to watch their daughters defiled by strangers grinding away inside them, leaving them forever broken and shamed. I have to remind myself that she consented and the purpose is for her to conceive. Even so, a tidal wave of shame, frothing with guilt—for her, for me, for him—sweeps over me.

Carlos keeps pumping away until he comes. He shudders and sinks on top of her, lying there for what seems a long time but can't be more than a few minutes. I want to grab him and pull him off her, attack him like a wild beast for violating one of my own. She stirs, moaning slightly, and I can't leave her.

He gets off and stands like a sated lion, swelling his chest. When he opens his mouth, I almost expect a roar to come out. "It would have been better if she'd been conscious," he says, "but it was good anyway." His eyes roam over her naked body as if he owned it. His ego is so big he thinks having sex with an unconscious woman is good. I eye his flaccid prick, the slug-like appendage that gives men so much power.

"You should be glad she wasn't," I say. "It's the only way she'd let you near her."

*

That act is enough for Claudette to get pregnant.

Our child will be born.

As her stomach grows, I put my head against it and talk and sing to the baby, imagining it can hear our voices blend in song.

We celebrate New Year's Eve 1973 drinking champagne, the two of us awaiting our baby's arrival on January 12. Carlos has taken the children to Big Bear to play in the snow.

All goes well with the birth, and Claudette comes back to the hospital room tired but glowing. The nurse brings the baby into the room, and I kiss her forehead. "Karla," I say, "welcome to our family. We will always love you very much."

*

We move to another house in the same neighborhood, and Gabriela and Karla share a bedroom. Their twin beds have white headboards with red borders. Their bedspreads are decorated with Snow White motifs, and they have stuffed animals—Mickey Mouse and Winnie the Pooh, Donald Duck and Daisy—that we bought when we all went to Disneyland.

Claudette's reaction to her child is similar to how she reacts to everything, childlike and playful. She treats Karla like a little live doll, fun to play with but ready to give over to someone else to take care of her. I hire a nanny, but I also feed her, change her, and answer her calls at night. I may not have given birth to her, but she's still my daughter. My children accept her as a part of our family, no questions asked. When, out of the blue, Claudette tells nine-year-old Armando that Karla is his little sister, he becomes big brother and protective of her.

Claudette wants to go back to nightclub singing.

"You have a baby who needs you," I say.

"You'll take care of her for me," she answers, with her innocent wide-eyed expression.

"You're her mother," I tell her. I don't want her going alone to obscure nightspots, and it's not possible to accompany her whenever she sings. She comes home in the early hours with a dazed look, reeking of alcohol. Seeing her in that state is too much to endure. She's attractive and desirable, and easily swayed when she's been drinking. What happens when I'm not around?

Fortunately, she follows my advice and accepts my decisions, much like a young girl with her mother. I'll convince her to give up singing and work in my dance school.

At first, she insists, "It's my career; I love singing too much," but my arguments against it wear her down. After Karla's birth and a long hiatus, it's not easy for her to find work and she has to settle for a seedy, low-down nightclub. She swiftly finds out that the customers don't go there to hear her sing, and when a persistent customer throws bills at her, she flees the premises.

I've seen Claudette practicing dance steps with Gabriela and how my daughter responds to her. Why not hire her to teach dancing in my school? She knows music and rhythm, is graceful, and has a charming way about her. She turns out to be a big asset. Her students adore her for the same reasons her audiences did, and the ranks swell. But she misses the stage and the applause, so I arrange for her to sing at gatherings and parties.

Occasionally, she gets nostalgic for her days as a nightclub singer and being the center of attention. The lure of those smoke-filled rooms still follows her, and the admiration of men and the high of performing. But after a while she settles into the fulfillment of being a teacher.

*

Gabriela and I come home from an afternoon at my dance school, and three-year old Karla runs to greet us. Gabriela, who's eight, goes to the record player, puts on a record, and dances around the room to the song's rhythm.

Her younger sister watches a minute and says, "Me too, me too. I want to dance."

"I'll teach you what I learned today," Gabriela tells her. "It's called 'Tequila,' and we're going to dance it at the recital."

My two little girls, one fair-haired and the other dark-haired, join hands. Gabriela leads Karla, with her chubby little legs, in a semblance of the dance routine she learned today. "No, Karla, this is the way you do it," and "Karla, that foot goes first," and, "You have to keep in time with the music," and finally, "You're doing great, Karla."

"I'm going to change," Karla announces, imitating her mother. She goes to her bedroom and comes back in her fluffy red dress and red ballet shoes, and twirls on her toes.

"Oki," Gabriela tells her, "you're so pretty in red."

Karla beams, pulls back her shoulders, places one hand across her chest the way her mother does at the start and end of a performance, and says proudly, "Oki is very *bonita.*"

An Emotional Conflict

Mexico City
1975-77

"I'm lonely," Carlos tells me when he comes by to leave off the children. "I miss being close to my kids and seeing them every day." This is leading up to something. I'm not sure I want to hear it.

"The kids are confused," he goes on. "They're wondering why all this has happened. They don't know the truth about you and Claudette, but before long they will."

"She gets on great with them," I tell him, thinking how Claudette has a talent to entertain children. "It's working, Carlos."

"I'm sure it is—for you." He smiles at Claudette instead of at me, and she smiles back. I don't like it. I sense he wants something from us and is trying to get her on his side.

"I have a solution," he says, "that I don't think would affect you two, but it would be good for the kids and help me. Why don't I move in with you? I'd have my own bedroom, of course. This way, the kids will have both their parents under one roof."

"No," I say, and shake my head for emphasis.

Ignoring this, he goes on. "It would be a big help for them, especially Armando, who's more affected by our separation. I won't get in your way. I'll respect you as a couple."

He glances at Claudette as if seeking her agreement, and she says, "I don't have a problem," and they both turn to me.

His request is more like a compromise. He wants to live with his children, and I want to live with Claudette. It will be good for the children to have both their parents living together, despite the unorthodox situation. But the picture of me, my lover, and my ex-husband living together appears more like a threesome than an ideal living situation.

"I don't agree," I say. "Claudette and I are lovers. If we're sleeping in the same room and you're in another, the children will find out."

"Maybe," he says, "but by then they will accept it. And think how delighted they will be to have us both under the same roof."

"But *I* don't like the idea. How will it appear, the three of us all living in the same house?"

"People don't need to know about our living arrangements. They'll think you and I are back together. We'll be a family, but a bigger one."

"Let me consider it." I ask Claudette, "What do you think?"

"You do whatever you want, Marina," Claudette says in her sweet, submissive way.

My mother thinks I should agree. "It seems like an excellent idea. He is the father of your children." Probably she's thinking of how society will view my living with my former husband as more respectable. Divorced women are still looked down on. Also it solves her concern that people suspect the friend who's living with me is my lesbian lover.

"This kind of arrangement isn't right," I say. "It's not what I want." Carlos and I are on shaky ground. He gave in too easily to separate sleeping arrangements. Knowing him and his sex drive, he has other intentions. But he refuses to let the matter go. He finds allies in my mother, who supports us pretending to be a big, happy family, and Claudette, whom he's managed to convince that it would be a good idea.

Months go by before I give in. Carlos and my mother gnaw away at my defenses. I hold out for as long as I can, but their constant pleading, pressuring, bartering, trying to persuade and even coerce me into agreement wear me down. "We can see how it works," I say, but with serious misgivings.

*

We settle into a four-bedroom house in the same neighborhood where Carlos and I lived before, near my dance school. He moves in and has his own bedroom, as planned. The children are delighted and stage a welcome back party. Little Karla runs around saying, "Papi's coming home!" Carlos is a good father who plays with the kids and takes the boys to sports events. On the outside we seem like the perfect family. Our gold German shepherd, Alex, rounds out the scene.

A month after Carlos moves in, while teaching a dance class, I'm overcome by a wave of dizziness. I have to stop and sit and ask Claudette to finish my class. I'm so shaky I can't see. I go home to rest.

For two weeks, I'm confined to my bed. After a series of tests, neither my doctor nor the specialists can find anything wrong. They suggest it might be work pressure or stress—a new word used to explain undiagnosed illnesses. "Take it easy. Don't work so hard" is their advice. Obviously, it's psychosomatic, similar to what I suffered as a child when we moved to Mexico City. All I can think of is that my current living arrangement may have brought it on.

I've tried hard not to give in to suspicions as to what is going on at home when I'm not there. Questions buzz in my head. Claudette and Carlos get on very well, maybe too well. Their behavior with each other and the way they interact have me on the alert. It's only Claudette being her charming self; she gets along with everyone that way. She would never betray me, and certainly not with a man. As a singer, she drew men to her, but their attentions had the opposite effect. She tolerated them only because of her work, she tells me.

Why, I ask myself, if she fearfully submitted to sex with Carlos to get pregnant, would she consider a repeat? Why am I so filled with doubts? Because I've found that Claudette is not truthful, or she exaggerates. Her years of struggle and fending for herself resulted in real and imagined fears. Occasionally, she slips into bizarre behavior, such as when I met her and she fought with her sister. Then I think how sweet and helpful she and Carlos have been since I've been indisposed, and I swat away my suspicions.

The next day I'm better, and the mystery sickness has disappeared.

One evening, after coming home from work, Claudette and I are in our bedroom talking about a couple of promising students at the dance school. "I think they both have a great future ahead of them," I say.

Claudette nods, but she has been too quiet and pensive throughout our conversation. Her mind tends to wander, and she gets easily distracted. "Were you listening?" I ask, irritated.

"Yes," she says, "you were talking about the school."

"About the students. Why can't you pay attention? What's going on?"

She gazes downwards. "Marina, there's something I have to tell you." She chews her lower lip. "When you go out and leave me here alone, Carlos wants to talk to me. He asks me to have sex with him."

"*Desgraciado!*" Fury mounts in me, the kind of fury that creates a fire in my gut, a fire so fierce that it flashes upwards and burns all thoughts except for one in my head. Get rid of him. Throw him out. But my fury transforms into cold anger. The horny bastard, it's what he's wanted all along. From that first evening when he salivated over Claudette in the nightclub. Typically, he'd think that one occasion when they had sex would lead to others. Didn't his mother warn me about his uncontrollable sex drive?

"I didn't want to upset you," Claudette says with an apprehensive note. She knows the signs when I'm angry. "Please, Marina, we haven't done anything wrong." She moves away from me as if afraid I'll hit her.

"What's wrong is that he wants sex with every woman he meets unless they're old and withered!" Or too young and virtuous. "Why did I let him back into my home with you here?" Didn't I realize a man like Carlos would be unable to keep his hands off a desirable woman like Claudette?

"I promise we didn't do anything," she says, her voice edged with panic, and she holds out a trembling hand. "I swear."

I ignore her outstretched hand. "I'm going to talk to him right now. I want him out of this house."

"No, please! Don't tell him anything." She backs away toward her dresser.

"You can't expect me to keep quiet about this."

"That's why I didn't tell you before. I knew you'd be furious." She leans on the dresser.

"I'm going to throw him out." I head for the door.

"Marina," she shouts and I turn. She's holding a gun and it's aimed at my stomach.

This does make me halt, not so much the gun as her expression. Her beautiful face is twisted and unfamiliar, and her mouth pulled back in what resembles a snarl.

"You can't … confront him," she says, gulping her words. "I don't want … problems." Her hand trembles, and the gun sways from side to side.

"Are you crazy, Claudette?" I feel a tightness in my stomach, as if she has in fact pulled the trigger. My hand flies to my chest but she hasn't shot me.

Calm down, Marina. You have to take control.

"Why don't you want me to talk to Carlos?" I try to keep my voice even, cover up the tremor in it.

"What's the use? He'll tell you I'm a liar and it isn't true."

"I know he'll say that, but I also know he's a liar. I'm not mad at you."

"You're not?" She's surprised; her bravado disappears, and she lowers the gun, though she still holds on to it.

"No, but I am very hurt that you'd pull a gun on me." I soften my voice. "I thought you loved me." The blood pumping in my temple is so loud I can hardly hear myself speak.

She gasps, and glances at the pistol as if she'd forgotten it. "With all my heart," she says in a small voice, and she has the expression of a kid who's done something she shouldn't have.

"I don't want to ever see that thing again." I'm trembling. If she can aim it at me over a stupidity, what more is she capable of doing?

Hastily, she turns and places it back inside a drawer.

"You can't keep it here," I say. "Anyway, why do you have a gun?"

She puts on her little girl face. "To protect myself."

"From what?"

"Men. To keep them away."

"But I'm not a man, and you have nothing to fear from me. Why threaten me with it?" I, who want to protect her.

"I don't know why," she says in a whispery tone. "Because if you tell Carlos what I said, I'm afraid he'll come after me."

In a way I can understand her twisted logic, but I must try to submerge my own sentiments and reason with her. "Claudette, I don't like having a gun in the house. It's too dangerous."

Her face sets. "I've always had one—for many years—and I'm not getting rid of it. Don't you see I need it to protect myself?"

"From whom, Claudette? You might have killed me with that."

She shakes her head vigorously.

"Then you have to get rid of it. Otherwise, after what happened I'll never feel safe with you." I sit heavily on the bed and hold my head in my hands. "If I see it again, I'll never forgive you."

"I'm sorry, Marina." She sits and puts an arm around me. In her soft, innocent voice she says, "All I wanted was to stop you from making a scene. It wasn't for real."

"How would I know?" I move away from her arm and lie down with my head on my pillow. "It's been too many shocks."

"I didn't mean it," she repeats, "and I shouldn't have done that, but I didn't want to create a problem with Carlos. I can handle him. You know I can."

"If you don't want me to intervene, then it's up to you to work it out with him," I say. "Promise me that if he comes on to you again you'll tell me."

"Yes, I promise." Her face is so contrite and sweet that I want to believe her.

"Now, leave me alone. I need to rest."

My mind is thrashing around from this double whammy. First, Carlos's behavior and then her extreme method to stop me from confronting him. She's hiding something, and I don't like to think what it might be. She's right: if I tell him what she told me, he'll accuse her of lying. Since she does lie, and so does he, it will be hard to find out the truth. Knowing him, I believe he's made advances to her, but also I want to believe that a worldly woman like her, a nightclub singer, would know how to fend off men like him.

As things stand, I can't trust either of them.

*

Claudette is changing. I thought I knew her inside out, but I'm not sure anymore.

We're in the bedroom having an argument. Perhaps it has to do with the school and the way she's been goofing off. It's not a heated argument; rather, I'm trying to make her understand that being my lover doesn't entitle her to certain privileges that other teachers don't also enjoy. She insists that she's doing something that I know she isn't.

"You're saying I'm a liar?" she asks with limpid-eyed, deceptive innocence.

"Not a liar but, yes, on this occasion, you have lied." My tone is harsh and accusing; her act isn't working on me anymore.

"I'm not a liar," she shouts, shaking her fist at me.

"You are," I say, and her expression, for seconds, warps into a person unknown to me, and she hauls off and punches me in the stomach. I double over, feeling like the blow has cut off my windpipe and my ability to breathe. For a brief moment, I panic, gasping, searching for an ever-dwindling supply of air, and when I get it, I scream.

Armando comes running. "What happened?" he asks.

"A bad stomachache," I tell him, which is the truth of sorts.

Fear flits across Claudette's face. She's never been physically harmful before, but it reminds me of the night I met her when she and her sister got into a fight. Is this her true self?

"I'm sorry, sorry," she says. I flick my eyes in Armando's direction. "That you have such a bad stomachache," she adds. She helps me to lie down, and when he goes for a glass of water, she kneels beside me and says, "Forgive me. Forgive me. I don't know what came over me." Something in my look or my voice or my accusation triggered this response in her—a trauma that she's never dealt with.

She's back to her kind, loving persona. Too late. If she's capable of hitting me over a minor disagreement, what's next?

Coming after the gun incident, it's a reason for concern.

*

A year after Carlos came to live with us in October, I get sick again. The same dizziness and weakness as before, but worse. I'm bedridden, without the energy to get up or do anything for myself. I'm unable to lift my arms, so my mother washes my hair. I'm as feeble as an old woman. Maybe it's leukemia—I have all the symptoms—but tests come back negative.

In desperation, my mother talks to a top doctor who recommends we go to Houston Medical Center. The next day, we fly there. As soon as we arrive, I seem to get better. The mirror no longer reflects an image as pale as a cadaver. My cheeks have a little color in them.

After three days of exams I get a diagnosis. Not what I expected to hear—or feared to hear. Almost a letdown after all the symptoms. "Your exams all came out normal," I'm told. "We couldn't find anything wrong with you physically. Emotional problems may have caused your disorder."

This corroborates what I suspected but tried to deny. I remember years ago reading about Freud and hysteria. How when fully functional people can't cope with emotional situations, they can turn into invalids. They may have all the symptoms of a life-threatening illness while physically there is nothing wrong with them.

What I haven't wanted to recognize is that the abnormal Claudette/Carlos situation has affected me to this extent. For one year we've been pretending to the children, to the world, and to ourselves that what we're doing is right. Covering up the problems with Claudette, the arguments, the fighting, the verbal crossfire between us, and Claudette's weird behavior that's becoming more evident.

My mother is beside herself with relief. "Thank God, Marina. I was so worried about you; not knowing what you had was driving me crazy."

"I'll phone Claudette and Carlos and tell them the good news."

No answer. "It's still early," my mother says. "We'll try again after dinner."

We go out for a meal. When we get back to our hotel room at 9 p.m.— 11 p.m. in Mexico City—I call the house. No answer. I keep dialing until one in the morning, but no one picks up. The children must be asleep, but where is Claudette? Carlos? They know I'm getting the diagnosis today. They should be waiting to hear from me, and instead it seems they both went out. They couldn't care less about me.

I end up crying in my mother's arms. She's the one person who's there for me when I'm sick or in trouble.

What are they up to in my absence? I'm afraid to find out.

Betrayal

Mexico City
1976

The following afternoon as I drive up to the house, Armando comes running out to greet me. "Guess what?" he asks in a voice loaded with excitement. "Last night Claudette had an orgy." He says it with pride as if divulging an important piece of news.

"An orgy? What do you mean?" He's thirteen, and "orgy" might be slang for a party.

"She brought your cousin, Elisa, home. They were in the bedroom, drinking and laughing, and making a lot of noise."

An "aagh!" clogs my throat, and I shake my head like a rattle. Claudette and my sixteen-year-old cousin? That chubby little girl with pimples? I've seen the way Elisa gazes at Claudette with adulation and shrugged it off as a teenage crush.

"What kind of noise?"

"Like when you and Claudette are in there. Laughing a lot, but also crying. Like Claudette's always sobbing over something. I can hear her."

Sobbing? It takes a moment to click. Moaning. The way she responds when we make love.

"And my dad was in the other room with two dance teachers from your school, and they were also laughing." His expression changes to guilty. "Mami, please don't tell them that I told you. I don't want Papi or Claudette getting mad at me."

I reach out to hug him, hoping that what he saw or heard wasn't too disturbing. "Don't worry, you did the right thing. I'm glad you told me." But his words have rocked my body and mind; it's too much to take in at one go. I feel like a house shaken by a nearby explosion that shattered its windows, raised a thick cloud of dust, and left jagged holes in the walls. The house is still standing, but only one retainer wall stops it from falling.

"Please, Mami, I'm sorry to make you unhappy."

"You're not the one who should be sorry," I say.

All those suspicions I brushed off as figments of my imagination fall into place. Even now, one side of my brain tells me it happened because I was too sick to want to face what was going on. The other side asks if the Claudette I care for is a fantasy who exists only in my mind. No amount of love can change her innate nature. It's not only Claudette, but Carlos as well. How little he cares for our children if he's entertaining two of my dance teachers in his room. Where were they all when I called? "Didn't anyone hear the phone ringing?" I ask.

"Yes, but I thought Papi or Claudette answered."

I'd rather go off to some hotel room to mull over the situation, but Armando is waiting for me to go inside. I can't face a bedroom sullied by Claudette and Elisa the night before. Or bear the idea of Claudette in there with my cousin—making love to her the same way she does to me. I can't stand the idea of Carlos, the father of my children, playing sex games with my employees, with the kids in the next room.

A pain spreads across my body—rage coupled with the pain inside me. I can't give in to it. I know what I have to do, for my children's and my own good. Get rid of Claudette and Carlos. Both of them.

Carlos arrives first. He stops and stiffens when he sees me, standing in the middle of the living room. There's no mistaking my anger, it's flaring out of me—in my stance, my expression, and the way my arms are folded. He must realize there's no getting out of this situation.

"What did the doctors in Houston say?" he asks.

If my eyes could stick spikes in him, they would. "I heard about what happened here last night. I will not tolerate such behavior in this house. I want you to leave at once."

He's unperturbed, even nonchalant. "It was nothing, really, Marina, just a few drinks with a couple of your teachers."

"That isn't how Armando saw it. He said it was an orgy."

"What orgy? We were having fun, that's all."

"In your bedroom?"

"Yes. Not here, not in front of the kids. What's wrong with that?"

What's wrong is that he will never admit the truth. Carlos is the master of denial. He'll wiggle his way out of anything.

"What were my teachers doing here?"

"They came back from the school with Claudette, but when Elisa arrived ..." He pauses, as if collecting his thoughts. "... I was left to entertain them. It was innocent, fun." He has the evasive look of someone guilty who's been caught but won't admit to the deed.

I ignore his excuses. "Do you and Claudette care so little for me that you both party in my absence?"

"That's not true," he says. "It all happened as I said." With a wheedling note in his voice, he adds, "You seem better. What did the doctors say?"

"Why ask if last night you didn't bother to answer my phone call?" I say, grinding my heel into the carpet so fiercely that the fabrics give way. "You don't deserve an answer. I don't care what you do when you go out, but not here in our home. Please pack your bags and leave."

"Calm down, Marina. What about the children? Our family?"

"They've seen enough. And we're not a family anymore. It's an amoral situation that I should never have accepted. Just get the hell out of here." He stares at me in disbelief, but he can't face down my determination. No amount of begging or persuasion will change my mind. I may not be sick physically, but he and Claudette have sickened me as much as if I had a grave disorder.

Next I confront Claudette. After five years it has come down to this. I trusted her, but her lies and deceit have eroded that trust. I chose to over-look the obvious, what was going on with Carlos, and even her craziness with the pistol. But she's gone too far seducing my young cousin.

Claudette arrives home from work and, seeing me, flings her arms around me. "You're back. I missed you." She doesn't seem to be aware that I'm rigid and don't hug her back. Drawing away, she asks, "What did the doctors tell you?"

"If you'd answered the phone last night, you'd know."

"You phoned? I didn't hear it ring."

"I guess you were too busy."

Fear and defiance flutter across her face. "Too busy?"

"With Elisa."

"Oh, her. She came by to keep me company since you weren't here. We were playing games."

"What kind of games? From what I heard, you were really going at it. And drinking. How could you? She's a kid."

"I swear nothing happened," she says. I'm not taken in by her faked inno-cence. I know when she's not telling the truth from the pained expression in her eyes and her mouth opening so wide I could shove an apple into it.

"You're a poor liar, Claudette," I say. "I don't believe you for one minute. If it were true, you'd have answered my call from Houston."

Her face droops. "I'm sorry, I forgot. Of course I care about how you are."

"You were too busy seducing my little cousin."

"That's not true, it's not true!" She comes at me, fists flailing, and I grab them and force them down. Still holding them, I say, "It's bad enough that you had sex with another woman in our room, in our bed, but did it have to be a young girl who doesn't know better? That's child abuse."

"She's sixteen, not a child anymore." The words come out before she can stop. Then, realizing what she admitted, she pulls away her hand and places it over her mouth.

"*A la chingada con las dos!*" I scream at her. To hell with both of them. "How could you and Carlos betray me at my most vulnerable moment?" I force back my tears not to show any weakness. "I asked him to leave this house, and I'll be moving out with my kids. Tomorrow, if I can find a place. Without you. You can stay here with the maid."

"But Marina, we don't have to end like this. We've been happy, haven't we? What about Karla? I can't let her suffer for my mistakes."

"She can live with me and my kids, but I'm done with you."

"No," she says, and her face hardens with the stubbornness I've come to know. "I'm her real mother, and she'll remain with me."

"I'm Karla's mother as well."

"No, you're not," she says, her voice like a vicious swipe. "You pretended to be, but you didn't give birth to her."

"I've treated her like my own child, and what have you done for her? Are you able to give her a home?"

She hesitates before she says, "I'll go back to singing."

"You gave it up four years ago."

"It's your fault that I stopped. I loved singing to an audience, but you were too jealous. You made me give it up when I was going somewhere."

I take a deep breath. True, it was her livelihood, but it won't be easy for her to find work after four years. "You can continue teaching at my school. You should earn enough to get by, and I'll ask Carlos to help with Karla's expenses."

In two days, my life has been overturned. First, a reprieve from what I thought was a serious illness, followed by my lover's betrayal and the realization that I've been living a lie for the past five years, to breaking up with both Claudette and Carlos, and the loss of my daughter Karla. No, I won't let that happen; I'll fight for her to the end.

*

The phone rings at two in the morning. I debate whether to pick up. It's a week since I moved, and picking up the pieces is not an easy task.

"Marina, I need to see you, talk to you." Claudette's slurred speech is an immediate indication that she's drunk. Another thing I should have noticed—she's drinking much more than she used to—and it's affecting her actions.

"I have nothing more to say to you," I tell her in a grim voice.

"Please, forgive me, *mi amor.* I love you, and I can't go on without you. Don't leave me like this."

"I can and I have."

"I'll kill myself. Cut my veins." I hear her despair. In her emotional, alcohol-fueled state, she's capable of going through with her threat. I can't take the risk. So I get up and go to see her and try to reason with her, but she's beyond reasoning. She babbles on about how she loves me, promises to be faithful, that the incident with my cousin was an accident brought on by too much alcohol and the girl's adoration. Oh yes, Elisa is far too young, she admits, and at a sensitive, uncertain stage, and she, Claudette, may have unintentionally hurt her, but I have to believe she hadn't meant to. She will leave the poor girl alone if my cousin promises not to keep calling her or trying to see her.

I want to believe her, but I want peace of mind more. My illness and her betrayal have depleted my resources. It took all my strength to move out of my home into this one.

"My decision is final," I tell her. It's five in the morning. "If you want to kill yourself, don't ask me to save you."

*

Two days later, around 10 p.m., I get a phone call from the maid. "*Señora* Marina, please come. We need you here."

"Calm down, and speak slowly. What happened?"

"*Señorita* Claudette and Miss Elisa tried to kill themselves with a knife. There's blood everywhere."

My heart beats so loudly it threatens to stifle my words. "Are they conscious?"

The maid can hardly speak. "Yes, but they are bleeding a lot. I called the police."

"You did what?" The worst thing she can do is to call the police. That means money—bribes—and possibly problems for Claudette, a foreigner.

"Why didn't you call me first? Or an ambulance?"

"They haven't come yet," she says. "I don't know what to do. They are hurt. They might die."

What possessed them to do such a thing? As I dash out to my car, I have visions of Claudette and Elisa, blood gushing from their self-inflicted wounds.

I arrive to find a police car outside the house and two policemen at the door. They haven't gone inside yet. I want to stop them from doing so because once they see blood, they will ask for a formal statement, and that means trouble. "*Señor policía*," I tell them, "they are my cousins inside. They were playing a game and had an accident. The maid got scared and called you, but it appears they are fine. Here's a little something for your trouble." I hand them each a hundred pesos, and they leave.

Claudette and Elisa are huddled on the sofa, glassy-eyed but conscious, bandaged with towels. Trails of blood streak across the floor, carpet, and sofa. I glance into the bathroom, and a rusty blood odor hits me. There are red pools in the tub, on the floor, in the basin, on the walls.

"Are you two out of your minds?" I ask them.

"We were making a pact of love like the Gypsies do," my cousin says, in a thick, unsteady voice. I glance at the empty vodka bottle on the coffee table. "We cut our wrists to join our blood."

"With what?"

She indicates a chopping knife, bloodied and lying on the floor beside her.

"Whose idea was it?" I ask Claudette, who cringes and shakes her head. "Didn't you think of the danger? You might have bled to death."

I pick up the phone and dial my doctor's number, tell him it's an emergency but we need to be discreet, so I'd prefer not to take them to the emergency room, where the story could get out.

"I'll be right over," he says.

I turn to Elisa, poor plain little Elisa who has the misfortune to have fallen for someone like Claudette. "I'm calling your mother to come pick you up. I'm going to tell her to forbid you to see Claudette again."

"I'll die if I can't see her," she wails. She rubs her tears with a bloodied hand, leaving her face splotched with red. "I've loved her for four years— ever since our first kiss."

A quick calculation. When Claudette and I were very much in love, or so I thought. "But you were only twelve! What kind of kiss?"

Elisa glances at Claudette, who glowers back at her.

"A real kiss," Elisa says dreamily. "It was my first."

I don't want to imagine it, but I do. Claudette, my loving Claudette, who kissed me so passionately, kissing this poor little girl, exploring her mouth, her emotions, her body as it came into puberty. My Claudette loving someone else. My bile rises and, like my tears, I force it back. I'll be sick, cry my heart out. Later.

"What more?" I ask in a cold voice. Claudette doesn't move or try to answer.

"She liked to rub my breasts," Elisa says, in a small voice. "She said this would help them grow more."

I turn away from them, from the ghastly scene, and gaze upwards, not wanting them to see the tears of anger that I can't hold in. So Claudette started seducing my cousin four years ago when Elisa was a little girl. What has she done to her since? How can I handle her betrayal of my trust? I'll have to work it out later. For now, I must be strong.

"I believed you loved me," I tell Claudette. "Or was it all a game for you?"

"No," she says. "My feelings for you are real. But I got bored waiting for you to finish work, and when you get home you're tired. You have no time for me."

"But why Elisa? A child."

"I don't see her that way," she says. "She isn't a child to me. I'd never hurt her."

"You didn't hurt me," Elisa says. "You're so sweet and tender."

"Shut up, you two!" I shout at them. Turning to Claudette, I say, "You can't see her again." I derive a weird satisfaction from her stricken expression.

"You're jealous and you can't stop us," Claudette says.

I know I'm jealous, but more than that, I'm appalled at Claudette's amorality. She seems to have no remorse for what she's done.

"It's not up to me," I say. My uncle and aunt are coming for Elisa; I'm certain they'll forbid her from seeing Claudette and will watch their daughter's every move from now on.

"Where's Karla?" I ask, hoping my little girl hasn't been affected.

"Asleep," Claudette says. "The maid put her to bed much earlier."

"I'm taking her home with me. She can't wake up and see all this." I wave at the blood.

"She can go with you tonight," Claudette says, as if giving special permission. "She's my daughter. Not yours."

The doctor arrives and attends to Elisa's wound. Then her very concerned mother comes to collect her. How can I explain to my aunt that the woman who lived with me for the past five years is the one to blame? My aunt doesn't know I moved out of this house and that Elisa wasn't spending the night with me. She had taken Claudette's word in good faith. I tell her we'll talk later at a more appropriate time. How will I explain all this to her?

They leave and so does the doctor after tending to Claudette's wound. He doesn't ask why I don't want to take her to the hospital, though he does recommend that she go see him at his clinic the following day. Taking advantage of Claudette's weakened state, I make her confess what happened. It seems that she, a woman in her late twenties, allowed herself to be persuaded by a sixteen-year-old girl to go along with this preposterous idea of cutting their veins in a love pact.

Since the incident with the gun, I've suspected she may have mental issues. Now listening to her drivel about her confused emotions, I'm certain. She's damaged, and damaged people like her can be dangerous to themselves and others.

I'm ready to face reality. She's ravaged my life, my family, and my health. For too long, I chose to overlook this and put up with her antics. What next? Suppose she seduces one of my students and causes a scandal at the school? Now that I think of it, she already tried. A few months before, a fifteen-year-old student came to me with a story about how Claudette had kissed and caressed her. Claudette denied it and I chose to believe her, and the student dropped out of the school. I can't let this kind of thing happen again. I could lose my business and everything I've built up.

Claudette will have to go, leave Mexico. It's not a decision I make easily, but for the past two weeks, I've deliberated this matter and reached this conclusion. If she's so destructive, what will happen over the long run? My children, especially, need to be separated and protected from her before she infects them with her craziness.

My uncle, Elisa's father, is furious about what happened to his daughter. He blames me and "my friend," as he calls Claudette. He'd like to contact the authorities about her, and maybe he will, though my aunt begs him to restrain himself and be discreet. "We don't want Elisa to get a bad name."

I go by the house early to speak to Claudette. She has just got up, and her face is bloated, her eyes red and watery. She reeks of alcohol. The maid brings her the strong coffee I asked for. Claudette sees it with disgust.

"You'd better drink it," I say, "because what I'm going to tell you is serious. Very serious. My aunt called this morning to inform me that Elisa's father knows what you did to his daughter and wants to put you in jail or have you deported."

"In jail? Deported? What for?"

"For one, child molesting. And physical damage, inciting his daughter to cut her veins."

"They can't accuse me of that. They have no proof, and at sixteen, in Mexico, she's not considered a child. As for cutting her veins, no one can prove anything. You sent the police away."

"I know." I was a collaborator of sorts. "But this is Mexico and you're a foreigner, which means they will take my uncle's word against yours. If you don't leave this country, you'll go to jail."

"But I don't want to leave. You'll make it all right, won't you, Marina?"

"Claudette, I can't help you. He went to report you this morning, and they could come with a deportation notice at any moment. You have no choice. Why don't you go to Madrid, where your mother and sister live?"

Her eyes search the room as if trying to find an escape. "I can't believe this is happening," she says.

"I'm sorry, Claudette, but you brought this on yourself."

"Do you want me to go?" she asks.

"Yes, for your own good." And mine. "I'll get your ticket for Spain."

"What about Karla? She's Mexican, but I can't leave her here."

"She can remain with us. We're the only family she knows."

Her lips tighten and she glares at me. "No, if I go, she goes."

"You'll have to take care of her." Until now, she's left her daughter's upbringing to me.

"I play with her a lot," Claudette says, with stubborn conviction, "and with your children. Karla knows I'm her real mother. You're too busy to spend time with them."

It's true. I'm busy working at my dance school while a less-occupied Claudette can play with the children. I thought it was a good thing—until now.

"It's your decision," I say sadly. "Just look after her the way we would if she stayed." What kind of life will Karla have with a mother like Claudette? For the three years she's been alive, I've arranged everything for her, or hired someone to do so, when all Claudette ever did was play games with her. Little Karla. My heart crumbles at the thought of losing her, but I have no claim to her.

"She'll need a passport, and her father's consent to travel outside the country," I say. "I have a friend who's going to Madrid in two weeks and can take her there."

Claudette doesn't know that I planned this. My uncle never went to the authorities. No one did. I took a page out of my mother's book when she got Manón deported. Forcing Claudette to leave is the only way my family can live a normal life. As long as she's in Mexico, it will be impossible to completely detach from her.

I still love her too much to let her go without a final farewell. We spend her last night in Mexico in a friend's home, a neutral place where we can be alone. She drinks a lot of wine and I don't try to stop her; this departure is too traumatic. Whatever she's done to me, she will remain in my heart for a long time.

We take off our clothes and lie naked in the bathtub. As I caress her beautiful breasts, I wonder if I will do so again. I study her face, wanting to keep the memory of her features in my mind—her dark eyes with their long lashes, her full lips, and her long, silky hair. I engineered this parting, yet I regret it with all my body and soul.

We go to bed and after all that wine, she falls asleep at once—as if she doesn't have a care in the world. I can't sleep, gazing at her, overcome by the knowledge this may be the last time I see her.

Letting her go is like cutting off my arm to stop her infecting the rest of my body.

*

We hold a good-bye party for three-year-old Karla. As usual, she insists on wearing a dress; it makes her feel like a little lady. "No pants for me," she says. "They're ugly and for boys like my brothers." She chooses to wear her favorite dress, a dark navy blue with red piping around the sleeves and skirt, and a red belt, combined with red socks and navy blue shoes. She stares at herself in the mirror and tells her image, "Oki, you're so pretty."

We take photos. Only I know they may be all we have to remember her by: her twinkling dark brown eyes, short black hair, upturned nose, and her mother's full lips.

Armando begs me, "Please, don't send her away. We already lost Claudette. Make Karla stay. She's our sister and she should grow up with us."

"I have to," I tell him. "Her mother wants her daughter. But Karla is part of our family, and I promise she'll come back to us." A promise that isn't mine to keep.

"I'm going to miss my little sister a lot," Gabriela says.

"We will all miss her," I reply.

"When will we see her again?"

"Maybe next summer she'll come to visit us," I say, knowing that won't happen. By then their pain will have dulled and Karla will be just another memory.

Late-Life Recognition of Sexual Orientation

MEXICO CITY
1976

Valeria, the doctor whom my mother recommended, gives me a long, thoughtful look. Her expression is one I've seen too often not to recognize. She's about to break some bad news to me. My mind races through a series of dire possibilities.

"I think you should know that your mother and I are lovers," she says.

My throat fills with incredulous laughter. My shoulders shake, and though I cover my mouth with a hand, I can't hide my chuckles. "It's not possible," I say, in a voice laced with amusement. Not my mother. I'd be the first to know.

Valeria's steady gaze is unnerving. Her clear brown eyes are serious. Why would this no-nonsense doctor with her short, mannish haircut and face devoid of makeup tell me such a thing? The laughter drains out of me, and I struggle to catch my breath as if, after running for miles, I'd come to a sudden halt. More like knocked to the ground and kicked in the stomach. I gulp in air. My words come out in a rough, throaty voice. "How long?"

"Six months," Valeria answers in her brusque manner.

I study her—she's the complete opposite of my mother's fastidious friends. "She never told me." Never hinted. I never suspected.

"She's afraid to tell you," Valeria says. "She thinks you'll be angry with her."

Anger isn't the word for what I'm feeling. Fury mounts inside me, touching off the harsh sting of resentment and all its accumulated venom. Is this why she fought against my sexual preference, blocked it, punished me, demolished me, and refused to let me be myself? When my mother interfered in my life years ago, was it because of her own repressed sexual urges?

I'd run out of Valeria's office if my limbs weren't unresponsive. I'm silent, trying to overcome the battle waging inside me. Valeria clears her throat a couple of times before I respond.

"Yes, I'm angry, not because she's with you, but because of what she did to stop me from being me. I'm glad she's found someone—she's been alone for too long."

"I'm not the first woman in her life," Valeria says, in her matter-of-fact manner.

So the mother I knew was an illusion, one she fostered through the years, deluding me, her own daughter, as well as the world. But I'll have to fight this battle later. Not here. Not in front of Valeria, whom I hardly know, and don't think I want to know.

"How long has she been having relations with other women?"

"You'll have to ask her," she says with a slight smile.

*

As soon as I get home, I call my mother. "Valeria outed you to me," I tell her.

A slight pause before she says, "I suppose we should discuss it."

"We should have had this conversation before. How could you conceal this from me? Why?" My voice breaks.

"You're upset, Marina."

"What do you expect? It sounds like you made your decision years ago. I want to know why you kept it from me and pretended to be someone you weren't."

"I'll explain it to you when I see you, but not over the phone." She hangs up.

How careful she has been to conceal her own preference, even from her own daughter. I would have understood, better than anyone else, and knowing the truth might have provided a means to staunch old wounds and start anew. I reflect on my surprise when she accepted my relationship with Claudette. At the time I considered it a kind of victory that she'd relented and acknowledged my choice of a partner, though she wasn't happy about my divorcing Carlos. Still, her big fear has been that people would find out and turn their backs on me and brand me as a degenerate for being with another woman.

It takes a while to realize how she had interred herself in the prison of her secret life. Social norms are such that she's been petrified for anyone to find out the truth about her, and she got used to hiding her true identity. My preference for women must have set off red flags in her head. She has dreaded society finding out about me, as all her efforts to maintain her secret would have been for nothing. We'd both be stigmatized as outcasts. Not for the first time I dwell on how unjust are the laws of society and the Church that condemn people for loving others of their own gender. Surely, if we're all made by the same God, we're entitled to our own identity.

When I see her several days later, I've worked through my anger. All I want is the truth. My mother, who's always brimming with confidence, seems to be taking this forced revelation in her stride, as if opening up to me somehow places us on the same level of confidantes.

"When did you start taking women lovers?" I ask as soon as she's seated. "You fought so hard against me loving a woman. I don't understand."

"You were so passionate about your affairs that I wanted to know why," she says, sounding flippant.

"Yes, right." Is this how she wants to handle the conversation? "Then, it was pure curiosity on your part. When did you find out that you liked being with a woman?"

Her expression turns serious. "Remember Kristen?"

It never occurred to me to question that friendship, unusual though it seemed. Even before I met Kristen, she sounded special but because she came from Vienna, Austria. When I met her, she turned out to be intellectual and cosmopolitan, and not at all like my mother's other friends.

She invited us to tea, English style, in the afternoon with sandwiches and little cream cakes that she bought at the Viennese bakery. An attractive woman in her late fifties, with her silver hair pulled back into a sleek coil, and steel blue eyes, she carried herself with the air of an aristocrat. Her gray suit had a timeless classic cut, subtly elegant, the same as the décor of her apartment. She spoke Spanish with a lilting German accent, and our conversation covered a variety of subjects from great cities to politics, psychology, and literature.

"How did you come to live in Mexico City?" I asked.

"I came with my partner ten years ago," she said. "Her family lived here."

She? I couldn't help glancing at my mother with surprise that Kristen should be so open about her sexual preference. Perhaps being European made it more acceptable. "Unfortunately, soon after we arrived here," she said, "she got sick and ended up in a coma."

"How sad," I said. "Will she ever come out of it?"

She spread gracious hands. "Who knows?"

When we left, I told my mother, "What an unusual friend you have."

"Then you liked her?"

"Of course. She's charming, educated, and well-read. What's not to like?"

The very next day, my mother called me, her voice strained, anguished. "Kristen had a stroke. She's in the hospital."

"That's terrible, Mami. But a stroke doesn't have to be fatal."

"In her case, the doctors say it's touch and go."

Kristen never recovered consciousness before she died three days later. The loss of her new friend changed my mother, for a while, from being cheerful and outgoing; she became morose, unhappy. She acted as if her sister had died. As I had no idea of the nature of their friendship I couldn't understand how deeply Kristen's death affected her. If there were signs, I didn't see them.

My mother had lost her lover and I never knew. While I can empathize, I can't help seeing the irony of her going down the very path that she fought so viciously to stop me from following.

"So Kristen came later. Were you trying to cover up your sexuality before? Was that why you fought so hard against my being with women?"

She raises her hands and swipes the air with them. "No, no, no. I was afraid for you, and that you'd be hurt because it wasn't acceptable behavior. You were very young."

"It wasn't because of your own sexual preference?"

"I swear to you, Marina, I couldn't let you ruin your reputation. I hoped you would find a decent husband and live a normal life."

"What about all the years you were alone, a widow?"

"After your father died," she says, and her voice hardens, "I never wanted to be with another man." I know the expressions in her eyes as well as mine. Better. They darken and her pupils almost disappear into their black depths. Haunted and troubled, they are the eyes of someone guarding a secret that she's on the verge of giving up.

"Because you loved him so much?"

She glances sideways, and up and down, and at her hands, with one folded tightly over the other as if protecting it, and then with resolve, says, "I never wanted to tell you or anyone this, but it's important for you to understand me." She pauses as if deciding to go on. "My wedding night was my first time with a man. I was scared, with only a vague idea of what would happen. When your father entered me, I didn't bleed, so he accused me of not being a *señorita* and of tricking him into marriage."

I listen in horror as she tells me how my beloved father, in a fit of *machismo*, ignored her protests and pleas of innocence. First thing the next morning, he sent for his mother, Nona, to accompany my mother to be examined by a doctor.

Her voice falters and she has to stop and take a deep breath before she can describe her young girl's humiliation at having to undergo a vaginal examination, spread her legs for a man to examine her private parts when she had never let anyone see them. The doctor assured Nona that she had been a virgin; there were signs of a torn hymen, but sometimes, as in her case, there was little or no bleeding. Nona, furious at her son for doubting his new wife's purity, told him: "You must beg for her forgiveness on your knees. Pray that she pardons you for humiliating her on her wedding night." But something other than her virginity was lost, and the scar of his accusation remained, a heavy shadow that would affect her sexuality from then on.

Her voice is stronger, but her eyes have the film of painful memories. "I hated having relations with him, and he wanted to almost every night. When he entered me, all I could do was submit to him and offer up the act as a sacrifice to the Virgin."

From the sounds of it, intercourse with my father must have been more like sexual abuse, especially since it resulted in a new baby every year of her marriage.

"After he died I never wanted another man to touch me," she goes on, and her voice is strong again. "I had some offers, and if I'd remarried, it might have been easier for all of us, but I went to work instead. With a woman I found true happiness."

"With Iris?" Your old friend."

She blinks. Normally I wouldn't notice, but there's a slight hesitation before she says, "With Kristen. I wouldn't have changed that, though it only lasted a few months."

"What about Valeria?"

"I'm happy with her as well." It strikes me she may be annoyed that Valeria was the one to out her to me. My mother likes to be in charge. I wonder how long they will remain a couple.

Later I confront my memory of my father, a man I've hero-worshipped since I was six, who did only good in life and left an inspiring legacy. Yet there were dark shades to him. I see my king as a man with flaws. I see my mother as another woman who has had to bury her true identity and live a lie. We share common ground. Her outing has brought us closer and made me see her other side, the one where I can finally relate to her.

*

"Marina, I have wonderful news," my mother tells me on the phone. I hear excitement in her voice. "I'm going to be sent to the Pemex office in Paris."

"That's great, Mami." Paris is the most desirable post for any employee. "How did you get this promotion?"

"I asked for a transfer, and as you know, I've been studying French for a while, so they took that into account."

I know how my mother manipulates and manages to get what she wants, which in this case, is Paris. I imagine she must have pulled some strings. Even so, for a woman her age, it's quite an accomplishment.

"Do you have any friends there?"

"Matilde, who's a diplomat, moved there last year, and her friend, Mireya. I'm going to rent an apartment in the same building where they live. I won't be lonely."

My mother spends a year in Paris. Her romance with Mireya starts there and continues when they both return to Mexico City and share a house. As far as the world and society are concerned, my mother is living with a female friend, a perfectly acceptable situation. I don't know if there are suspicions about them, but if so, they are never voiced. Two middle-aged women living together is the ideal cover-up in a hypocritical society.

PART III
THE
STRAIGHT
LIFE
Mexico City and
San Diego, California

BARRIER EIGHTEEN
A Powerful Man

MEXICO CITY
1977-79

Running my dance school takes up most of my time. I work long hours and get home late, too exhausted to think about a social life. Occasionally I go out for coffee with a student who tells me about the fascinating people she meets at gatherings she goes to. When she asks me to go to a party with her, I'm reluctant. It's Monday and I have a busy week ahead.

"Come on, Marina, there's such a thing as too much work. You need to get out more. I promise you'll have an interesting evening." She's twenty-eight and single and doesn't have the responsibilities that I have.

"I'm sorry but not tonight," I say. I've never been a party person, and she wouldn't understand that my idea of entertainment is reading or going to the movies.

"Why do you always say no to my invitations?" I detect a hint of hurt in her voice, which is why I say, "Okay, I'll go tonight."

The party is in a mansion in Pedregal de San Angel, one of the more upscale areas of Mexico City, where homes are built on lava rock. High walls surround a huge garden where lava has been used for sculptural effect with fountains, rock gardens, and pathways.

When we arrive, others are getting out of cars, and about fifteen people are already there. A romantic trio is playing.

I sense someone staring at me. A tall man, probably in his mid-forties, with striking blue eyes that follow me as I move around. His light brown hair streaked with gray is cut fashionably long, and he wears a tailored suit the shade of sleet. He crosses the room with the obvious intent of joining me. His walk, as he approaches, is strong and decisive.

"Señora," he says, holding out his hand, "will you dance with me?"

We dance slowly to José José singing "*La Barca.*"

"My name is Juan Alberto," he says and asks for mine.

He's a good dancer, but dancing is not what is on our minds. He's the kind of person who makes me feel like we've known each other before and are just getting together again. We fall into easy conversation about current events. How the American president, Jimmy Carter, committed a major gaffe when he told a bunch of high-placed politicians, including the Mexican president, that he was afflicted with Moctezuma's Revenge.

"He must have meant it as a joke," I say.

"If so, it was in poor taste, and people were appalled," he says.

After a couple of dances we head for the buffet table. Most of the items are appealing, except for the shelled oysters, which look disgusting. "They're like gobs of snot," I say and he laughs. "I like your laugh," I tell him. It's warm and spontaneous.

People keep coming by, saying hello to him, and giving us meaningful glances. So we find a nook overlooking the garden where we can sit and talk about travel and books, authors and politics. We explore each other's impressions of our favorite European city, Paris. Imagine being there with this charismatic man.

Stop. I only met him a couple of hours ago.

He consults his watch. "I'm sorry that I have to leave."

"I'm sorry as well," I say.

"Marina, I enjoyed talking to you. May I see you again, take you out for lunch? Here's my card. Please call me."

I stare at him, taken aback. Giving me his card seems presumptuous, not what I expected from a man like him. Why give it to me rather than ask for my number?

He takes off. Disappointment clouds the evening. Maybe I should have given him my card as well.

When we introduced ourselves, I didn't catch his last name. It isn't until the next day that I glance at his card and recognize him. He's an important politician, a cabinet member. I'm not surprised he gave me his card. That's what politicians do, give out their cards to everyone. He must be full of himself—high-placed politicians usually are. And most are married.

Forget about him.

"You made a conquest last night," my friend says, a teasing note in her voice. "Are you going to see him again?"

"I don't think so. Isn't he married?"

"He's separated. I heard he and his wife are getting a divorce. So, will you see him?"

I shrug. "I doubt it. He didn't ask for my number, gave me his card instead, and I don't call men. They call me."

"He's a powerful man. People call him."

"I told you, not me."

"Don't be so old-fashioned. Did he ask you out?"

"He mentioned lunch."

"Then call him. What's the harm in that?"

He's charming, interesting, powerful, and we got on great and I was attracted to him. But why should I have to call him? It takes two weeks before I give in and dial his number.

He comes to the phone at once. "I've been waiting to hear from you," he says. "How about lunch tomorrow at the Champs Elysée?"

I hoped for this, but when he asks, a shiver runs through me. "Yes," I say, elated at his swift reaction but a bit fearful about what I'm getting into.

It's six months since Claudette left, and this is the first time someone else has such a strong effect on me. Am I ready to take a chance with him? He's very attractive and charming, but I must be careful. A handsome politician can have his pick of women, and he probably has several in tow. I don't want to be one more. I'll make it clear that all we're doing is having lunch. Nothing else.

After two hours of invigorating conversation, we both have to get back to work. I'm relieved that he didn't try to prolong it or turn it into something else, but also vaguely disappointed.

Later that afternoon, he calls me. Would I like to go to Acapulco with him for the weekend? I thank him for his invitation. Tell him, "First, I want to get to know you better." Grit my teeth, waiting to see how he'll take my refusal. Will it be the end of our—friendship?

He says, "Forgive me, maybe it was too fast, but I want to spend more time with you."

I mention that I left my dark glasses in the restaurant, and he sends me a case with six pairs of designer glasses in it. The accompanying note says, "A token of my thanks for a wonderful conversation."

At forty-eight Juan Alberto is well up the ladder to holding one of the most important positions in the country. His appearance, charismatic presence, and assured manner differentiate him from other politicians. He knows what he wants, and what he wants is me.

He sends a large basket of flowers; it's so big that I place it on the floor. The following week, another one arrives, and so on every week. He's making a big effort to conquer me. I know I'm a challenge to him; I hold my own in conversation and don't give in easily.

After two months we fly in a private jet to Las Hadas, a seaside resort in southern Mexico. He reserved the presidential suite, which has a king-size bed, a marble bath, and a Jacuzzi. The suite faces the ocean, with a view of waves lapping the sands at low tide. Everything here, from the summer robes and slippers, to the shared bed and bathroom, implies soon-to-be intimacy.

My stomach quivers the same way as when I was young and inexperienced. All through dinner in the hotel's French restaurant, I keep thinking, *What if it doesn't work out?*

We return to the room, flushed with wine and good food, after a meal filled with shared glances and desire. We go outside onto the terrace, and the full moon rises in the sky above the dark, quiet sea.

Juan Alberto kisses my lips, fiercely, as if trying to imprint his lips on mine. "I can't wait any longer," he says and leads me to the bed.

His hands and mouth travel across my body, his lips moving across my breasts and down my belly, exploring, teasing, until ripples of feeling seize hold of me, and I draw him to me with an animal need. He straddles me, at first slowly and then with rising excitement, intent on giving me satisfaction before he takes his own. I come wildly, desperately, urging him on so that we both can come together, and he thrusts inside me and again as our need for each other heightens, intensifies, and escalates into a climax so strong that I can't stop coming after he withdraws. I must have more of him, and he responds.

He's a potent lover, and we make love over and over—even after we're both exhausted we can't get enough. I doze off and wake to see him watching me, and this time we make the slow, easy love of two people who have come to know each other's bodies. We fall asleep in each other's arms.

Early in the morning, while he's slumbering, I go outside and watch the waves as they break in large, frothy white surf. He's demanding, all about physical satisfaction, wanting to give the same enjoyment as he gets. And I responded, more intensely than I ever have to a man. Juan Alberto is so different from Carlos, who wanted only his own satisfaction. I marvel at the ease with which I switched from a woman to a man. When I was with Claudette it wasn't easy to respond to Carlos's lovemaking. But Juan Alberto knows how to awaken my sexual side and take me to a point of excitement where all I want is for him to go on and the feeling to magnify and crescendo inside me like an explosion that has to out. He's awakened a dormant physicality in me, and I want more.

"He's a man worth falling in love with," I tell myself.

An unbidden image springs into my mind. Claudette. One last time—for this must be the last—tears fall. I reflect on how her gentle touch aroused the hidden corners of my mind as much as my body.

Good-bye, I whisper, and picture her spirit carried away by the waves, by the tides, to other horizons.

I turn from memories of her, back to Juan Alberto and a day when we don't leave the room.

After three months he asks me to dinner in the elegant Restaurante del Lago in Chapultepec Park. On this mellow evening, the picture window opens to a view of the lake, where colored waters dance to the rhythm of soft music.

We're meeting his friend Ernesto and his girlfriend. I know Ernesto a little, and I don't like the way he regards me, his eyes moving down, resting on my breasts, mentally stripping me. A chubby, dark-skinned little man with a bristling mustache, he's a fawning underdog to his top politician boss, showing off his importance in his *jefe's* shadow. Once I saw Juan Alberto lose it when Ernesto didn't do something he ordered him to do. Sudden rage spewed out and he verbally crushed his underling. I don't know how Ernesto wormed his way back into Juan Alberto's good graces.

Ernesto arrives with a Nordic belle, Ingrid, from Sweden. In her late twenties she has long, straight blond hair and big blue eyes. She's wearing a tight black skirt and embroidered vest that show off her large breasts and curvaceous body. To me, she resembles a beauty queen more than the newspaper journalist she claims to be.

We drink a bottle of Dom Perignon while we dip into appetizers. I'm enjoying the conversation when a hand glides up my left leg. I rear back in surprise and reach down to remove it, but there's nothing there. I glance at Ingrid, sitting next to me. She's chatting in fluent Spanish about her impressions of Mexico. Maybe it was accidental.

Five minutes later, the hand travels up my thigh. Ingrid's arm is positioned under the table while she keeps up her conversation without a pause.

Why is she coming on to me? All I did was admire her appearance. I'm with Juan Alberto, and I can't imagine why she'd think I'd respond to her. The way she's rubbing my thigh leaves little doubt what she's after. Grabbing her hand, firmly, I remove it. She keeps on talking to the two men as if nothing happened.

Ernesto is watching me intently, with a glint in his eye. It reminds me of Carlos's tiger expression when he'd watch Claudette. I turn to Juan Alberto and see tense anticipation on his face.

They know what Ingrid is doing.

The air around us is thick with male sweat and lust and expectation. The truth hits me. They put her up to it. Maybe hired her. They planned a foursome.

I catch her barely visible headshake. Ernesto chews his lower lip. Juan Alberto smiles and gives a slight nod.

The champagne I drank rises to my throat, and a bitter taste invades my mouth. Dizzy with disgust, I say, "Juan Alberto, I'm not well. Can we leave?"

"What's wrong, *mi amor?*"

As if he doesn't know. "Please, take me home."

As we leave the restaurant, I say, "I don't like this kind of game."

"Game? I don't understand." His pretended bafflement makes me nauseous.

"You know that Ingrid came onto me. I saw your face—and Ernesto's—drooling at the idea of what? Seeing me naked and screwing with a prostitute. How could you?"

He has a furtive, caught-little-boy expression. "I'm sorry, *mi amor*, if it offended you, but you're so liberal and I wanted to see how you'd react."

I ball up my fingers and dig my nails into the palms of my hands. "How could you think I'd degrade myself that way? Is it your perverse fantasy? Or did that little pimp set it up?"

He puts his arm around me. "*Cálmate, mi amor*," he says. "Nothing happened. We didn't mean to upset you."

"Upset me? Shut up and take me home."

We get into the car and he uses his smooth politician's voice to persuade me that he didn't mean to hurt me. He's glad I didn't rise to the bait, and no harm was done. "Now I know your feelings for me are real."

I'm silent, staring straight ahead, not acknowledging anything he says. My anger has turned to cold resentment that we should end this way.

"I don't ever want to see you again," I say as I climb out of the car. "That was a disgusting thing to do to me."

Afterwards, I go over this incident, studying it from every angle. Why did he expect me to be attracted to another woman rather than another man? Suppose Ernesto insinuated himself back into Juan Alberto's good graces after unearthing personal information about me, and about Claudette?

Juan Alberto sends me flowers. Every day. More flowers with more "Forgive me" notes. He leaves messages at home, at my school. A couple of times he gets through to me on the phone and apologizes, begs, promises it will never happen again. He's constant in his persistence and won't give up until I agree to see him. He gives me his word that he will never disrespect me again. Ernesto is no longer in his employment.

Our affair becomes more intense. As if the fear of losing me has increased his passion. We see each other several times a week and go away on weekend trips to resorts like Cancun, Zihuatanejo, and Cabo San Lucas.

Our trip to South America is unforgettable, in both the best and worst senses of the word.

Machu Picchu, the first capital of the Inca Empire in Peru, is an exhilarating, magical adventure. Juan Alberto rents a private helicopter so that we can see the ruins from above. This way we can appreciate their layout from a viewpoint not visible for people coming up by train. The mystery is how the stones for the construction were carried up to the top of the mountain. What possessed a nation to build a wondrous city on a mountain ridge in such an inaccessible place? Religion? Security? To escape their enemies? Guard themselves against interlopers and the outside world? The Spaniards never found or reached Machu Picchu. Why was it abandoned?

At 7,970 feet above sea level, we have trouble breathing. The guides give us a coca tea to help steady us. I'm overcome with exhilaration; it's like being at the top of the world, somewhere both mysterious and sacred, where I can sense the spirits of the last Incas all around us. We find a place and make love with desperate, searching passion.

From there, we go on to Argentina to Buenos Aires, a gracious, European-style city. One evening we're watching a show in a nightclub, and Juan Alberto tells me, "After this I've made plans for us to go to a place where we can watch some women."

"What do you mean by 'watch some women'?"

"You know what I mean. I'm sure you'll like it."

"What? Have you forgotten why I broke up with you before?"

"No, Marina, this is different. What's the matter with you?"

"You low-down bastard. You promised to respect me. I should have known you politicians break your promises all the time." This is the biggest insult I can tell him.

He's trained himself to stay calm on the surface while, underneath, his anger mounts up. His skin darkens and his eyes turn to slate.

I'm too angry to care if he gets riled up. "You think you're a big shot and can get away with anything. But not with me."

"Shut up," he says. "*Cállate.*"

I aim my eyes like deadly beams at him, and say, "You're an animal, a scumbag *politico* crawling in filth."

He slaps me. The shock hits me first, but I don't move. Rather, I raise my head and sit up as straight as I can. I taste rust inside my mouth. I wait a minute, or two minutes. "Let's get out of here," I say.

We leave and start walking toward the hotel. He's walking along as if nothing happened after insulting me, humiliating me, and hitting me in a public place. "Coward," I yell at him. "You're not a man. Asshole. Woman beater."

"You're hysterical," he says and slaps me again.

I march on, my head zinging from the impact. Silent. As soon as we get to the hotel, I go straight to the main desk and ask the clerk to accompany me to my room. "I need your help because this man is hitting me." I show him my red cheek, and he agrees to stay with me while I pack my suitcase.

Juan Alberto offers a barrage of apologies. "Please, don't go. I don't know what came over me, but you got so angry, so insulting in front of other people."

"I don't give a damn. I won't allow anyone to hit me."

"You were out of control." He's blaming me?

"I don't want to see you anymore. I mean it," I tell him.

"I swear, Marina, I'll never hit you again."

I laugh, a dry, bitter sound. "The damage is done."

"Please, don't leave. Don't leave."

I stare at him in disbelief, this man whom I've been with for two years. Who is he? The lover who took me to Machu Picchu? The man who's always trying to please me? The politician who gets his own way? Or simply a *macho* who wants to be in control.

While I'm waiting for a taxi, he thrusts a wad of hundred dollar bills at me. "I don't want your money," I say, flinging them back at him.

I leave him, arm held out to me as if begging for something he just forfeited.

I go to another hotel, where I discover that all I have is fifty dollars in cash. Fortunately, I also possess an American Express card, which I use to pay my bill and purchase my ticket back to Mexico City the next day.

On the plane, I reconsider our relationship. I thought I could trust him, but my wonderful Juan Alberto has a creepy side that he keeps undercover most of the time. When it emerges, as it did yesterday, it's too unexpected and damaging.

Our story should end in Buenos Aires but for one of those unforeseen occurrences that intervene in our lives. At thirty-eight, I find out I'm two months pregnant. It probably happened when we went to Machu Picchu, where, exalted by that experience, the lack of oxygen, and the coca tea, we made love and failed to take precautions.

There's no question about having the child, but I call Juan Alberto. He agrees with my decision not to have it.

He tells me that after I left the hotel, he searched for me for three days all over Buenos Aires. "I thought I'd lost you forever," he says.

"You did." I say, but I open up to him about Claudette and how much she meant to me. "She meant the world to me," I tell him, speaking from my heart. "You have no idea how much you offended me when you twisted my love for her out of context, thinking it meant I'd be willing to have sex with another woman."

Juan Alberto's face displays a gamut of emotions from surprise to bemusement to compassion when he hears about her betrayal. Three days later he comes back and tells me how much my story moved him, and how it took him to a new level of understanding me. "I truly admire your honesty, and now I respect you more than ever."

*

Juan Alberto decides to run for governor of his state. As a public figure, he needs to be accompanied by a wife. He's been living on his own in an apartment in Mexico City while his wife kept the family home in a provincial city. They are still married; she never agreed to a divorce, and he didn't want to have a scandal. Now they will have to get back together to keep up appearances. "For political expediency," he says. "As soon as the campaign is over, we'll split and I'll find a way to make it definite."

With her playing the role of the wife of the soon-to-be-governor, she becomes possessive toward him. We have to be careful not to be seen in public, which adds to the strain he's under.

It isn't long before his wife finds out about us. She asks one of Juan Alberto's friends to "tell my husband's whore that if she doesn't leave him, I will shoot her in the legs so that she can't ever dance again."

I get nasty calls at my school, insulting me and threatening my well-being. A blackened duck leg is left in my mailbox—a sign someone is working witchcraft on me. I find offensive messages under my door and scrawled on my car window. A man waits in a car parked outside my house when I get home until after I go to bed. I can see the glow of his cigarette. I receive late night phone calls from friends telling me an unknown person called and I'm in danger.

Juan Alberto takes me to Japan. It's an opportunity to be with each other without stress. The trip is part business, as he's traveling with fourteen Mexican delegates interested in new communications methods. One morning he's at the Japanese phone company with all the Mexicans and their Japanese counterparts when they decide to try the new system of speakerphones. He volunteers to call his home in Mexico.

His wife answers the phone. He says hello and she shouts at him, "You bastard! I know you're with that woman."

The new system is working perfectly and everyone can hear her. "I wanted to go to Japan," she screams, "but you told me it was only men. I'm taking a plane tomorrow. Get rid of that whore before I arrive."

The Japanese may not understand, but the other Mexicans do. This incident will probably leak out and may affect Juan Alberto's chances of being elected governor.

That night he drinks too much. He'll give in to his wife's demands and get a divorce. Then he'll marry me. "*Mi amor*, I want to be with you forever," he says, emotional from the drink and her shadow hanging over us. "I don't want to lose you. I'll do anything to keep you."

"It's better if I leave tomorrow," I say. "We'll talk it over in Mexico City once things have calmed down."

On the flight back I ponder the situation. A divorce at this point would be a black mark in his political career. His wife will not let him go easily. She wants to be the governor's wife. She's out for revenge, and I'll be living in fear. What about my children, who are teenagers, and their safety? She'll have no compunction creating havoc with our lives. I can't take that risk.

After three mainly good years, this ugliness has turned our relationship into something sordid, to be hidden, and not open as before. Anyway, he's not going to give up his political future for me.

How about moving to the US? A cousin suggested San Diego and opening a dance school in Tijuana.

I'll make a new start in another country.

A Different Reality

San Diego, California
1979

My first date after joining the Singles Club is Mark. In his early forties he's divorced and a business owner. I like his clean-cut appearance, his all-American appeal, and his obvious sincerity when he talks. What I don't like is the way he's dressed, San Diego style—T-shirt, jeans, sneakers—as if we were going to the beach rather than to a nice restaurant.

I can't help comparing him with Juan Alberto. We ended a year ago. Yet how can I forget that suave, elegant man, perfectly attired in his tailored suits, or the way he treated me like a princess?

"How about we meet at the restaurant?" Mark says rather than "I'll come by for you." It's the American way. Women here expect to meet a man on the same terms, especially on a first date, with the underlying idea that if one doesn't like the other, they can depart. I miss Latino courtesy where men compliment and try to give women a good time.

We talk about our different backgrounds, mine in Mexico City and his in Denver. Mark likes talking about himself and his business, and for me to listen. Anything I say, he follows with a story of his own; they are amusing at first but boring after a while. I don't know the people he talks about, and I don't know him well. When I mention Mexico City, he's dismissive. "I've been to Baja," he says, as if that's representative of the country. "That's like saying you've been to San Diego, so you know what the US is like," I say, which seems to annoy him and he changes the subject to baseball. "I'll take you to a Padres game, and once you catch on, Mari," he says, using his new nickname for me, "you're gonna become a fan."

I try to find mutual ground. Movies? He likes action and horror films. Books? Doesn't have time to read. Europe? Never been. New York? Not for him. Wine? Can't beat California *vino*. History: World War II, Vietnam. "Don't care for all that old stuff." The world? "Hawaii's a blast." Business? He blabs about his latest deal.

115

The waiter brings the bill and hands it to Mark. He glances at it and says, "Thirty-six dollars plus tip. Let's say your share is eighteen. I'll take care of the tip."

I hand him a twenty-dollar bill. "Here's my share, including the tip," I say.

Is this the norm here, for each to pay for his or her own dinner? Or is he a cheapskate? To me, it's embarrassing but probably because I'm not used to splitting the bill on a date after years of the royal treatment with Juan Alberto. Even Carlos, who was frugal, never expected me to pay for anything.

Different cultural mores.

If this is the American way, I'll have to get used to it. But not with Mark. I won't see him again.

*

There's no reason to feel depressed and lonely, but I'm homesick for Mexico City. I've heard this happens—something like buyer's remorse.

I miss my lifestyle there. At thirty-nine, moving to another country and culture can be daunting, especially when the cities are complete opposites. Mexico City, with 16 million inhabitants, is situated in a valley ringed by mountains. With more than a thousand years of history, it overflows with movement and is colorful, modern, and cosmopolitan. San Diego, with eight hundred thousand inhabitants, has been predominantly a Navy town with a laid-back beach atmosphere, though the influx of young people and immigrants has turned it into one of the country's fastest growing cities. Before, on trips here, I came as a tourist and saw only the sights, the sea, the clear blue sky, the shops with a myriad of choices, the clean streets, and the modernity. No crumbling buildings or shacks; order and respect for the law; people living in harmony; and no poor or beggars like in Mexico.

I didn't foresee that living in San Diego would be another reality. This is an early-bird city, where most places are closed and dark by 11 p.m. At that time of night, Mexico City is throbbing with activity. I miss its liveliness and the theater, ballet, concerts, and good restaurants. There, I had a large circle of friends. I was somebody. Here, I'm anonymous, with just my work to keep me busy, and my kids for company.

On the positive side, our three-bedroom house has a large yard and a pool. My children, already fluent in English, have settled in private schools and made friends. The difference hits me again when I come home to find a bunch of kids around the pool. Only one of the boys says, "Hi." The rest ignore me or look away. Mexican kids, whether or not they knew me, always greeted me with a handshake or a kiss.

I lease a studio in Tijuana to set up my dance school there. My cousin, who belongs to a country club, sends invitations to all her friends for the opening. The mayor's wife cuts the ribbon, and the event comes out in the newspapers and on local television. Almost at once, I have students enrolling.

Every day I cross the border to teach classes and run my school in Tijuana, but I don't derive the same personal satisfaction from it as the one in Mexico City. It has only one classroom versus the other's three and 150 students versus 600.

Despite my absence, my school in Mexico City is doing well. When I go back to check on it, I'm more like a visitor. I've lost the personal attachment that motivated me to make it the best dance school in the city.

What I need is a new challenge.

The US is the home of audacious, inventive, and progressive people with phenomenal ideas. Why not take advantage of the opportunities this country offers and become part of this culture? I pick up a brochure from a community college and leaf through it until the page offering Psychology 101. It reminds me how, as a teenager, I avidly read Freud and Jung's theories on human behavior.

This might be the *something meaningful* I'm searching for.

*

Five years later, I stand in my cap and gown waiting to receive my BA from San Diego State University.

I'm one of hundreds of graduates, yet I feel like I stand out, though not because I'm older than most. I'm overflowing with pride and so elated that, like a superhuman, I could rise to the skies. This must show in the way I walk, the way I hold myself, like an athlete winning gold. Or a Nobel prize-winner in the ranks of glory.

My mind returns to my first day at community college. Going back to school after twenty years. The exhilaration of my first A. Changing my focus. My decision to go for a BA and transfer to San Diego State University. Finding the combination of studies and work too demanding. Coming home one evening at nine, exhausted. Hungry, but nothing in the fridge to grab and eat. Five messages on my answering machine—all dance school and business related, all requiring action from me. Sixty pages of homework to read and analyze by the next day.

My mind crashed inwards as the opposing forces of my studies and my work battled each other. I flung my books on the floor and screamed, "To hell with all this! I've had it."

I was trying to do too much and carrying too heavy a load. My dance school across the border was a full-time job. I didn't have the energy to do homework. I'd be up all night studying everything the professor left us to read.

I took several deep breaths, the way dancers learn to do, and it helped calm me—physically. But the battle went on in my head. I never expected my studies to be so time-consuming. Perhaps going for a BA was too ambitious, and I should settle for the courses I enjoyed. Why kill myself studying? What was I trying to prove? I was a successful businesswoman. I didn't need another career except for personal fulfillment. But—that was the point. My dance school was running smoothly, while my studies, and my aim to get a degree in psychology, had become my focus. I couldn't not finish what I'd started.

I'd make it in this country. Become somebody again. If I were willing to make stiff personal sacrifices for the next few years.

Yes. No. Maybe.

Don't be wishy-washy. Either yes or no. If yes, make a commitment.

All I had to do was accept there were obstacles to overcome in order to achieve it.

What the hell? I'd been overcoming obstacles all my life.

*

I clutch my diploma, hugging it to me as if I can't bear to part with it, then extend my arms and study it, engraving the words on it in my mind, kiss it, and hold it up, displaying it for photographs, show it to my kids and my boyfriend, Rod, and my mother and to anyone who's taking photographs on my graduation day. I could dance across this quadrant except that it's too crowded with people.

"What do you plan to do next?" my mother asks.

Without hesitation, I say, "Get my MA in Counseling Psychology. Close my school and concentrate on my new career."

Leading a "Straight" Life

SAN DIEGO
1981-1996

In the five years since Claudette, I've been heterosexual. These days I even question if being a lesbian was a phase I went through, a way to get back at my mother, a reaction to Carlos's infidelity and his notion that female lovers didn't count. Or I had to find affection when he gave me none. What appealed to me about Claudette? Her beauty, or her neediness and my desire to protect her? My attraction to women seems to have ended with her departure, and since then I've dated only men. The fact I can be straight after a long, meaningful relationship with a woman disproves, for me, the theory that people are either straight or gay with no in-between.

During my third year of studying psychology at San Diego State, a couple gives my class a lecture about male and female homosexuality. I study the woman: in her thirties, pretty, slender, with short, curly hair. The way she stands, moves, her mannerisms, her voice are all mannish. She's not at all like Claudette, yet I'm reminded of her—and not in a good way.

It might be what the woman is saying, how a homosexual couple is much like a heterosexual one, with the same lifestyle and facing the same every-day problems and delights. But the way they describe the sex act between women, a clinical and dispassionate description, makes it sound dirty. Nothing like what I remember with Claudette—her tenderness, her touch.

I shiver, hunching in my chair the way I used to when I was young and felt dirty. I glance around to see if my boyfriend, also in the class, or anyone else has noticed. My self-disgust is coming at me like a wave I can't outrun. I gulp back nausea and try to concentrate on the lecture and listen to the pretty, young lesbian speak about things I never want to think about again.

I make it through the lecture, stumble outside, and suck in fresh air. Why such a strong reaction? Because those memories are so painful they are better forgotten, or because I'm ashamed? Is this what happens when you stop being gay and become straight?

My boyfriend comes up and puts his arm around me. "At least we know we're not gay," he says jokingly. "Let's go prove it."

Slowly, I nod. He's right.

*

When I first see Joe in a restaurant in Tijuana I know I have to meet him.

As he walks past our table, I tell my friend Lisa, in Spanish so that Rod won't understand, "What a gorgeous man!"

He sits at the table facing us, and I study him openly. Exotic, dark hair, olive skin, and a hook nose that might indicate Middle Eastern descent. But he's American— the way he walks and his air of entitlement. He catches me looking at him and smiles. Full-lipped, sensuous. I smile back, and he raises his glass to me.

I have to meet him. How? Rod's here with me, and Lisa. We're celebrating my birthday.

Be resourceful.

In an aside, I tell the waiter, "Ask the man sitting at that table to give me his phone number." I hear my mother's voice. *Marina, you're shameless, trying to pick up a stranger with your boyfriend seated next to you.*

The waiter comes back and says, "The gentleman would like to invite the three of you for a drink at the bar."

"That man over there wants to invite us for a drink," I say to Rod, pretending it's because he's interested in Lisa, who's alone.

"Sure," Rod says, "if he's paying." Typical. Rod is several years younger, and after three months living in my home, he'll take any freebie coming his way. I'm thinking about asking him to move out.

Up close I see that Joe has steely gray eyes with flecks of green in them. "Where are you from?" I ask, and his chin dimples with a smile. "My father's Italian and my mother's from Lebanon," he says. An educator, he works for the County of San Diego. Before long, we're talking about beliefs, and equality, and prejudices.

After an hour of conversation, I nudge my friend and tell her *sotto voce* to ask Joe for his phone number. I want to see him again.

"I already did," she says, "but he wouldn't give it to me."

He told us where he works, so I know where to find him. Several days later, I go to his office to look for him. He's out of town but will return the following day. I leave a message with my name and phone number.

He calls me as soon as he gets back, and we see each other the same evening. The start of a seven-year affair. Joe has an MA in Education, and we connect on an intellectual level. But it's the strong sexual attraction between us that keeps us together.

He introduces me to American politics. Except for foreign policy, I haven't been interested. I don't understand the difference between conservatives and liberals. An ardent Republican, he continually talks about Reagan, his policies, and why he admires him. How Reagan reduced government spending and advocated reducing tax rates to spur economic growth. Later

I learn that Reagan's spending cuts affected social programs such as mental health, letting loose thousands of mentally sick people to fend for themselves, thus creating a whole generation of homeless.

Joe criticizes liberals for their social programs and people on welfare for living off the government and not trying to find work. He goes on for hours until I hardly listen, and when I do, I'm not certain if I agree with him. In the end, I stop sharing his views and beliefs. I've learned from his speeches and harangues not what he wanted me to but, rather, that liberal values and ideas fit more with my core beliefs.

Despite Joe's radical stance about politics, personally he avoids conflict. I find this out early on when he tells me, "Italian women serve their men."

"I'm not Italian," I say. "Don't expect me to serve you."

He stands and, without a word, leaves the room, and the house.

For two weeks I don't hear from him. I assume he's finished with me over what seems an inconsequential matter. Then he turns up and without a word of explanation behaves as if nothing happened. He repeats this pattern whenever we have a disagreement—absent for a couple of weeks, and refusing to talk about the issue.

It's impossible to be close to someone like Joe, who will disappear rather than face a conflict. This inhibits us from becoming truly close, and I know it's the end when he disappears for three weeks. On this occasion, when he returns I refuse to let him into my life again. Within a few weeks I'm going out with a fellow therapist who is the complete opposite of Joe.

*

Matt also works in the child abuse agency where I'm gaining experience while I get my MA. I first notice his compassion and empathy for our patients. He tries to help them and be there to provide support and advice. We go out for coffee, and he listens and responds to what I say. I open up to him about my past with women. He seems to understand. I'm attracted to him and to his deep commitment to combating social injustice.

I know he's attracted to me, but his background is very different. He grew up poor in Georgia in the early fifties when blacks were still discriminated against, and he experienced this at an early age. He tells me hard-to-believe true stories in a voice thick from the effort to restrain his emotions. "I was seven when I started questioning God's love for us. I saw white men drag a black man out of his house and hang him up, and the only reason was they didn't like his black skin. I asked myself, where is God?"

He says this with sadness and frustration. This big, six-foot-four ex-Marine is tough on his exterior and yet so tender inside. We spend the night together. He's soft as a teddy bear. Much as I like him, I'd prefer not to let this develop into more than a friendship. He has other plans. It doesn't take long for me to give in.

"How can you consider marrying a black man?" My mother's voice shakes with indignation. "The very idea makes me sick."

"That's insulting." I derive satisfaction from her frustration. She can't stop me from going through with this. "He's one of the nicest men I've met. Your prejudice is blinding you."

"True," she admits, "but I can't help it. All our family is white, and we've never married anyone dark-skinned, let alone black. Why can't you just live with him?"

"I want to marry him." Again I ask myself, *why?* I enjoy his company, and the sex is good, but I don't want to be the woman who's living with a black guy. He's from the South, from Georgia, where people are more traditional. "When a man respects a woman, he marries her," he says. Maybe I'm lonely now that my children have grown up and left home.

"Make an effort," I tell my mother. "Come to the wedding. Get to know Matt. You'll like him."

"Marina, I don't know why you're doing this."

"He wants to get married. And so do I. I'm at an age when I need the company of a man."

"How will you bring a black man to family functions? What will they think?"

"I don't care what they think. If you're embarrassed, it's because you let their opinions influence you."

Her tone changes. "Remember, Marina, I was alone and needed their moral support. And it isn't just the family that should concern you. What about society? You'll have big problems in the US. People here are very racist."

"Matt and I talked about this. We'll take it as it comes. Are you coming to the wedding?"

"I'll try," she says. "I don't know about your brothers."

Her reaction, and my family's, is not surprising. I expected it, and I'm prepared to face their dismay. Why can't they see past Matt's skin color and appreciate what a good person he is?

*

I marry Matt, defiantly scandalizing my family, though my mother and three of my brothers come to the wedding. The one in Mazatlán lends us his house in La Jolla for the ceremony but can't attend; he says he has a previous engagement. An Army chaplain who was with Matt in Vietnam officiates at the ceremony.

I wear a tight, pale pink suit that shows off my figure, perhaps too much. My mother gazes at it in horror and says, "*Ay, mi hija.* Is that an appropriate wedding outfit?"

"It goes with my hairdo," I say, glancing at my reflection and my new golden blond, silver-streaked short cut. I'm going on fifty, but people tell me I look forty.

My mother's been crying since she arrived, and her tears flow during the ceremony. She walks out as Matt and I exchange vows. In her mind, what I'm doing is an embarrassment to her. She still feels responsible for my actions.

We go on our honeymoon, a Caribbean cruise for a week. It's 1990, twenty-six years after the Civil Rights Act*, but people stare at us with curious and occasionally annoyed expressions. A mixed-race couple is still an anomaly, and I imagine they're wondering what a white woman is doing with a black man. Or vice versa.

One afternoon on the sun deck, four black women eye us, me in particular, so fiercely that I shudder. One of them raises her hand and shakes her fist at me. They keep staring at me for a long time, their steady eyes filled with venom, all four making what seems to be a concerted effort to send their dagger vibes to intimidate and threaten me.

I nudge Matt. "Those women there, what's going on with them? They look like they want to murder me."

"Black women often get angry when they see a couple like us," he says. "In the black culture there's a belief that once a man is educated, he wants to find a white woman."

"Is that true?"

"It happens," he says. "Like us. You're going to find blacks discriminate more than whites against mixed couples, especially when it's a black man with a white woman."

In the years we're married we encounter discrimination in one form or another. Black people, especially women, confront me and demand to know why I stole one of their men. I learn that discrimination is very much alive, in a more muted form, a defanged beast lurking in the shadows of hatred and ignorance.

*

From Matt I learn about cultural aspects that I hadn't previously considered. "Maybe the minds of whites don't even register the suffering they cause others," he says. "The white race is superior in two aspects: they're greedier and more aggressive. And that explains their power."

He also says, "No white can bear what blacks endured." It makes me think of the Mexicans and how the cultural imprint of the Spaniards left them oppressed and suffering. Why, in places like the South, can an ignorant, illiterate puny white man consider himself superior to an educated man like Matt?

His bitterness toward white people doesn't extend to me; I'm Mexican. When I think of my mother and her fixation on our fair complexions, I have to laugh. The irony is that both she and Matt are prejudiced against the other race.

Over the years I discover that Matt, a Vietnam vet, has many emotional scars. His experiences haunt him—ones like killing a kid who had a bomb and was threatening to blow up Matt's buddies. The blood and death. "You don't know what it's like to have to pick up body parts," he says.

Matt's political views are completely opposite to Joe's. Joe liked Reagan because of his social policy, and Matt dislikes him for the same reason. "All the social problems he caused," he says. The dominance of white privilege, evident in the difference in public schools in rich neighborhoods versus poor ones. He points out how education has deteriorated, resulting in more teenage crime and vagrancy; how the working poor and the blacks were the most affected, as were the mentally ill and Vietnam vets. I learn more about the political parties but from a Democrat's point of view. Matt supports the feminist movement, and we watch the Anita Hill* versus Clarence Thomas* debate. It's infuriating to see how she's mistreated, and proof of Clarence Thomas's harassment of female personnel is largely ignored. What happened to female liberation?

*

During our five-year marriage, Gabriela has marital problems. She separates from her husband, and she brings her five-year-old son and seven-month baby girl to live with us. I buy a house so we can have space for them, and finance it myself. Matt doesn't have much money and isn't good at handling finances, so I'm in charge.

He's been a university psychology professor for years. One of the subjects he teaches is institutional racism. He's a big help to me when I start teaching multicultural counseling at Chapman University. So it's hard to understand why a smart, educated man like Matt isn't successful until I realize his background is a hindrance. His ambition is to go into politics, but his color is a drawback.

To be successful in business, men have to be driven, materialistic, and often ruthless, none of which is in Matt's nature. He's a man with a mission that he's unable to fulfill.

*

What is wrong with our marriage?

Everyone warned me that our different backgrounds and cultural differences might become an issue. I was brought up as an upper-class white girl in Mexico. He has a lot of bottled-up resentment about what he endured as a black man in the South and seeing his ambitions dashed because of his color. Vietnam was a hellhole from which he returned, the same as many other veterans, damaged and angrier than before. I try to understand and support him, but his emotional baggage is too heavy.

I'm health conscious and exercise every day. I find it hard to tolerate Matt's bad habits. He's a big man when we marry, but because he eats piled plates of fried food, he puts on another thirty pounds. He smokes two packs a day. He starts coming home late and going straight to bed. He has no sex drive.

When I ask him if he's all right, he's vague or devious. Finally, I demand to know why he's going to bed so early.

"I didn't want to worry you," he says. "I'm diabetic."

"You should have told me before so I can help you." I'm sure he's hidden his condition because he doesn't want to change his diet or give up smoking, and he knows I'd hassle him about it.

After that he keeps saying he's worn out or his blood sugar is low. He uses this excuse too often. Something else is wrong. He's apathetic, tired, has lost interest in subjects he was passionate about, or has sudden bursts of fury about some law or problem affecting blacks.

"Matt," I say, "it's hard for me to be with someone who's so self-destructive and doesn't seem to care."

He glares at me. "Self-destructive?"

"Yes, you're overweight, you smoke too much, and you're too tired to do anything. You've become a couch potato, and you spend all your time watching TV."

"That's unfair, Marina. I work very hard at a stressful job. When I get home, I want to relax, take it easy. Surely you can understand that."

I also work at a stressful job, but on the contrary, I'm full of energy. All he wants to do is lie in bed or on the couch. Where's the brilliant man I married? We used to do things, go out with the kids or friends. Now I go out on my own, like a single woman. I might as well not be married.

His depression, I assume, is related to his inner torment, so when my maid says, "I found this in the trash can. Matt left it there," I'm shocked. An empty vodka bottle inside a brown paper bag.

I never suspected Matt might be a closet alcoholic. He's got drunk at parties, but he doesn't drink at home—or where I can see him. He's good at covering it up. I'm relieved to know the reason for his behavior, but can I—do I—want to help him? I'm a therapist, but I don't deal with alcoholism.

When he comes home, I show him the bottle.

"It was only this one occasion," he says. His eyes focus on a point behind me.

"I know you've been drinking on your own. What do you do, buy a bottle after work?"

"No, I swear," he dips his head, "it's not that. I was upset. Something happened, and I needed to relax before coming home. I didn't want to burden you with my problems."

As a psychotherapist, I've learned to tell when people are lying. At first, Matt insists it was only that once. "People don't suddenly buy a bottle and drink it all in secret," I say, and I don't back off. His shoulders sag and he sits in his chair, thoughtful, as if considering what he has to say. "Matt, our marriage is at stake," I tell him. "I need to know what I'm dealing with."

"Yes," he says. "I admit I have a drinking problem. I drink every day, in my car, on the way home, or stop somewhere and knock back a few. I've been trying to keep it out of the house until it got to the point where I couldn't anymore."

"Where do you keep your bottle?"

He shows me how he's stashed away two bottles, both at the back of cabinet shelves high up where they are not visible and are out of my reach.

He promises he'll try to stop drinking. No good. Within a week he's lolling on the bed with that absent expression that tells me he's had a few. I don't know where he's keeping his bottles, not in the same places as before, but he definitely has access to a bottle somewhere in the house. Later, I find a bottle tucked inside the toilet basin.

Our marriage is going downhill, and I'm not prepared to deal with his alcoholism.

A colleague calls. "Would you be interested in going with me to a women's conference in Beijing? In three months? We'll leave from LA and tour China three weeks before it starts."

"I might be." I want to visit China.

"Hillary Clinton* will be a speaker," she adds.

I need no further persuasion. "Then I'm going. You know how much I admire her."

Little do I suspect I will meet the woman who will change my life and turn it upside-down.

PART IV
JULIA

A Heterosexual Woman

SAN DIEGO
1996-2006

On this warm, muggy August afternoon I close the door on the woman who told me, "I want to be with you always and to grow old with each other."

Our good-bye embrace is like a child's farewell to a parent after a divorce. *I can't let you go. Please stay with me.* "I don't want to lose you, because I love you," she says, and I feel her warm breath on my cheek, and the shudder running through her becomes my own.

Gently, I pull away. "We have to do this. For our own good. We already mourned the end of us."

She grasps my arm. "This can't be the end." Her face reflects her inner struggle. Both accepting and rejecting an unalterable decision.

"I have to go." My voice is firm. I know how to handle good-byes and conceal my pain. If I show a sign of weakness, we'll both break down and give in again.

I force myself to turn and walk resolutely to my car before glancing back. Our eyes lock, wordlessly communicating our love. I get into the car and drive away.

Once on the road, I open my window for the air to come in. Sunlight has crept through the overcast LA sky; it covers the green verge at the side of the road and glitters off oncoming cars.

As I settle into the two-hour drive ahead, the deep sadness of our good-bye hits me. The way we looked at each other in mute desolation. Her face filled with the bleakness of loss.

On our last days, a kind of desperation seized us. A frenzy to capture and hold onto all the moments we would never share. Two doomed lovers consuming each other before the dark curtain of separation came down between them. We'd lie in each other's arms and watch the water play in the fountain outside our bedroom. She'd run her hand across my face as if memorizing my features. "I'll never find anyone as pretty as you," she said.

The memory so overwhelms me that I slow down and search for an exit. I can still go back. On the point of turning around I reconsider. Another new start isn't the answer. On previous occasions, after a separation and reconciliation, we'd be aflame with the joy of a new start. Only to return to old patterns of damaging behavior to each other.

After ten years I have to leave her. If not, our bond will turn into an emotional monster that will destroy us both. To survive we have to remake our lives, separately and on our own. It means saying good-bye to our dream house in Pasadena. Five years ago, when we first entered it, we knew it would be ours. "Are you experiencing what I am?" Julia asked. "This house has the wisdom of a house that's witnessed many lives and happenings."

It's old, by LA standards, built in the 1920s. The patio is cobbled with paving stone, and it has a Mexican tiled fountain. A row of organ cacti surrounds the courtyard, where plants sprawled in pots and vines clamber up tree trunks. The garden is shaded by old wisteria and orange and lemon trees. Hummingbirds hover over red flowers.

As I drive toward San Diego, tears blur my vision. I rub them off with my fingers, but they keep falling, these watery messengers of grief for what we had and for what we will never have. I swipe them away, grab a tissue to soak them up, and make them vanish like my memories. Later, I can give in to them, let them run freely and reflect on the sadness of our end. Right now, I must concentrate on my driving, and the road ahead. Make sure the moving truck containing my belongings is behind me.

For five minutes I turn my attention to the road and what lies ahead— then memories catch up and overtake me.

*

My mind goes back fifteen years to a warm August afternoon at the Los Angeles airport. Julia is one of our group of forty-nine women and three men on our way to China to the 1995 International Conference on Women. Forty thousand women, and some men, from around the world are expected to attend.

Both of our husbands take us to the airport. We say good-bye to them and join our group. We're all thrilled to be going on this trip and to the conference, but Julia's exuberance outranks everyone else's. She bounces around, welcoming her fellow travelers, introducing herself, and distributing buttons to the people in our tour group.

"Are you in charge here?" someone asks her.

"No, just giving these out. To show our solidarity with women around the globe." Her smile is warm and welcoming.

She comes over to where I'm seated and asks, "How are *you* doing? Aren't you excited to be going to this conference?" She greets me like a friend she hasn't seen in a while, and the thought darts through my mind that I might have met her somewhere. My eyes flit to her badge with her name on it. Julia P. When I agree this will be a unique event, she goes on. "It's a great opportunity to push our agenda for female empowerment."

From what she says I get the impression Julia is another ardent feminist—probably every woman at the conference is a feminist of sorts, but she's gung ho and ready to battle for women's rights. She doesn't seem to care about her appearance. No makeup, hair pulled back in a ponytail, her eyes almost hidden behind glasses, and in sloppy, casual clothing.

"Where are you from?" she asks.

"Mexico City."

"The first women's conference was held there in 1975. Did you go?"

"No, but I had friends who did, and they told me about it." I had other things on my mind. My young children. Carlos. Claudette. My dance school. How my life has changed in the twenty years since then.

"It was before my time." She must be in her early forties. "Here, take one. I'm giving these out." A button with "Fourth World Conference on Women, Beijing 1995" on one side and a picture of Eleanor Roosevelt on the other. "She's my role model," she says. "And Gloria Steinem.*" She shows me another button with her famous quote: "The truth will set you free. But first it will piss you off."

*

China is unlike any country I've seen, and for the Chinese, I must be unlike any other tourist they have seen. Old and young people, teens and children follow us around, pointing at me and my Hispanic companion. Some come up to us two and ask to have their photos taken with us. They trail us everywhere to the point of frustration or, as my companion points out, "Now we know what it's like to be celebrities."

The different customs, values, and beliefs are evident wherever we go, but the marketplace is where they clash most with mine. Huge dead rats, furry pelts gleaming, hang on hooks, displayed alongside dogs and cats in cages. The seller gestures at the rodents, then touches his fingers to his lips, makes kissing sounds, and pats his stomach.

I turn my head and retch.

"Rats taste like chicken," someone says.

*

The Fourth World Conference on Women in 1995 gives women from many countries the opportunity to share their stories. Each country has its tent where, inside, they can discuss their strategies to advance women's rights in their countries. Beliefs vary from traditional to progressive to polar opposites.

Islamic women show their pride in their religion and their role as wives, relating to their men by being obedient and submissive. Women from Argentina have a message: "Violence is not just one blow" ("*La violencia no solo es un golpe*"), and how this comes in different forms such as verbal and psychological violence. African Muslims want to put a stop to female genital mutilation. Europeans have taken up causes concerning women's protection and prevention of abuse.

The high point of my trip is Hillary Clinton's speech, one of the reasons, if not the main reason, why I came. I admire her competence and self-discipline and for her work, along with Marian Edelman*, with women and children.

I get up at 4 a.m. and ride a local bus for two hours to the city of Huairou, where Hillary is scheduled to speak. An experience that, despite being half a world away and culturally different, reminds me of a trip in a bus in rural Mexico. Shoddy vehicles, disorganization, hair-raising moments, roads in need of repair, passengers carrying animals, caged chickens, work tools, battered suitcases, and boxes of belongings. I arrive to find a crowd of early birds waiting in the heavy rain. Still, I obtain a seat in the fifth row.

Hillary's speech conveys her passion for a cause she's been fighting for since her university years. She ends with the words: "Human rights are women's rights, and women's rights are human rights, once and for all." She utters them with such fervor that there's a huge murmur of assent, a cumulative drawing in of breath that crescendos into an outbreak of applause such as I'm unlikely to experience again.

*

Four of us Latina therapists and a Chicana university professor form a group. We're louder and more expressive than other ethnic groups, which draws attention to us.

"Can I join you?" Julia asks. "You guys sound more interesting than those other boring people. They're too serious."

We all hesitate. Eyes signal to other eyes. Unease flickers across faces. Our group has bonded because we're all Hispanic. She's a fair-haired American from the Midwest. But how can we turn away someone like Julia with her eager, open smile?

"Of course," I say.

She plops into a seat. "I'm so glad I found you guys. I've been stuck with a bunch of academics."

By the end of the evening she wins us over. Intellectually, she can challenge the best of minds among us, but it's her laughter that does it. She has a way of flinging back her head and roaring with laughter so contagious we can't help laughing with her.

"You're like us," I say, "loud and lively."

"I never knew Latinas could be so much fun," she says.

At the end of the evening we're in someone's room, drinking wine, and getting raunchy about the physical differences in ethnic groups. How Asian women's breasts tend to be small while African women's are more spectacular.

"Hey, we Latinas aren't far behind. *No nos quedamos atras.*" The Chicana professor lifts her shirt to show off hers. "Here's the proof." We all clap.

Julia stares at her as if making a comparison, then pulls off her shirt. Mimicking a model's sneer, she raises her head and arches her back, showing off her own breasts. "American white woman," she announces.

The room erupts in laughter.

"You're all so funny," she says. "I've never been around Latinas."

"*Guera,* you've missed a lot," I say.

"I've lived in LA for years, but I had another impression of Latinos—I haven't met people like you guys. You're all outstanding women."

"You're like one of us," I tell her. I find her delightful, with a winning personality.

"For a gal from the Midwest, that's some compliment," she says, "specially coming from one of you."

Next morning, I see her in the hotel hall, but she hurries past without saying hello. Later, our paths cross again and I stop her. "Did we sleep with each other last night?" I ask.

"What?" a frown appears on her forehead, and she gives me an incredulous glare.

I chuckle. "That's a popular saying in Spanish when somebody doesn't say hello to you."

"When did I cut you?"

"Earlier. You were in a hurry and didn't stop."

"Oh, I'm so sorry." Visibly embarrassed, she gushes, "I was late for a meeting, and I didn't see you. I do apologize for being rude. It was never my intention. Please, Marina, forgive me. I hate for you to be annoyed." She clasps her hands like a penitent, begging for forgiveness.

She's turning a small oversight into an incident threatening our friendship. "Don't worry about it. I was teasing you."

"Oh." Relief covers her face, then concern. "So you're not annoyed at me?"

"Of course not."

Julia takes everything seriously.

*

On the flight back I'm seated next to a friend and colleague who was part of our group at the conference. But when Julia comes over, she ignores my companion and directs her words to me. "Marina, I'm going to miss you and all the fun we had."

"I'll miss you too, Julia." Her laughter. Her witty conversation. Her crackling sense of humor. And her extreme feminist attitude.

"Let's keep in touch. How about meeting for lunch when I go to San Diego?"

"Sounds like a great idea." She's become a good friend and I'd hate to lose her.

*

Three months later she calls me. She's coming to San Diego to see her niece. Can we have lunch on Friday? We agree to meet at Anthony's Restaurant, overlooking San Diego Bay.

At first, I don't recognize the woman in a turquoise blue outfit as she walks toward me. The way she carries herself, head held high with her shoulder-length golden hair flowing behind—like a celebrity in the spotlight.

Then I see her big smile—brimming with enthusiasm—and I know it's Julia.

"Marina, it's so good to see you!" She embraces me tightly, jiggling us from side to side. "I'm so excited. I don't want to let go of you."

I don't know what words I use to greet her. Nothing I say can rival hers to me.

She moves away but holds onto my arm, studying me. "You look great. Red suits you." She hands me a box of candy and a card. "I usually don't do these things, but you're special to me."

Special? Why?

"That blue you're wearing goes with your eyes," I tell her. They're a sparkling azure blue, the same blue as a late-afternoon sky in summer. I hadn't noticed them in China, maybe because she didn't make them up. Now, I see they are wide and so expressive that when we talk they range from desolate over the plight of women in the third world to fervent when discussing self-defense techniques.

She tells me about her work as a writer and a columnist on women's issues, and how she came to LA from the Midwest hoping to become an actress. "I got off to a promising start, had my own TV show. I thought I had it made." She fingers her wine glass, rubbing the stem, surveying the contents. "Then the producers didn't renew my contract and they started turning me down for roles. You hit forty and you've had it in the TV business." Resentment creeps into her voice. She lifts her eyes—darkened like pools at dusk. "Only a few female actors overcome the age factor, while men go right on into their sixties romancing younger women. Where are women's rights in that?"

Our eyes lock and hold for long seconds. A surge of excitement ripples through my body. We both turn away at the same time. I reach for my wine glass and she for hers.

"Cheers," we both say.

"Tell me about yourself, Marina," she says.

I pull my mind back from where it's reaching out to her, beyond this table, into an area where I fear to tread. Tell her about my dancing schools in Mexico, my practice here as a therapist, about Matt and our marriage.

"Your life has been so different from mine," she says.

I dally with the idea of telling her about my affairs with women. Hold on. Why did that occur to me? It's a part of my past that I'd rather not share. Why with her?

Because there's an obvious connection between us.

My breath comes out in a jagged gasp. I'm attracted to her in a way that I haven't been to another woman in twenty years.

When we say good-bye, we both mention we'll have to see each other again.

I felt the energy between us and recognized it for what it was. Better discard it as a passing notion, a harking back to my youthful inclinations. Nothing to do with the person I am today. And she's married. Showed me pictures of her husband and her dogs. Forget about it. Let it go.

*

The invitation is more like a flyer. Impersonal. Julia's throwing a party in her Los Angeles home to celebrate the one-year anniversary of our trip to China. I'm one of forty people invited.

I might go, yet I don't know if I want to.

A couple of days later, she calls to ask if I'm coming.

"I'll try, but it's a long drive for one evening. I'd be going on my own. I broke up with Matt."

"Then why don't you come and spend a week with me?" she says.

"I don't know," I say. It's too sudden, too off the cuff. We haven't seen each other since our lunch eight months before. If she hadn't called and jolted my memory, I might have passed on her invitation.

"I'm also on my own now," she adds. "My husband left me seven months ago. He took off right in the middle of couple's therapy. I was really depressed. Now, I'm over him and getting on with my life."

An invisible hand grips my stomach. "I can't spend a week, but I can stay the night, and the next day."

My body tingles at the thought of seeing her again. For only one night? On second thought, I'd like to see more of her. I get excited remembering the physical attraction between us when we met. I want to go forward—if she feels the same about me. This is the moment to act, while she's alone and has a week to spare.

I call her back and ask her to go with me to Puerto Vallarta, where I have a time-share.

"Oh yes, I'd love to go." Her voice overflows with enthusiasm. She sounds like a little girl who's been given a special gift. "I adore Mexico. Give me the dates, and I'll get my ticket right away."

*

"You're seeing someone," my mother says.

"How do you know?" I ask.

"I'm your mother, I know." I can't hide anything from her, not even now when I'm older and independent.

I have no idea that Julia, who's not a lesbian, has been attracted to me since China but held off since we were both married. Before the party she asks her lesbian friends how to go about seducing me. "I met this beautiful woman, but I'm not sure how to approach her."

"Get her drunk," they tell her.

Good advice, except that I don't drink much more than a glass of wine.

The night of the party, a flirtatious expression dances across her face as she greets me. From her first slow kiss on my cheek and whispered, "I

134

missed you," her intentions are obvious. She's dressed like a femme fatale in a dress with a butt-length skirt and so low-cut that when she leans over, her breasts almost fall out. While I'm talking to people about the women's conference and its repercussions, she keeps sidling up and giving me quick kisses, openly coming on to me. This makes it easy for me to ask, "Will you visit me later?"

"Yes," she says, in a breathless voice, "as soon as all my guests leave."

Around midnight she enters the guest room and, without a word, slips into my arms. We kiss on the mouth. A long, lingering kiss that leaves no doubt where we're headed.

We stop and I lean back against the pillows. My body is whirring with sensation; it's been so long since that last evening with Claudette. Her memory still fills me with pain.

Julia reaches out to me.

"I think we should go slow and get to know each other first," I tell her. "I haven't been with a woman in twenty years."

She moves away and lets out a sigh. "I'm glad you told me. I don't have experience in this area."

"Then, let's agree to wait," I say. "I'll see you tomorrow. Good night, sweetheart."

"Good night, honey. Sleep well."

We spend the next day talking about our lives and our loves. Getting to know each other. We kiss and make out. "Wait," I keep telling her, when she gets eager to take it to another level. "It's too soon."

I return to my home, warm with the feeling that my life is starting again. This happiness seems alien to me, as if, emotionally, I've been dead for years. I haven't wanted to recognize what a dry and empty existence I've been leading.

Our week in Puerto Vallarta becomes our honeymoon. I want to kiss every part of Julia, to own her if only for now. I run my hands through her hair, separating strands, feeling the texture with my fingers, kissing its smooth surface. My lips brush her face and graze on her cheek, her brow, and her throat. I trace along her skin with nibbling kisses, and her body writhes, coiling and uncoiling, responding to my touch. Her breasts grow taut as my tongue plays with her nipples, teasing them into hardness. Her breath is rushed, panting, and she moans. I want to learn every curve and inlet of her body, and play in her soft places, and make her shudder with delight and let out those little moans and mews of enjoyment, and yearn for me as I do for her.

I pull her against me, and her body cleaves to mine so closely that I feel the pounding of her heart. Our body heat is one, entwined as we are with each other, pressed together at the hip. We kiss, and my fingers make their way to the mound between her legs. I stroke her wetness, slowly, until I find her object of desire, and she comes in one long, sobbing gasp. I continue to excite her until her sobs subside and she can come no more. Spent, she lies against me for a few minutes.

135

With a gentle move to my side she caresses and kisses my face and lips and then slowly travels along my body, going on for many minutes, heightening my arousal, taking me to the edge of exquisite pleasure. She lowers her head between my legs, and my excitement deepens and sharpens and magnifies to such an intense pitch that I come with a scream of joy. I want to love Julia until we disappear into the next world. To always sense the tenderness of her body after being together. Every touch and scent and sigh of those nights together draws us closer. Exhausted with happiness, we fall asleep pressed in a knot of arms and legs.

BARRIER TWENTY-TWO
The Complexities of Loving Another Woman

Baja Malibu, Mexico
1997-2000

For the first time I can love another woman openly without fear of censure or ostracism. I can share Julia with everyone, with my children. I don't have to hide my happiness or my feelings from them as before.

I have some misgivings about Armando, who has become a fundamentalist minister in a church that preaches homosexuality is a sin. "Mom, I don't approve of your lifestyle, but my love for you won't change," he says when I tell him.

"Will you meet her? Give her a chance?"

He gives me a reassuring hug. "I'll treat her the same way as any friend of yours."

Jaime is free and easygoing, a pilot like his father. He sends me a letter from South Korea. He's surprised at my choice of partner but doesn't have a problem.

With Gabriela, it's different. She's still living with me, and we're very close, tell each other everything. I wait until my first evening back from Puerto Vallarta to talk to her. After dinner when the children have gone to sleep. Late so no one will disturb us.

In her thirties, Gabriela is like many grown daughters—more sensitive to my feelings. "You found someone?" she says before I can start.

"How do you know?"

"From your smile, your laughter, the gleam in your eyes. Who is it? What's he like?"

I hesitate, suddenly reminded of when my mother came out to me—or rather, when her lover, Valeria, outed her. But that was different. Gabriela and I are much closer.

"He is a she, a woman," I say and wait for her reaction. "You'll meet her tomorrow at lunch."

137

She stares at me as if my words are difficult to comprehend. "This isn't the first time you've been with a woman," she says, as a statement of fact. "I want to understand, Mom, why you've kept secrets from me."

Where's this coming from? "You and I have been honest and open with each other."

"Not really. I'm connecting the dots. Claudette, who lived with us when I was a little girl, was also your lover. Why didn't you tell me the truth about *her*?"

"You were too young to understand."

Gabriela is staring at me like an accuser. "I don't agree," she says. "She shared your bed. Not my father. It might have seemed more natural if I'd known."

"We had to stay in the closet and keep our relationship secret. For your good as well."

She twists her lips. "I don't get it. For my good?"

"What I did reflected on you. If people had found out, I'd have been a social outcast, and also my children. Some parents wouldn't have let their kids be friends with you. Society used to be very narrow-minded."

"You didn't think that I could keep a secret? Did my brothers know?"

"No. To them she was a friend who worked with me. But you were a very talkative child, and you might have told someone. That's why I had to lie to you, and to everyone." My voice shakes. "For me, that was the hardest part. Claudette and I could never show affection openly, even with you."

It all comes back in a rush. Hiding my feelings for Claudette had been exhausting. The pretense. The subterfuge. The dishonesty. I rub away my tears.

Gabriela leans over and takes my hand. "Mom, I wondered why you never confided in me."

"I tried to put it behind me. It was so damaging that afterwards I convinced myself I wasn't gay, that it was a phase I went through. I came to believe that loving another woman was wrong. As you know, I went out with many men, had male lovers, and remarried, but nothing fulfilled me until I found Julia."

"I'm thrilled for you," she says. "I'm sure I'm going to like her."

For years, I've been like an undercover agent who has gone so deep for so long that she's almost forgotten who she really is. With Julia, I can retrieve my identity and love a woman openly. Be my real self. No more pretending.

*

When Julia laughs, everyone laughs with her. From the moment she arrives for her first weekend, her arms loaded with goodies she baked, she's intent on winning over my family. It isn't easy. She has to get used to sharing me with my kids, my grandchildren, and my mother.

"She's young and intelligent and *simpática*," my mother says. "A much better choice than that black man you married."

Even Armando overcomes his objections. Julia wins him over. They discuss having a debate on the radio, with a feminist versus a religious point of view.

My pretty, blue-eyed *guera* is a hit with my family when I take her to two family weddings in Mexico. She's so entertaining that my brothers, even the uptight one in Mazatlán, are won over by her.

I show Julia the true Mexico, the one I know. It's important that she sees and understands my Mexican side and my lifestyle before I came to the US. She finds Mexico City overwhelming and chaotic, but she's impressed by the glamour of being chauffeured around in my brother's car, eating in elegant restaurants, visiting beautiful homes, and being treated like a princess. "I can't get over how everyone dresses up here," she says, "just to go out. They wear makeup and stockings and high heels every day. I couldn't do that on a regular basis."

"Why don't you try?" I ask, verbally giving her a gentle nudge. "You're so pretty when you fix yourself up." Makeup enhances her features and her eyes. What a difference between her drab appearance in China compared to when she gets all done up now.

We attend a family wedding at an old hacienda, a lavish do with five hundred guests, coiffed women in designer outfits, and a banquet that outdoes any Julia's seen. My family takes to her, finds her attractive and entertaining. Male cousins, not knowing about us, flirt with her. At the post-wedding dinner, Julia tucks into the food with such gusto that my sister-in-law comments, "*Tu amiga tiene muy buen diente*," meaning she's someone who likes to eat a lot.

On the plane back to Los Angeles, Julia is crying.

"What's the matter? I thought you had a good time." I'm not used yet to her changing emotions.

"It was wonderful being with you and your family." She wipes her eyes only to have fresh tears fall. "But to think you'll be going back to San Diego and I'm going to LA. It's just killing me. I hate to be separated again."

My heart aches as well. I don't want to leave her. We've been with each other for ten days.

I miss her so much that two days after getting back, I drive two hours to spend the night with her and four hours back to San Diego in commuter traffic the following morning.

We have to find a solution. This commuting situation is not working out for us.

"Why don't we live together?" she says.

*

We consider Laguna Beach. She will be close to Los Angeles, and I can move my practice to nearby Oceanside. Sunday morning we're on our way to Laguna to view houses when Julia says, "Honey, I saw an ad in the *LA Times* for a beach house in Rosarito. Let's go see it."

"Are you crazy? That's in Mexico."

"I know, but I'm curious."

"Okay," I say, laughing. "For me, it would be very convenient because I wouldn't have to move my practice."

"And we'd be living in Mexico, your country."

It's one of her fanciful notions; she can't be serious, but I play along. She turns the car around and heads for the border.

Neither of us likes the house—too many things wrong with it. Maybe this will cure her fantasy about living here. But the agent insists on taking us to a cozy, pretty community, Baja Malibu.

"How pretty this is," Julia says when she sees the white houses and rust-color tile roofs overlooking the sea. "Honey, this is the place for us. I know it is." She claps her hands when we arrive at a house right next to the ocean.

As we enter the living room, we see a high red-brick ceiling and a rich, maroon tiled floor. The panoramic ocean view from the tall windows is a thing of beauty, and we stand there, enthralled by the scene before us. Cascading waves nuzzle the coastline.

The kitchen is poorly equipped with a stove that's seen many years of use. "I'll bring mine," Julia says. "Won't my furniture be just right for this living room?"

Downstairs is an unfinished suite with marble bathroom walls and floor and a spa. "We'll finish it and call it the honeymoon suite," Julia says. "Our friends can spend weekends here. We'll have house parties." She constantly entertains. "People like visiting Mexico. When I tell them about this view, they'll come running."

"Don't count on their coming as often as you'd like," I say.

"It will be unbelievable to live here." She gazes out the window. "This view is to die for." She turns to me. "This house is just right for us. We'll buy it."

"Julia, why don't we find a house to rent first?" I'm alarmed to see her carried away so easily. "You don't know if you'll like it here."

"You know I will; I like everything about Mexico."

"You've never lived in Mexico, and things are very different. Much slower than what you're used to."

"That doesn't matter. More relaxing. I can write in peace."

"What will you do when the telephone doesn't work or you can't get on the Internet? Or you're cooking or bathing and you run out of gas and have to wait hours, or days, for them to deliver a new tank? Or the constant water problems?"

She turns a puzzled face to me. "Marina, why are you so negative? Don't you like this house?"

"It's amazing, but I'm being realistic."

"You agree that it's an incredible, a one-of-a-kind house," she sticks out her chin in a show of stubbornness, "then I'll be realistic. This is a unique house with a great view. I like Mexico, and it's close to San Diego and your work. And I have to have it."

She turns to the agent. "I want to buy this house." To me she says, "I'll talk to my parents and borrow the money from them while I sell my house in Los Angeles."

As I watch her make arrangements with the agent, my mind reels from the shock. I can't believe she's willing to go for this without thinking it over. Impulsively discard her life in LA, sell her house, pull up roots, and come here to live. Get herself into debt with her father. All for a dream. Again, I try to dissuade her.

"I agree it's a gorgeous house, but why's it been sitting there empty for seven years? There has to be some drawback." When we go to see the attorney in charge, we find out it belonged to a drug dealer, now incarcerated. The government confiscated it, and it ended up in the hands of the attorney. There's a tunnel, he tells us, built by the drug dealer, that is 1,200 meters long, with electric lights, and it extends from this house to another next door. The authorities closed the entrance, but if we want to unblock it, we can.

"Just think," Julia says. "We have our own underground tunnel."

*

True happiness. Living as a couple.

Images of our first months in Baja Malibu. Both of us seated on the living room couch gazing out on the view for hours. Watching dolphins leap in the sea and whales pass by as they travel south. She, jumping to her feet, exclaiming, "A whale! I can see a whale from my living room window!" We watch them; six go by, or a couple, dark blobs the size of gas tanks, churning the water and leaving ripples in their wake.

In our bedroom, we listen to the waves breaking, their rhythm, the unbroken movement of the sea. We have a growing awareness of the power of the universe. Of the beyond.

Julia and I on the beach gazing out to sea, and up at the night sky, pledging ourselves to each other. "Honey," she tells me, "I love you with every cell of my body."

Julia in my arms at night. She, loving me. I, loving her. Touching, caring, moving as one.

Julia, waiting for me when I get home from work. The house rich with the odor of the food she cooks on her vintage stove. "Honey, try this. I made it especially for you."

Smells of sand, sea, of scents brought in on the wind mingle with the aromas of her kitchen.

My family becomes "our family," as Julia puts it. Her own is distant, emotionally and geographically. They rarely see each other. She talks about her mother's reserved nature, her inability to show affection. How this drove Julia to seek it elsewhere. She doesn't have children of her own. So she adopts mine. "I'm so lucky to have found a family," she says. "I never thought I'd be a step-grandma."

My mother is delighted with Julia, and Julia showers her with attention, more so than I've ever done. My family comes over often. The kids play on the beach with Julia's retrievers.

The one thing she can't understand is the Mexican inability to be punctual. She prepares special dishes for my family, and when they arrive late, she gets hysterical. "All this preparation for them and they can't arrive on time?"

Her friends come from the US to our housewarming party. Some return for weekend visits and stay in the newly refurbished honeymoon suite. "You see," Julia says triumphantly. "Everyone will be coming here." But after a few months the suite is empty more often than it's occupied.

*

I ignore the signs. Or discard them as worthless. Sure I can handle her quixotic personality. Her sudden loss of temper. Her mood swings. Little things. Like when we're at the courting stage, and she's eating a slice of pecan pie, and without asking her, I fork off a small piece.

"Don't do that." Her voice is sharp, shrill.

"Sorry," I say, but shocked by her lack of generosity.

"No, no, wait." She cuts off half and places it on my plate. "It reminded me of how my sisters did that to me."

We're in the car, driving away, when she says, "My sisters took everything away from me. I could never have anything of my own. They wanted everything for themselves. I didn't count at all." Her voice rises as she vents about the past, and how she was deprived growing up, and how nobody took her into account. She's so loud that at a stoplight people in a nearby car stare at us. I have to roll up the window so that drivers and passersby won't hear her.

I thought it an isolated incident, but it should have been a warning of what was to come.

*

During our first year in our beach house, Julia keeps busy working on her motivational book. She becomes involved with a group of American writers who live in the area, but has few other friends or social activities. "I don't need them," she says. "I have you. And I'm too busy writing."

Besides the book, Julia writes a weekly column for a newspaper in LA. From her, a champion of female empowerment, I learn more about feminism in the US. What happened in the seventies and the Equal Rights Amendment. A Democrat like Matt, she comes from a privileged white background, so her perspective is different. She doesn't share his ingrained resentments, and her opinions are balanced and objective.

She gets compulsive about the book, writing long hours, well into the night. When I get home, she's at her computer. "Honey, let me finish this part, and I'll be with you." Or, "Honey, would you mind eating yesterday's lasagna?"

Her moods go from high when she has a good writing day, to frazzled when it's been slow, and to the verge of depressive when her output is poor. She frets about finishing her book and meeting her publisher's deadline. She has outbursts over things that distract her from it. Running out of gas. Getting cut off from the Internet. People knocking on the door. Distractions. Interruptions. Her inability to communicate with others here.

Once she finishes her book, during her second year, she has less to do. I'm away all day, leaving her alone. "Here, I have only you," she says. She misses LA. She misses the US. Living in Mexico is not what she'd envisioned. "Nobody works in this country." Her mood sways from excited about her book's publication to depressed when things aren't working out as she'd like. "I can't do anything stuck out here," she says.

The elation of having her book published wears out fast. She expected more fanfare, more sales. More reaction. To become an overnight success. A best seller. Selling the book is much harder than she'd foreseen. She expected that her many friends, fans, and followers would swamp the bookstores asking for it, but sales are much lower than estimated. It doesn't help that she lives in Mexico and has book signings in the US. Her publisher assures her it is doing well for a first book. She's snagged a core group. If more interest in it can be aroused, sales will increase. She has an intense series of radio interviews to promote it. More tension. Sometimes the Mexico-US connection doesn't work or breaks off in mid-interview. Frustration heaps upon a mound of other frustrations. "How will I sell my book and do PR if I'm living in this fucking place?"

Her book is one passion of hers that I can't fully share. I've followed its progress closely, and it's a large part of our conversation. Too large.

She gets angry about what is going wrong and why. She blames living in Mexico for her problems. Much as she tries, she can't adapt to a culture that doesn't respond to her demands. Too many things about Mexico are too strange or unacceptable, especially for someone used to the pace of a city like LA.

Her problems are compounded by loneliness. I cross the border to work and am gone all day. I keep up my dancing. When I get home, she's ravenous to talk, while all I want is to unwind. As a therapist, I've been listening to people's problems for seven or eight hours.

I lead a full life away from Julia. She's a part of mine, not the whole. Sensing this she tells me, "I'm not your priority. Your work and your family come first." She's moody, eats junk food, puts on weight—more than she's ever weighed before—wears the same tracksuit for days, and flies into rages over what seem to be insignificant things. She takes out her frustration and unhappiness on me with a barrage of insults and hurtful words.

I think I can be strong and put up with it all. Her sisters tell her, "Marina is like a brick. A solid person." Julia will come round and we can be happy again.

My health suffers. I have tachycardia, an accelerated heart rate. I see a cardiologist and take all kinds of tests, but the same as years ago in Houston, they find nothing wrong with me. "It's stress," the doctor says. I develop stomach problems that won't go away. More tests. Nothing wrong that they can find.

*

Our love has become as fragile as a pot of fading once-bright flowers. Each fight and every insult leave holes until our love is wilting, drying up as it receives too little nurturing.

We give up on living in Mexico and move to my house in San Diego. We're there for six months, but things don't improve. "I never thought I'd end up a housewife in Chula Fucking Vista," she says. More than ever, she misses her social life in Los Angeles. "In San Diego, no one returns my calls."

We're in the canyon behind the house, walking the dogs, when she tells me, "You don't have any dreams. Your world is too small. I don't fit in it."

"Then why don't you go back to your big world?"

"Do you want to break up?" she asks.

"Yes," I say. "Let's break up. Maybe you'll be happy in LA."

Her eyes cloud over. Mine don't. Not until I'm alone.

BARRIER TWENTY-THREE
Different Directions

LOS ANGELES
2001-2006

Julia stands out in a crowd of several hundred at my class's graduation from Landmark.* Author, actor, journalist, and playwright, she's such a vital force that a group has gathered around her. She radiates enthusiasm and energy and is every inch the star. She's lost weight, and her snug, green dress favors her trimmed-down figure. When she throws back her head and laughs, her hair billows out around her like an aura.

She must sense my gaze because she glances over and waves frantically for me to join her group. Everything slows down as I walk toward her—the noise, the other people fade away—and it's only the two of us. Julia spreads her arms, and her embrace erases the six months since we've seen each other. We're both overflowing with enough happiness to fill this room and beyond. After a long minute, we separate and stare at each other, and embrace again, wildly, crazily laughing—until the sadness of reality hits us.

"We really tried," she says.

"I know, but we failed," I answer.

We search each other's eyes. I see hope in hers.

"It's too hard being apart," she says.

"Too hard to let go." I reach out my hand, and she takes it and holds it to her heart.

"We should try again," she says.

*

This time, we both swear, we'll live independently and avoid conflicts overstepping the other's boundaries. I drive to LA weekends and holidays, but it becomes a drag. On the way back to San Diego one Sunday evening, it occurs to me that I should consider moving to LA and building a new practice. The buzz of excitement is on me, similar to when I decided to go back to school. A larger, more complex, and fiercely competitive city would be a major challenge and offer me more opportunities for growth.

By the end of my drive, I've made my decision. I call Julia. "I'm going to move to LA," I tell her.

"Want to play in the big leagues?" she says jokingly.

I buy a one-bedroom condo in Playa del Rey near the beach and install Armando in my San Diego home. I rent an office near Beverly Hills, and while I build my business, I work for AIDS Project LA*, giving therapy to terminal patients.

Who knows how it will go with Julia? The essence of our love never died, and it's growing again, unspoiled. This break made us understand that our bond is worth nourishing. We must work on overcoming the emotional barriers and deep wounds we left in each other.

I've never been much of a partygoer, but as her partner, I accompany her to the social events that are important to her, and a continuous round of parties and gatherings. I don't mind; seeing how comfortable and confident she is on her home ground is all that matters. She's always inviting people over, a diverse crowd of predominantly writers and activists or ones associated with the arts. At first I enjoy talking with them, but after a while I realize the more high-sounding they are, the more superficial their conversation. They're pretending to be something they're not, and in their pretense, they have convinced themselves that they're what they're pretending to be, like actors in a surrealist movie where everyone is wearing a mask. After all, this is LA, where role-playing is the main industry. Some are amusing, others well-read, a few very talented, an occasional brilliant one, but others are more like hangers-on who feed off Julia's hyped-up personality.

She attracts followers—they admire her as a political columnist, as author of a book that enhances her feminist stance, and for her past successes as an actor. I find them annoying—the way they surround her and demand her attention at these functions. I should be at her side and not some high-sounding activist or gay singer chanting her praises. But each one of them is important to her. If I want it to work between us, I'll have to share her with her admirers.

She introduces me to her friends as her love, her partner, her soul mate. Often when people learn I'm a therapist they want an on-the-spot consultation. They think I can read their minds, know what is wrong with them and how to fix it. I try to be polite, hide my irritation, remind them this isn't the right place and that I reserve my time for my patients. Some accept this, but others get pushy, desperate to surmount the barrier of my reluctance. Do they really think I can cure their emotional ills in an impromptu session during a party? "I don't have a crystal ball," I tell them.

How people repeat themselves. "So you're a psychotherapist?" they ask. "You've come to the right place. Everyone in this town needs a shrink."

"I'm a family therapist," I say, frost dripping from my words.

146

"That's what my ex-wife/husband needs." They ask for my card, but it's only for show. Neither of us is interested. My clients come from word-of-mouth recommendation, and my list is growing.

Julia is open about our relationship with friends and family. Not so with her audience. In an interview, when asked whom she lives with, she answers, "With my dogs." Afterwards she feels guilty and begs me to understand how coming out of the closet would have a negative effect on her public image. I understand her point, but even so, it's a hard pill to swallow that she can't be open about us—or me.

I'm enjoying LA with its buzzing social scene, multicultural ambiance, and focus on the arts. I become a board member of LAGPA* (Lesbian and Gay Psychotherapists of Southern California). I have other therapist friends. I'm making a name for myself in this community.

"I must go home," I tell Julia at the end of another weekend at her place. We're lying on the couch, after reading newspapers and watching old films and nibbling on crackers and cheese and fruit, and laughing at the same things. A couple who enjoy being with each other.

"Do you have to leave?" she asks in the teasing tone that can make me stop at the door and turn back. "C'mon, relax."

I try to compose myself, not allow her to woo me into staying another night. "I have to prepare for tomorrow," I say, gathering up my belongings.

"Honey, why don't we buy a house together?" she asks. "We can't go on like this, dating. It's been nine months."

I go rigid, stuck in mid-motion until slowly I shake my head. "I can't believe it."

Her bright smile fades. "You don't want to?"

"That same idea just occurred to me, but you said it first." I drop my things and walk back to her. "Yes, yes, and yes!"

We hug and kiss and I decide not to leave. I want to spend every moment with her. "What do you have in mind?"

"I like Pasadena," she says. "It has charm, personality, interesting people, and we can walk around there. Or would you prefer somewhere else?"

"Anywhere will do as long as it's us from now on," I tell her.

We find a gracious old place with a garden and a patio, in her environment, close to her friends and her activities. The choice is mutual, nothing like the impulse purchase in Baja Malibu. I'm as eager to live there as she is. It's easier for me to adapt to her world as long as I have my own work, my own office, and my own income. My business has taken off, my schedule is full, and I see around thirty patients a week. Coming to LA has turned out to be an excellent career move.

We join a group of American activists as volunteers with The Hunger Project* in Oaxaca*. Mexico. The aim is to teach indigenous women to be self-sufficient, how to make clothes and sell them. A similar group of Mexicans is also working there. Being in Mexico in this archetypical pre-Columbian, colonial, and modern city, it's natural to lapse into Spanish and spend time with my fellow countrymen. Culturally, I relate more with their crackling wit and tuned insights than with the well-intentioned Americans.

After a week the Mexicans leave, and I'm bereft. Julia finds me crying. "They were my connection to my culture," I say. With the Americans, I'm like an outsider; I need to remind myself they are the outsiders here in my country. I avoid them, wanting to be alone. How can I explain to them that it's a culture clash? Julia understands how it's impossible for me to adapt to her world in my country.

The rest of the time we're as close as when we first started going out. When we go to the theater she always grasps my hand. She needs me to be near her, and I respond to her need. I'd love her without pause forever if not for her emotional ups and downs.

"Honey," she calls to me from her office. "You have to read this. Another person is telling me how my book changed her life." Whenever she receives fan mail, she's ecstatic, so high that it sends her into the clouds. "I should get a talk show," she says. "I'm pitching the idea to a producer I know." She has several friends who claim to be producers and a couple who have established names. They all make promises that they don't follow up on or brush her aside with excuses and delays. Her glow wears off, leaving her with the dull tarnish of rejection.

Then there are the critics, the snakes in the grass.

"What's wrong, sweetheart?" Two hours before, she had acted as if a golden ray had descended from heaven. Now her eyes are shadowed and her face stormy. "I thought you were happy about the letter," I say.

"I was, until I saw this." She shoves a paper at me. "Look what this reviewer says about my book. After I made such an effort to win him over."

She hatches an idea, contacts people, throws a party, invites them, and they turn up, seem to enjoy themselves, drink her liquor, eat her food, and load her with praises. She's sure her efforts will bear fruit, and they do, but often the response is not what she hoped for. "All that work for nothing," she complains or rages or sobs. "I feel like I'm beating my head against an enormous wall while they keep throwing darts at me."

I try to comfort her, hold her in my arms when she's in pain or weeping, understand what she's going through, and her frustration when things don't work out for her. She's under too much self-imposed pressure to succeed, to be visible, to be a star, and it's not happening.

Her loving nature helps me put up with her verbal assaults, her changing moods, and her rages. Affection is healing. The payoff comes when she gives me what I want—the kisses, the hugs, the touching. In her excitement when I get home and she rushes to greet me. Her expressive way with words and endearments. I touch her skin and kiss her lips and sense the warmth of her body against mine. I bury my face in her hair; it smells like tropical fruit. Every hurt is gone. A gentle slope of peace recovered.

As she gets older, the casting calls are few and far between. "It's like they forget about you after you're forty." Then she receives one. She's exultant. "This will be my new break," she says. The audition went well, she says, she's sure to get the part. But no call back. Some actress less talented, less appealing has been given the role that should have been hers. We go to the show. Fifteen minutes in, Julia whispers to me that the actress is lousy and the show is no good. We walk out, and she storms about it all the way home, trying to force me to agree with her and getting angry at me when I don't. "I could have done a better job," she says, "and they knew it. So why give a third-rate actress the lead? Hidden interests?"

"Maybe because she was in a recent hit film," I say. It's as if I were agreeing with the producers' choice. She lights into me.

After our fights, I detach, give her the silent treatment. The worst thing I can do to Julia is not pay attention to her, behave as if she were a shadow. For me, it's painful as well, but I need to recoup my defenses. After two to three days, I can't bear not being close to her, and in the night I'll creep into bed with her. She puts her arm around me and everything is all right. Making up almost makes up for the small distance between us.

Before, it was her book and now it's work events. Even for someone who cares for her very much, it's hard to put up with her roller coaster of moods. As before, she flies into rages, yelling at me. I fight back, using my knowledge of psychology. I know how to calm high-strung patients and soothe them. But our bond corrodes a bit more until the cracks are beyond repair.

*

She's seated at the little wooden desk in her office. Light comes in through the portico doors facing the courtyard. She's content in that room, her hair drawn back in a ponytail and no makeup. Cute. Natural. She's put up a sign. "I'm not self-absorbed, I'm just an artist." There, she shares her next week's column with me. She writes about feminist and political issues and her opinions about local politics, prejudice and discrimination. What do I think about her piece on Eleanor Roosevelt? About local politics? Prejudice and discrimination? She's writing a one-woman play based on her childhood experiences, and it's funny and poignant and intense, as Julia is herself. A friend, Michael, is with her. The three of us talk, or rather, Julia talks about her plans—where she's going next—and all her projects and talks and trips. She's going to do this and go there. Until Michael says, "What about the two of you?"

"That's right, let's plan a cruise," she says. We reminisce about our travels, our Caribbean and Mediterranean cruises. How we enjoyed *The Phantom of the Opera* in London and again on Broadway in our favorite city, New York. Our visits to Mexico. Sharing my country with her. How she loves my culture, the food, and the way Mexicans respond to her. For a while we pick up the threads of the life we've made together and embroider another pattern.

For a while.

"Honey, I'd like us to go to therapy," she tells me. "We can work on our issues."

Her pressing issue is "I'm torn between pursuing my career and my relationship."

During our year in therapy, little changes. Her play has been quite successful, and Julia goes out of town more often to perform it on stages across the country. I come back to a home that's empty without her. She has to do things on her own, go out and do PR as part of her business. Hers isn't like my profession, where clients come to me through referrals. She has to bang her own drum, and the louder she bangs it the more attention she gets. She doesn't have much time for me.

I stop going to events with her.

"Why don't you want to go to parties?" she asks.

"They bore me," I say.

She's mystified. "You used to say what interesting people go to them."

"They're your friends, not mine," I say. "I'm tired of making an effort to get on with people who pretend all the time. I don't care about the same issues." In my own world, I'm a recognized authority. Why should I live my life through hers?

Her expression turns sour. What about her? What about when we lived in Mexico and she had to stay alone at home all day? What about my family? They're more her family than her own. She's tried to live up to my expectations, but whatever she does, it's never good enough. "You think your work is more important than mine?"

"I can't be a social butterfly," I say.

Her voice rises, gathering the anger inside her and venting it at me. "You think I'm superficial? My work is PR, dealing with people." And, "You don't understand that I'm an artist." And, "You think you're perfect. I should call you Miss Perfect. Who can live up to your high standards?" She's the one who's spent thousands of dollars on self-improvement seminars.

We've come to another impasse, the same that constantly seems to stop us. I level with her, as if speaking to a patient. "Julia, you want to be the center of the universe. I can't be your satellite revolving around you. I'm my own person."

Her brow wrinkles and she shakes her head. She doesn't get it.

She isn't fulfilling my needs, and I'm not fulfilling hers. She doesn't want a partner; she feeds on social events.

Memorial week starts with frustration and disappointment. A celebrity couple invited us to brunch, but they haven't called to confirm or taken her calls. Apparently they forgot or dumped us. For Julia this is the worst kind of rejection, and she takes it out on me.

"I'm tired of being the target of your frustrations," I shout at her.

She closes her hands into fists, lifts them like a boxer, and asks, "Want to fight? Want to fight?" in the aggressive tone of a street fighter challenging me.

"No, Julia." My hands go up in a defensive gesture. "I don't want to fight." I feel disrespected and bullied. "I can't handle any more of your dramas." Sudden dizziness hits me. My muscles contract, my heart beats faster, my breathing becomes rushed, preparing for fight or flight. "I can't take it," I say, and the sentence sounds garbled and distant. I might be on the verge of a stroke. I retreat to my room.

Julia has scratched my soul. Raked her nails across it so deeply that it can't heal.

For three days I go deep into my mind and analyze the situation. Is this pride or pain that's keeping me from leaving? There's too much "me" in this relationship. She acts like she's lost interest, concentrating on her career, and her play. Whatever happened to "we"?

For distraction I go out shopping and buy Julia a present, a small shoe for her collection. When I get back, I find a mile-long letter on my computer—most of her written and phone messages go on and on. In it she admits she feels responsible for her frustrations and begs me to give her another chance. It ends with, "Honey, I don't want to break up. Losing you would be like losing a limb."

I leave her a note. "I'm spending this weekend with my family in San Diego. Why don't we discuss it on Monday in my office?" My home ground.

*

Monday, Julia appears wan and sad, her face puffy. Her big smile seems forced, fixed in place, a pretense smile for when she has to deal with a difficult issue or person. I know her too well not to see she's hurting. Probably as much as I am inside. We hug but something makes me hold back. She seems to sense this, so that instead of our usual effusive embrace, it's more like a greeting between two casual friends. She moves away, seats herself, and waits. Her smile is unsteady, though her eyes are alert, questioning.

Outwardly I'm calm, deliberate. "I've decided to go back to San Diego in two months," I tell her. "I believe it's best for both of us. This isn't working anymore."

Her smile disappears and her lips fold, the lower over the upper, and she nods once, slowly, and lowers her head as if mulling this over. Silence fills the room, and the space between us seems to expand, and I'm on one side of a cliff edge and she on the other, separated by the enormous ravine between us.

After long minutes she looks up, her eyes expressionless. She sighs deeply and says, "I saw it coming and stayed in bed all weekend crying about it."

"Sweetheart, we have different needs. You've made your projects your priority."

"Relationships have never been my priority," she says with a flash of defiance.

"We" used to be her priority.

"I don't want a part-time partner," I say, making an effort to keep my composure, talk to her the way I would to a client.

"You're telling me that you're done with me?" Her voice trembles.

"I'm not done with you. It's better for our own good to be apart."

151

"You're right, it's not working, Marina, but I don't want to lose you as a person." Her voice holds such sadness that it's difficult not to try and comfort her.

"Nor do I, sweetheart. But we can't stay together. It's harmful for both of us."

"I know," she says. "I won't stop loving you."

"And I won't stop loving you, sweetheart." My voice breaks. "When is this going to end?"

"Never," she says.

I think of all the laughter we had, Julia and I, and how for a long time it outweighed the tears until, like a swollen river, they crashed over their banks and ravaged all around, breaching the walls we had constructed together, until everything that sheltered us disintegrated and fell away. We're both tired, so very tired of trying to stave off the inevitable flood, and now that it's left us in ruins, we'll have to walk away, each on her own. But freedom smells like bristling sea air after a storm—the kind that smacks your face and gives you a glow—and the cool tang of early morning, and the simmer of late afternoon, and the glory of the setting sun all rolled into one.

PART V
MARINA

My Lost Child Returns

SAN DIEGO
2011

The woman comes out amidst a throng of travelers and hesitates, appearing both confused and expectant. Her eyes are dark, her nose upturned, and she has her mother's mouth. She's wearing a summer dress with a short skirt. *No pants for me.*

Armando calls, "Karla, Karla." Gabriela joins him, and I make up the chorus.

Her head turns toward us, eyes wide, startled. I realize she's not used to this show of Mexican enthusiasm and tug at Armando's arm. "Stop. She's seen us."

She heads our way, pulling her case behind. Tall, she has the proud walk of a woman who knows attention is on her and that she's worth more than a glance. With a slight flaunt, her swaying hips remind me she lives in a black community in New Jersey. The resemblance to Claudette is there but transposed onto another face, one with the hardened, aggressive-defensive features of a survivor.

"She's had a difficult life," Gabriela had told me after talking to her on the phone. "Claudette was always gone, working around Europe, and Karla was raised by her grandmother in Spain—she died when Karla was twelve years old. At that time, Karla hadn't seen her mother in four years. She was sent to Switzerland to live with Claudette and her husband, a grouchy old man who didn't want her."

I have spoken to her on the phone several times. Our first call was tense, hard to communicate, trying to find a way to relate to her, someone whom I don't know at all except that I'm partly responsible for her coming into this world. "I'm not your biological mother, Karla," I told her, "but I took care of you when you were a baby. You were like my own daughter, and you were part of my family. It was very hard to let you go." I have to convey to her how happy I am—we all are—to know about her and be in touch again.

Her voice was cool, flat, with a wary sound to it. As if I'd caught her on a bad day. Or she didn't care.

"My mother told me about you," she said, "and about my brothers and sister, and the dog, Alex. I know I was happy with you, but I can't remember much except for the Disney dolls and my sister teaching me to dance."

She's the same on the second call. Distant, unresponsive. I have to remind myself that I'm a stranger to her.

The third call, she opened up more. "I couldn't get along with my mother," she told me. "We fought all the time. I was very unhappy living with her and her old husband." At sixteen, she dropped out of high school, left home, and went to work in a chocolate factory. She saved some money and decided to go with some Puerto Rican friends to New York. She was seventeen. At eighteen, she married a drug addict who died of an overdose, leaving her with a one-year-old baby girl. "We were homeless, living on the street; we didn't have a place to sleep."

Shaken, I thought how all this could have been avoided if only Claudette had relented and left her with us. Or if Carlos had been successful when he went to Spain hoping to bring her back to Mexico, but her grandmother refused to let her go.

It wasn't easy to find the right words to say, and "I'm sorry" was hardly enough to cover all she'd gone through, but they were the only two words that occurred to me. "Karla, I'm so sorry this happened to you. A widow, with a baby, and homeless. If only we'd known we would have helped you. What a hard life you've led."

She made a sound like a short laugh—or a snort. "Marina, those hardships have made me strong and resilient. I'm a well-known DJ in New York, and I like what I do. My daughter, Aisha, is going to college." She sounds proud and self-confident, having achieved a measure of success and become a known personality in her area.

This conversation remains in my mind long after we hang up. Little Karla walked out of her happy life with us into one of deprivation and not much affection. Why didn't I fight to keep her with us? I tear my mind apart trying to remember. I did what I thought was right. Sent away Claudette, who was on a destructive path, and her child became the victim of her thoughtless actions. But I should have taken a stance and refused to let Karla go with an unfit mother. Fought for her custody. In retrospect, it's always easier to right yesterday's wrongs once the passion of the moment has died out.

*

Armando is the first to greet her, giving her a bear hug, and she retreats a little. "Remember me—Armando?" he asks, as if he hasn't changed from a boy of thirteen to a middle-aged man. Meanwhile Gabriela is filming everything.

Karla has a dazed expression as she shakes her head. She's lost her child's mischievous twinkle and seems shocked at this noisy welcome. When I greet her, she accepts my hug but doesn't respond. She responds more to Gabriela, whom she's got to know over the phone and Internet. This has given Gabriela some insight into Karla's, "my sister's," background, so different from her own.

Karla has made her home in a black community and both her daughter's father and her current partner are black. To me, the throaty way in which she speaks sounds black, and the slang she uses, though Armando says it's probably more like a "Joisey" accent. She seems uncertain and overwhelmed, but who wouldn't when meeting an effusive Mexican family?

We go out to lunch to a Mexican restaurant, and I can see she isn't finding it easy to relate to us. I understand why she'd be distant after the long estrangement and probably some resentment about being sent away with her mother. And our affectionate family can be overwhelming.

Armando is so moved that he keeps hugging and kissing her. She blushes and says, "I'm not used to all this."

"You'd better get used to it, Karla," he says. "You've come back to your family, and we're going to give you a lot of loving."

I wish this were so and that Karla could fit in again with us, become part of our family, but I doubt this will happen. She seems to have attachment issues as a result of her deprived youth. She knows how to handle herself in her own ambiance, but taken out of it she becomes the lost daughter who has finally turned up—a completely different role that I'm not certain she wants to accept.

"You're lucky to have the mother you have," she tells Gabriela. "I was ashamed of mine and how people talked about her."

Her life might have been very different if she had stayed, but she didn't, and the "might have been" doesn't exist, and what happened, happened, and nothing can change that. The only important fact is that she's content with the life she's chosen, and that she has come back to us.

BARRIER TWENTY-FIVE
Repeated Patterns

The black and white photo shows two young women in bikinis cavorting on the beach. Young, good figures, great legs, beautiful faces, seemingly without a care, or any idea of what lay ahead for both of them.

Claudette is a ravishing woman in her twenties, with a slender, curvaceous figure and long, well-toned legs that she would show off when singing—flaunting them, arching them, and flicking her dress against them. Her perfect oval of a face draws my attention, and her beguiling eyes and sensuous lips. What the photo doesn't show is her long, shiny, jet black hair or her mischievous smile as she flips it over her shoulder. Or her full breasts that made me ache with pleasure when I caressed them.

I want to hug her, hold her close, feel her body against mine. Study her face so as never to forget it, and see the expression in her eyes. Only then will I know that I've found her again.

How will she see me? My hair is still curly, though not fair anymore, with a reddish shade. My figure is still good, though I won't wear a bikini again, and my movements are lithe and easy due to my dancing.

Fear is lifting its ugly head and picking like a crow at my excitement, raising questions and doubts I'd rather not bring up. Claudette must have changed; she can't be the same person who betrayed me thirty-five years ago. Yet when we talked on the phone, she couldn't remember why she left Mexico City. Nothing about the horrifying circumstances that destroyed us and affected everyone around us. "I recall feeling like a victim," she says.

"What about my cousin?"

"I remember her vaguely. A nice kid."

"You abused her sexually."

"I wouldn't have acted that way." Her voice is indignant as she squeaks out her denial.

"For years she hung onto the hope that you'd return," I tell her.

157

"Why would she do that?" she asks.

Perhaps she's pretending to have no recollection of what happened or why she had to leave Mexico. Or she's hidden it in the back of her mind for so long that she's erased the memory. Even so, it must linger in her subconscious. Once I'm there with her, I'll find out. I'm an experienced therapist, and I can tell if she's lying or if it's what she's come to believe. She may have erected a barrier of guilt; if so, it's going to come down.

*

After traveling eighteen hours, I arrive at Zurich airport. Claudette's nephew, Eduardo, and his boyfriend pick me up there. Claudette isn't well and couldn't come. Eduardo, balding, late thirties, has the same easygoing charm as his aunt. On the forty-five-minute drive to where Claudette lives, we go through what Eduardo tells me is the heart of the Alps. The mountains' snowy faces, pure and solemn, remind me of ranks of grand old men who, for eons, have overseen us mere mortals.

"That one," Eduardo says, pointing at a peak, "is near where we live. It's also a popular area for older people to retire. We have many foreign residents."

Claudette lives in an old, Swiss chalet-style building with dark timbers that overhang its whitewashed spaces and large framed windows. In front is the town square, and behind, mountains add to its rugged scenic charm.

As I step out of the car, the church bells peal. I stop and breathe in the fresh mountain air, let it fill my lungs with its pure goodness. This would be a good place to live.

I'm in good shape, but the steep stairs to her second-floor apartment wind me. Or it's the prospect of seeing her, having her in my arms, these arms that haven't held her for many years.

She opens the door and stares as if I'd startled her. "*Hola, mi amor,* I'm here at last," I say. She doesn't move, so I put my arms around her and give her a heartfelt hug. Now she reacts and cradles herself into me.

"Dear God, thank you for bringing Marina to me." Her voice is gravelly.

I kiss her lips, her cheeks, her forehead. She's smaller than I remember, and skinny. I can feel her bones through her thick sweater. Where are her breasts? Become soft little pouches against her ribs.

"See you later," Eduardo says and puts down my suitcases. "If you need anything, I'm right next door."

Arm in arm, Claudette walks me into a spacious living room, with hardwood floors and light coming through large windows. Pictures line the walls. I gesture to them. Some are scenes similar to the ones we drove through coming here, and others are colorful landscapes in Mexico.

"What wonderful paintings," I say, indicating a mountain scene that must be from around here. Next to it is one of the Mexican volcanoes, Popocatépetl or Iztlaccíhuatl.

"I did them," she says, "they're mine. I've been painting for years."

"I never knew you were a such talented painter." But they're all different styles.

"I was a late bloomer, as they say in the art world." She gives me a shy little smile. So unlike her bravado-filled smile when I knew her. I can't envision lively Claudette, who could never keep still more than a few minutes, painting scenes that must have taken long hours of diligent work.

This is not the Claudette I knew. This woman bears no resemblance to my memory of her. Her skin is pale, sallow, as if what is flowing through her veins is transparent liquid. Her eyes are the color of mud, sunken behind protuberant cheekbones, and her scarred neck has sagged into her shoulders. Her lips have faded into a pout. Her hands that grasp mine are cold, with so little flesh that every bone and vein in them is visible.

Gently, I loosen her grip on mine and sit on the couch. Tiredness washes over me—I hardly slept on the way over—but I push it away. She sits in a large, comfy armchair next to a table with a pack of cigarettes on it.

What turned her into this wreck? She told me on the phone that she'd had a good marriage to a much older man. There must be more to the story.

"Tell me more about yourself," I say. "What about your marriage?"

Her small smile is barren of happiness. "To be truthful, I married for security. As I got older it was hard to get by singing. He was well-off, forty years older—eighty-two when we were married." She coughs, a deep, chest cough, and another, and lets out a long, ragged breath. "We had separate bedrooms, and I never slept with him." She's already told me this. Is she trying to reassure me there was no sex in her marriage? But I've met horny old guys in their eighties; I'm not convinced.

"Then why did he marry you?"

"He wanted a companion in his old age. He was good to me and let me do whatever I liked." She pulls out a cigarette and stares at it.

"Sounds like you had a good arrangement," I say.

"We were married twelve years, until he died." Her hand trembles as she lights her cigarette. "He was good to me and let me do whatever I wanted."

Didn't she just say that?

She takes one puff and lays her cigarette in an ashtray. "I've given up trying to give up smoking," she says, and glances out the window. "What a great day."

We talk about the weather and the scenery while the shadow of her marriage seems to hover over our conversation. She keeps rubbing the back of her neck as if something is bothering her. Then she picks up her cigarette, draws on it, puts it down, and stares at me. Her features are set, with no trace of sadness in them. Her hands grasp the sides of her chair.

"I lied about my husband," she says in a rasping voice. "He wasn't good to me. As he got older, he became stingy, irritable, and his health got worse. I can still hear him yelling, 'Claudette! Claudette!' and getting furious if I delayed. Even when I was in the bathroom." She pauses for another puff. I'm silent. This memory must have been poisoning her for a long time.

159

"He expected me to wait on him hand and foot. He didn't like my going out except when I had to buy food and medicines. It was so awful being shut up with him that I started to drink. I kept a bottle in the kitchen. Alcohol became my refuge from this daily torment. It made everything easier until it started to work against me. I went into a depression and did crazy things, like cutting myself."

My mind flashes back to the knife incident with Elisa. Was that the start? Or had I missed other clues?

Claudette rolls up her sleeve and shows me the scars on her arm. "And my throat." She moves her hand across it in a cutting gesture. "Eduardo found me passed out and saved me. I went into alcohol rehab."

She stops, and her face is as full of venom as a coiled snake. My body goes rigid with primal fear. "I went into my husband's room one morning and found him dead. He wasn't breathing. I said a quick prayer for him, and thanked God that he'd gone. My tears were for me, not for him. For my lost years. He was ninety-four." Her face puckers in anger. "If I had known he'd last so long, I'd never have married him. I got his pension. Not much payment for all the years I put up with him." This admission seems to take the feistiness out of her. Her body droops and curls up in herself. She becomes so small and fragile that I have to go over and hug her. Like the first time we met, I want to protect her.

Her eyes brim over with happiness. I hold her hand while she goes on about those years, sometimes babbling and repeating things in her desire to let it all out. Even when she smokes, cigarette after cigarette, I don't move away.

"What about your health?" I ask. "When we talked on the phone you told me you had problems." I have to find out why she's so run down, and why she smokes so much.

"I told you I had throat cancer six years ago," she says. "They gave me radiation, and I have to blend all my food. It hurts to swallow. I eat like a baby. That's why I'm hoarse and drink water all the time." She waves a hand at her empty glass, and I take it to the kitchen and fill it and another for me. Swiss mountain water. Delicious.

We have our first meal together. Hers is all mush. She puts everything in the blender—vegetables, meat, and eggs—and adds yoghurt to it. She takes an hour to eat it, little by little, swallowing with effort. She heats frozen vegetables for me. I'll have to buy some food for myself. "Is there a store nearby?" I ask.

"A small market a block away. We'll go after we finish eating. I don't go out much anymore. I'm alone except for Eduardo. My sister and my mother are all dead, and I never see Karla or her daughter."

I'm trying not to weep over her state. Has she any idea how harmful her smoking is for her health? It's obvious in her constant coughing, her hoarse voice, the way she has to stop and catch her breath, her jerky movements, and unsteady walk.

Her voice becomes a croak; it's an effort for her to talk. She must rest it. "What about you, Marina?" she asks. "What's your story?"

"As you know, I'm a psychotherapist."

"What is that? What exactly do you do?" she asks as if I hadn't told her in our phone conversations.

"I help people to understand themselves and their problems. Try to make a difference in their lives."

"It sounds fascinating," she says. "Tell me more."

She seems to be attentive, but as I speak I notice her eyes go blank and her mind is elsewhere. She's not listening to what I say. Did she ever? I used to go on about my dance school and the students, but perhaps she didn't pay much attention, which is why she made mistakes.

"You're as pretty and shapely as I remember," she says, verifying my suspicions.

I switch subjects. "I keep active, dance hip-hop, and go to the gym. Take good care of myself." I don't want to sound like I'm showing off or making comparisons with her apparent lack of personal care.

She brightens. "I discovered Jesus Christ. It gave me a reason for living."

"That's important," I say. "I'm not religious myself, but comfort in Jesus can be a strong emotional support."

"I study the Bible with my sisters from L'Armée du Salut*. They pick me up and take me to Bible study and bring me home. I don't go anywhere else. I only feel safe here."

I should have seen the signs: sending her nephew to meet me and not coming herself, not coming downstairs to greet me, her seeming reluctance to go to the store. I'll try to persuade her to take a leap of faith.

"Claudette, how about going to see your brother, Gastón, in Greece? I'll invite you. Think you can leave your home?"

"I'd *love* to see him again," she says, a slight glimmer in her eyes. "He lives on an island called Paros. It would be like old times, you and me going to the beach together."

"You're certain?"

"I told you, it's a wonderful idea. Why don't we call him right now and tell him about our plan?"

Gastón is delighted to talk to us, and Claudette sounds enthusiastic about visiting him. "It's been too long since we last saw each other," she says. Her hand goes to her throat as if realizing how destroyed it is with all the scars on it. She should cover it with a scarf.

We retire to her bedroom. Her medications overflow on her night-stand—an army of little bottles and boxes of pills: antidepressants, anti-anxiety pills, sleeping pills, thyroid pills, and aspirin to prevent stroke. In addition, she wears three morphine-and-opium patches on her chest. "I have to use them because I'm in a lot of pain. In my throat, my back, sometimes all over my body. They make me sleep a lot. Some days I don't have the energy to get out of bed."

"What about all these pills?"

"My doctor insists I take them; the nurse comes once a week to make sure I do."

The first night we spend together, we kiss lightly, embrace, and hold hands. Even then she is not at peace. "I have sleep apnea," she tells me. "Trouble breathing. I have to wear a mask so as not to deprive myself of oxygen. The machine is in my nightstand." She slips a mask over her face.

It's hard to sleep; I doze more because I'm tired from the flight and the different hours. Seeing her again in this state fills me with anxiety. When she goes to the bathroom and doesn't come out, I go for her. She's asleep on the toilet, snoring, with her panties down around her ankles. The following night the same thing happens. This seems to be a common occurrence whereby she's too drugged to go back to bed. Suppose she fell over and hit or broke a bone? Would she realize? How long before anyone would find her lying there?

Church bells wake me; they ring every fifteen minutes all day and night long. If I were here long enough, I might get used to them.

In the morning I say, "We have to make reservations for our trip."

She tilts her head to one side and wrinkles her brow. "What trip? I've forgotten what we talked about last night."

"We're going to visit your brother, Gastón."

"I'd like to see him," she says, "but he lives on the island of Paros in Greece. I don't think I can go that far to a place where I've never been."

"Why not? You were excited about it last night."

She gives a slow headshake. "We spoke to him, didn't we? But I can't go all that way to see him. I'm afraid to go out at all. I get sick. So how can I travel to another country?"

"We called him to say we were going. He was so happy about seeing you again."

She tries to speak, but the words seem caught up in her throat, and they come with an effort. "I'm sorry but I can't do it."

"Claudette, you'll be fine. I can help you. I'm trained in this. You may have agoraphobia, fear of open spaces."

"Agoraphobia?" she repeats. "Yes, it might be that. I take pills for anxiety when I go out because my heart beats so fast I can't breathe. I want to run back here and hide."

"Panic attacks," I say. "But you don't have to worry if you're with me. I know how to calm you down; I am a psychotherapist."

She hesitates, and her face takes on the stubborn expression that I've seen with patients who don't want or mean to follow my advice. "I don't think so," she says. "I'm too afraid of what might happen if I'm far away from my home."

"Why don't we go out somewhere and see how you manage?"

"Marina, I have serious health problems. I have to be very careful, and I have trouble moving around."

"We'll get a wheelchair."

"No, it isn't a good idea."

She shrugs off all my efforts to motivate her. Yesterday's excitement and happiness have disappeared and are replaced by obstinate refusal. Nothing I say changes her mind. She's stuck inside her home, and the very idea of venturing far away is too hard to contemplate. The only place where she seems at ease is in the little grocery store/gourmet deli. I offer to pay, and I'm shocked when Claudette, who eats so little, buys a bunch of fancy patés and cheeses. "It will be like it used to be," she says with a hint of her former self.

If all her problems were physical, I might be able to deal with them, but her mind is also affected; it wanders without focus. She has memory lapses, can't concentrate, and in the middle of a conversation diverts to other subjects. We may be talking about the view, and she suddenly mentions Karla. When we discussed going to Greece, she wasn't thinking of a journey but more like her brother lived nearby and we were planning a short trip across town.

I go next door to talk to Eduardo about my concern for her fading mind, her lack of recall, and her physical problems.

"I have to agree with you," he says. "She's also self-destructive." He found her when she slashed her veins, her arms, and cut her throat with a knife. After this last incident she spent a year in a rehab program to help with her alcoholism and drug addiction.

"She's still addicted to pills," I say.

"The doctor prescribes them, and she really needs them," he says.

"One of these days I'm afraid she'll overdose, or have an accident when she's walking around in a daze. Or when she gets up at night; she's too groggy to go back to bed."

He rubs his chin. "I'm afraid of that happening as well. She'll have to go to a nursing home. Unless she finds someone to live with her and take care of her."

"I'm afraid that won't be me," I say. "I thought I might help, but she needs more than what I can give her."

"I'm sorry to hear that," he says. I gather he'd hoped otherwise.

The third day she tells me, "Remember how I used to like to rest my face on your shoulder, and how I kissed you?"

"I do remember." I kiss her tenderly. "Claudette, I believe you need to stay here in Switzerland. I can't take you back with me to the US. You have too many health problems, and your doctors here take good care of you."

"But when will I see you again?"

"I'll come back," I say, "and we'll be in touch." I have to distance myself before she becomes too dependent on me. I can't repeat my old pattern of responding to her neediness. She's already got inside me, filling me with the same tenderness toward her as before. But only the embers of her old self remain, and what we had together has become a fading glimmer of a once-vibrant fire.

*

Rain interrupts my all-day tour in Bern with Eduardo, so we come back earlier than expected. I turn the doorknob, trying to open the door to Claudette's apartment. It's locked but I hear voices just inside the door. Claudette must be Skyping with someone whose voice, halting and high-pitched, sounds suspiciously like my cousin Elisa. Maybe it's my imagination, but I'm going to find out.

I knock again. I hear the click of the computer turning off and Claudette's slow steps to the door. She opens and says a nervous, "Hello." I caught her off guard; she's obviously agitated—her flustered expression gives her away.

I walk straight to her computer and turn it on. My cousin's face appears on the screen. The same girl—now a middle-aged woman—whom Claudette remembered "vaguely."

Claudette is twitchy, her hands shaking. She says, "Your cousin contacted me."

It's as if she took out a knife and ripped out my guts. I'm still alive but bleeding to death. I slump into a chair. The same reaction as years ago when I caught her cheating on me with the same cousin. My neck muscles tighten in an involuntary convulsion. I can't speak for several minutes, while Claudette watches helplessly.

"So it's still going on between you two?" I say finally.

She simulates innocence. I remember that expression well—wide-eyed, artless, and her childish pout. "It wasn't anything, Marina. She got in touch with me."

"Why couldn't you be honest and tell me the truth?"

"I swear, Marina, it was just today that we spoke." She sounds shifty, with a scared note—a guilty person trying to convince me of her innocence.

"How can you deceive me when I came all this way to be with you?"

"Marina, it's nothing. You don't have to be concerned about it."

Not concerned with that face on the screen? Perhaps, since I told her I couldn't take her with me to the US, she's trying to hook up with my cousin. Or she's desperate for a companion, someone to take care of her.

I have to get away. She may be hell-bent on destruction, but I'm not going with her. "I'm going for a walk," I say and slam the door on my way out. I go next door to see Eduardo.

"I didn't know Elisa was your cousin," he says.

"She's also the reason why Claudette and I broke up. What do you know about her?"

"I didn't want to say anything," he says, "but, yes, I thought something might be going on between them. They've been talking on Skype every day for hours."

"Every day for hours?" More than we did. It seems like Claudette has been playing me.

"Before you arrived," he says, "I thought Elisa had been Claudette's big love. She told me Elisa has always been in love with her, and she became a flight attendant so she could search for her all over the world. She's been talking about selling her house in Mexico and moving to Switzerland to be with Claudette."

While I made plans to be with Claudette, my cousin was also making hers. "I can't believe Elisa would do such a thing. She must be crazy. She doesn't even have a job." From what I know, she's capable of taking this step because she's been locked in her fantasy of Claudette for all these years.

Claudette catches me packing. "Why are you doing this?"

"I'm going to Eduardo's for the night and leaving for Rome in the morning."

She gasps. "Why? You can't do this to me."

"Of course I can."

"Marina. Please. Let's talk." Her beseeching expression that used to be so charming now makes her resemble an old crone begging for a handout.

"What is there to talk about? You betrayed me before, and you're doing it again. With the same person, while I'm here in your home."

"It's you I care about," she says. "Elisa is a good friend. I swear, Marina, that's all."

"I hope it's true, for her sake."

"Marina, I love you, only you, and I don't want you to go. Or, do you find me so unappealing now that I'm old and sick?"

"Claudette, when I first saw you and heard about your problems, I wanted to help you get well. It's your lack of honesty I can't take."

"All I did was talk to her. On Skype."

"You'll never own up to the truth. I know you've been doing it for hours every day."

"We can try," she says. "Remember all there was between us?"

"Why would I want to?"

Years ago I was in pain long after I broke up with Claudette. Today it's anger because I allowed myself to be hooked again by the same person who betrayed me before. Once a liar and cheater, forever a liar and cheater.

I leave her huddled in a chair. "I don't understand," she's saying as I go out the door. "I don't understand what I did to make you angry."

Separating Self from Mother

Sᴀɴ Dɪᴇɢᴏ
2004-2005

My mother and I are sitting on the small patio in her home. Water tinkles in the fountain, and the air is filled with the aroma of her garden roses. The atmosphere is soothing, in tune with my senses.

She is eighty-five, but her skin is fresh and rosy. Her hair, a brown mahogany, is colored every month in the beauty salon. Her body is slender, her posture good, her walk brisk, and in her blue-and-white pantsuit she could be a decade younger. Her appearance still matters to her, and she's as choosy as when she dressed to go to work.

Her mind is taking a slow good-bye on the way to the long one. At first she keeps forgetting things and repeating herself constantly. We think it's old age and make excuses for her forgetfulness, even joke about it. Then I come home to find twenty phone messages from her. "You should know," and "I have to tell you," and "I'm not sure if I called you," all about the same piece of news. The following week she does it again—leaves thirty messages—as if she can't remember she's already called me. When she visits, she puts her handbag in odd places, like in the pantry and in the fridge, and we have to search all over the house to find it. We're on our way to the airport when we find out she's left her dentures at home. She goes into a panic, and we have to return all the way for them. "Mami," I say, "it's like going out without your underclothes. Why didn't you miss them?"

"I suppose I'm getting forgetful," she says. Not my mother, who was so sharp that she'd remember the slightest detail.

I've gone through a ladder of emotions—refusal at first and then frustration at her vagueness. I get angry at her, at myself, at God, or whatever fates are causing her to turn into a shell of her former person, and because I'm powerless to help her despite all my therapist's knowledge. Finally, sadness. I miss her sharp tongue and what I never thought I'd miss—her controlling mind. I'd do anything to have another argument or fight with her; it would mean she was herself, but that part of her is gone. She can carry on a conversation, but it's brief and vague before her mind closes. Or she appears to be in a reverie only to come out of it and make a comment.

"Marina, I never understood you," she says after being silent for twenty minutes.

I stare into her dark eyes, which hold a peculiar glow in them as if she's imparting some newfound knowledge. "Mami," my voice quivers, "I've waited most of my life to hear you say that."

"You are a serious person," she says.

I have to make her stay with the thought before it becomes a wisp blowing away on the breeze.

"Why did you never understand me?" I try to jog her memory.

"You were complicated," she says.

"You tried to control what I thought, what I did." I have to anchor her faltering mind to this point before it's too hard for her to hold onto it.

"I did what I considered best for you," she says in a defensive tone, sounding more like herself again.

"Why, when I was exploring my feelings toward women, did you drive them away?"

"Which women?" she asks. "I liked Mireya most of all." Her lover. "You married a good man, and you had three beautiful children with him."

"You persuaded me into a marriage because it was the 'right thing to do.'"

"Why blame me? You walked down the aisle with him," she says with the canniness of the failing mind.

"You're right, Mami, you never understood me."

"You didn't understand yourself, Marina. You wanted to be with women, then you wanted to be with men, and then with a woman again."

How can I answer her? She, of all people, should know what it's like to love both women and men.

I can't win, not even now. It's always been her way or no way. How often I tried to confide in her, but she'd brush it aside and keep on talking about inconsequential matters. I wanted to tell her how much I admired her hard work. I learned discipline from her. "It's for your own good," she'd say, but I didn't understand then. It takes discipline to deal with the rigors of work.

"Mami," I say. "My happiest moments as a child were with you."

Her face softens into a smile. "Is that so? I never realized."

"Your charm, your smile. I wanted to hug and kiss you whenever I saw you, but you'd tell me, 'Leave me alone. Enough.'"

"You were too clingy," she says.

"I needed you, and you weren't there for me."

"I don't remember," she says. "Didn't we sleep in the same bed until you grew up?"

On that note, her memory shuts down, and we never have a real talk again.

My mother is in the hospital. Helpless, she depends on all the tubes feeding liquids into her body. She is so pale, as if the tubes, rather than sustaining her, are vampires, sucking the life out of her. The dark blue circles under her eyes announce the end is near. Her chest hardly moves when she breathes. Her face is drawn in taut lines. I'm a witness to torture, standing close while nurses search and stab her seeking a vein to stick yet another a needle into. My body shudders in response to her agony, and when she screams, "*Ay, ay, ay, ya no más!*" invisible darts pierce my being. They have to clean the wounds on her feet, infected because of her diabetes, and her face twists with the same agony I've seen in paintings of hellscapes. How much longer can they afflict pain on her, and for what? Her mind is almost gone. Let her go.

She gazes upwards, and a softness comes over her face. She focuses on some point beyond me, beyond these walls, and her lips open again. She calls to her mother and father, both long gone, "Come here to me," and to her sister-in-law, dead for the past fifty years, and to her sister who passed away two years ago, "Meli, I'm tired. I want to go with you." She seems to be connecting with the spirits of the departed. "Roberto, Roberto." He's the only one of her five children whom she calls to, and he died last year, but we never told her.

Is this what happens when it's near the end? Can she see all of those people? Are they coming for her? I hope so. She won't be alone.

Will death be a relief? But then, what is death? It is the Nothing—a peek through the crack to the not being beyond. No more pain or loss. I'm sure everyone thinks about death sometimes. It's human nature—a sick neurosis when we're depressed or find ourselves near the end of a road. Is death the discovery of something bigger than this existence? Another stop on the way to a new incarnation?

Then, as she quiets down and seems to be sleeping I think back to when I was very young, after Papi died, and when she left me on my own. How I'd sit at the window until late at night, watching the street, waiting for her to come home, and hugging her pajama top against my chest. I'd put it to my nostrils and breathe in her strong, elegant, self-confident scent.

I'm seated on an uncomfortable hospital chair. The doctor has asked me for permission to stop the antibiotics, which aren't working anyway. I make the decision.

Am I prepared to watch her die? Yes, she's suffering and helpless—she who was so strong. She's not going to recover—ever. My brothers would not agree with my decision, but they're not here to see how she's already gone. I've been near her throughout her slide down. I started mourning her loss two years ago when her mind failed.

Over the years, my affection for her was tainted with anger for her ill-fated attempts to turn me into what she wanted and not what I wanted.

We were both strong-willed, and we challenged each other. I always thought about how she'd tried to control my life rather than all the ways she was there for me: sending me to dance lessons and supporting my performances; demanding that I become an outstanding student; teaching me how to be a hard worker, caring for me when I was sick or unable to cope; showing me how to face up to and overcome obstacles. Importantly, she taught me self-discipline. Finally I recognize my mother was my role model.

In later years my heart opened up to her, and I learned to be patient. Perhaps after I became a strong, independent woman with a mind of my own, after becoming a wife, a mother, and a successful businesswoman, perhaps when I found out the truth about her own sexual battle, I began to understand the workings of her mind.

Mami, now that you're not here anymore, I hope you will forgive me for revealing your secrets. You pretended to be someone you were not and hid the real you. I know you had to do this because the very society you esteemed so much would have reviled and abandoned you. Because you preferred to keep yourself private even when you appeared to be so open with everyone. I remember you telling me, "Dirty linen is washed at home, not in public." I hope wherever you've gone you can finally be yourself."

THE LAST BARRIER
My Struggle to Be True to My Bisexual Identity

S̲a̲n̲ D̲i̲e̲g̲o̲
2012

"It is the courage of the human spirit and the relentless persistence of life all around us that give me faith." – Oriah Mountain Dreamer*

Today I danced off hours of therapy, of helping couples and singles heal their wounds, their hurt, confusions, and secrets. Sometimes their vibes attach to me like sticky sores that I need to medicate, sanitize, eliminate before they turn into tumors. My healing is in the dance that takes me into another world of joy, creativity, and fulfillment. Jazz is my passion, moving smoothly to the beat while executing turns with grace and balance. These dance expressions give me great confidence—I'm the queen of the dance floor. I project my emotions through dancing. The same as a writer has her spirit in her mind, a dancer has her spirit in her body.

Afterwards, I'm more powerful, granted remission from the dark corners of my mind. A time to reflect and meditate and understand—above all, understand—the complexities in my life and uncover depths in my past. I contemplate my life as a bisexual, and how it unfolded: my initial struggle to be myself and be with whomever I wanted, male or female, and the influences and social pressures that prevented me from being myself until middle age. Experience shows what a hard road I chose to follow.

Bisexuals often have to pay a high price personally if we want to be true to our identity. It takes courage and, as my son says, "three balls" to outrun the bisexual gauntlet. We have to contend with the stigma attached to our sexual preference.

Unfortunately, bisexuals are still misunderstood because people are unable to categorize us as either straight or gay. We are often marginalized because we are seen as degenerates, or discriminated against out of ignorance or intolerance. Just as gays formerly concealed their homosexuality, most bisexuals have to do the same, many for their entire lives.

I have had feelings for both women and men, and why not? Why should there be a gender distinction? The spirit of the person is what moves me, where I find that deep connection. When I loved a woman, there was a deep emotional connection, a need to merge with her, to possess her, and fill the void of her/my emotional needs.

With a man, I felt safe and accepted. I enjoyed being with him in the straight world: going out in public, being at his side, openly showing affection, and having challenging discussions. I liked being held in his strong arms.

My relations with women were more intense emotionally, and harder to let go. For me, physical pleasure and sex can be spiritual when emotions are present. Sex gives meaning to life. Through sex, I revealed my feelings more than through language. Those attachments belong to the complexities of my past. Often we have to endure emotional pain and loss to enjoy the freedom of age and experience. Now I long to set out alone and do what I want, rather than play another's tune.

We need to envision a world that celebrates affection in any form regardless of sexual orientation or gender expression. As more bisexuals come forward, more knowledge and information will be provided about this identity. Perhaps then we will see a change in attitude toward others like me.

I'm not in a relationship, nor do I want to be—they can be draining and suffocating—though sometimes I meet an attractive man or woman. If one day I'm attracted to a man and the next day to a woman, it's not a problem, which, sadly, was not the case when I was young. I have a sense of self-peace and self-understanding. Mostly, I prefer to be left to do my own things: my practice as a therapist, my family, my reading, and my dancing. Always my dancing.

I will keep on dancing. It is my last connection with the joy of youth. The shadows of the past fall away from me—I toss them into the air, kick them in the belly, slap them off me, batter them, stomp on them, tread them into nothing, and banish them into the ether. Peace swoops down, and I clutch the moments of happiness, to be guarded, nurtured, nourished, cared for, perfected, and cherished. After all, it is my spirit, unique and free, that I must recoup from the wilderness where my life took it.

Therapist's Notes

Myths and Realities of Bisexuality

Sexuality runs along a continuum. It is not a static "thing" but rather a process that can flow, changing throughout our lifetime. Bisexuality falls along this continuum. As Boston bisexual activist Robyn Ochs says, bisexuality is the "potential for being sexually and/or romantically with members of either gender."*

Myth: *Bisexuals are promiscuous/swingers.*
Truth: Bisexual people have a range of sexual behaviors. Some have multiple partners; some go through partner-less periods. Promiscuity is no more prevalent in the bisexual population than in other groups of people.

Myth: *Bisexuals are equally attracted to both sexes.*
Truth: Bisexuals tend to favor either the same or the opposite sex while recognizing their attraction to both genders.

Myth: *Bisexual means having concurrent lovers of both sexes.*
Truth: Bisexual simply means the potential for involvement with either gender. This may mean sexually, emotionally, in reality, or in fantasy. Some bisexual people may have concurrent lovers; others may relate to different genders at various time periods. Most bisexuals do not need to see both genders in order to feel fulfilled.

Myth: *Bisexuals cannot be monogamous.*
Truth: Bisexuality is a sexual orientation. It is independent of a lifestyle of monogamy or non-monogamy. Bisexuals are as capable as anyone of making a long-term monogamous commitment to a partner they love. Bisexuals live a variety of lifestyles, as do gays and heterosexuals.

Myth: *Bisexuals are denying their lesbianism or gayness.*
Truth: Bisexuality is a legitimate sexual orientation, which incorporates gayness. Most bisexuals consider themselves part of the generic term "gay." Many are quite active in the gay community, both socially and politically. Some of us use terms such as "bisexual lesbian" to increase our visibility on both issues.

Myth: *Bisexuals are "in transition."*
Truth: Some people go through a transitional period of bisexuality on their way to adopting a lesbian/gay or heterosexual identity. For many others,

bisexuality remains a long-term orientation. Indeed, we are finding that homosexuality may be a transition for bisexual people.

Myth: *Bisexuals spread AIDS to the lesbian and heterosexual communities.*
Truth: This myth legitimizes discrimination against bisexuals. The label "bisexual" simply refers to sexual orientation. It says nothing about sexual behavior. AIDS occurs in people of all sexual orientations. AIDS is contracted through unsafe sexual practices, shared needles, and contaminated blood transfusions. Sexual orientation does not "cause" AIDS.

Myth: *Bisexuals are confused about their sexuality.*
Truth: It is natural for both bisexuals and gays to go through a period of confusion in the coming-out process. When you are an oppressed people and are constantly told that you don't exist, confusion is an appropriate reaction until you come out to yourself and find a supportive environment.

Myth: *Bisexuals can hide in the heterosexual community when the going gets tough.*
Truth: To "pass" and deny your bisexuality is just as painful and damaging for a bisexual as it is for a gay. Bisexuals are not heterosexuals, and we do not identify as heterosexual.

Myth: *Bisexuals are not gay.*
Truth: We are part of the generic definition of "gay" (see Don Clark's *Loving Someone Gay*). Non-gays lump us all together. Bisexuals have lost their jobs and suffer the same legal discrimination as other gays.

Myth: *Bisexual women will dump you for a man.*
Truth: Women who are uncomfortable or confused about their same-sex attraction may use the bisexual label. True bisexuals acknowledge both their same-sex and opposite-sex attraction. Both bisexual and gays are capable of going back into the closet. People who are unable to make commitments may use a person of either gender to leave a relationship.

It is important to remember that **bisexual**, **gay**, **lesbian**, and **heterosexual** are labels created by a homophobic, biphobic, heterosexist society to separate and alienate us from each other. We are all unique; we don't fit into neat little categories. We sometimes need to use these labels for political reasons and to increase our visibility. Our sexual esteem is facilitated by acknowledging and accepting the differences and seeing the beauty in our diversity.

– Sharon Forman Sumpter
"Myths/Realities of Bisexuality"

Therapist's Insights

BARRIER ONE: Consequences of Past Actions

We are free to choose our paths, but sometimes decisions are made without thinking of future consequences. Our past actions remain a part of us. They're part of the tapestry of our lives. Their consequences continue to live on and impact us. We cannot undo what we've done along the way that creates dilemmas or challenges. But we can learn to accept the consequences that remain alive. We can learn and grow from them. It is valuable to accept the flow and change of life. Instead of fixating on the sadness, regret, or guilt over past actions, we can put our energies into other venues and other experiences and create greater fulfillment and positive energy.

BARRIER TWO: Hidden Memory

Sexual abuse of children by women is a subject most parents and caregivers are not familiar with. Sexual abuse by females rarely gets reported or acknowledged, or is minimized because of a lack of awareness by the public. Females may be more likely to use mental coercion than physical force.

Research on female sexual abuse perpetrators indicates that many suffer from low self-esteem, antisocial behavior, poor social and management skills, fear of rejection, passivity, promiscuity, mental health problems, and post-traumatic stress disorder. Victims often don't understand that what happened to them was abuse until years later when they are adults. – **Hunter et al., 1993; Matthews and Spelt, 1989**

BARRIER THREE: Loss of My King

For a young person the loss of a father is extremely difficult because she is losing a mentor, the person who would help guide her to maturity. It may feel as if the loss of a father has taken away the person she is inside and removed a piece of herself that was integral to making her the person she was meant to be.

Experiencing the death of a parent is traumatic at any age, but it is particularly harrowing for young children. With the death of a parent young children are deprived of not only the guidance and love that the parent would have provided as the children grow up but also the sense of security that the parent's ongoing presence in the home would have bestowed. More often than not, the child feels terribly vulnerable, especially when the death is accompanied by the relocation of the family. – **Greg Harvey**

Psychological research has shown that a person's age affects his or her ability to cope with the death of a parent, according to clinical psychologist Maxine Harris, PhD, in her book *The Lifelong Impact of the Early Death of a Mother or Father*. The loss of a parent before adulthood has a profound effect on the rest of a child's life. It may affect personality development with the surviving parent and significant others.

BARRIER FOUR: A Symbiotic Relationship

Emotional incest is one of the most pervasive, traumatic, and damaging dynamics that occur in families in this dysfunctional, emotionally dishonest society. It is rampant in our society, but very little is written or discussed about it.

Emotional incest occurs when a child feels responsible for a parent's emotional well-being and the parent does not have healthy boundaries. It can occur with one or both parents, same sex or opposite sex, when their emotional needs are not met by their spouse or other adults.

This type of abuse can have a devastating effect on the adult/child's relationship with their own sexuality and gender, and their ability to have successful intimate relationships as an adult.

Jungian analyst Marion Woodman describes emotional incest as "unboundaried bonding" in which parents use the child as a mirror to support their needs rather than mirroring the child in support of her/his emotional development.

BARRIER FIVE: Left on My Own

Sometimes a child or adolescent continually complains of a discomfort or a pain for which a physician cannot find a cause. The pain or the discomfort, however, is very real to the sufferer. Physical complaints with no apparent medical basis may be a reflection of a stress, such as nervousness in a social situation, a demanding school setting, separation from parents, or other stressful situations.

Stress, as it affects the body and the mind, has an effect on some illnesses and can influence how a person perceives the symptoms of the illness, how she or he deals with the illness, and the rate of recovery.

Somatoform disorder is the term used in the *Diagnostic and Statistical Manual of Mental Disorders* (*DSM IV*) to describe a group of disorders characterized by physical symptoms that cannot be fully explained by a neurological or generalized medical (organic) condition, direct effect, or a substance, or be attributable to another mental disorder (e.g., panic disorder). For people who have a somatoform disorder, medical test results are normal or do not explain the symptoms.

To address this illness, it is imperative to tackle the underlying causes that are buried in the subconscious mind. When managed effectively, such as with psychotherapy, the disease regresses and becomes quiescent, and the patient experiences immense relief.

BARRIER SIX: Interrupted Sexual Development

Sexually abused children are exposed to focused and excessive sexual stimulation that interrupts their normal sexual development. They are denied the opportunity to learn about sexuality at their own pace. Sexual arousal is paired with feelings of fear or confusion or pain.

Sexually abused children become confused about sexuality, and negative associations are formed between sexuality and care-getting and care-giving.

In addition children's normal development in the sexual sphere is thwarted by inappropriate and excessive focus of feelings and behaviors that would usually surface gradually during the child's development.

The emotional climate in which "these lessons" are taught may further create fear and anxiety in young children not yet capable of understanding the varied aspects of sexual arousal. – **Eliana Gil, PhD**

BARRIER SEVEN: Sexual Feelings Are Wrong

Children and adolescents who have been sexually abused can suffer a range of psychological and behavioral problems from mild to severe, in both the short and long term. These problems typically include depression, anxiety, guilt, fear, sexual dysfunction, withdrawal, and acting out, depending on the severity of the incident.

Victims of sexual abuse may also develop fear and anxiety regarding the opposite sex or sexual issues or display inappropriate sexual behavior. It is important for victims of abuse to relinquish any guilt they may feel about the abuse. Victims report that attending workshops and conferences on child sexual abuse and undergoing psychotherapy have helped them feel better and return to a more normal life.

Healing

There is an assumption in society that people who have been sexually abused in childhood are "damaged" or not capable of living a normal life. On the contrary, many adult survivors find ways to resist the effects of the abuse, earn strategies to help with healing, and succeed in a range of professions and in all strata of society.

BARRIER EIGHT: The Wrong Prince Charming

When a love relationship ends it can cause injury to a person's ego, a sense of failure, and a diminished sense of self-worth, more so if the loved one leaves or breaks it off. This is particularly true with the loss of first love. There are nagging questions about what went wrong and fear about the future. This loss may result in disruptive or contradictory behavior, with one or both of the lovers seeking love with anyone who shows them affection, often misplaced or damaging to their emotional stability.

Love is the state in which man sees things most widely different from what they are. – **Nietzche***

The heart is the place where we live our passions. It is frail and easily broken, but wonderfully resilient. There is no point in trying to deceive the heart. It depends on our honesty for its survival. – **Leo Buscaglia***

BARRIER NINE: Infatuation with a Woman

Emotional vulnerability: A state of being in which your brain is able to perceive and communicate emotions back to your conscious mind, and you are able to freely communicate those emotions to another person. The more emotionally vulnerable you are, the more perceptive you are of other people's emotions, unspoken or not. The desire for physical intimacy (touching, hugging, and caressing) is normal. It has been shown to increase the "feel good" chemicals such as oxytocin, dopamine, and serotonin while decreasing stress-related hormones. Emotional vulnerability makes this stimulus necessary for validation of worth.

Controlling mothers, a boundary issue. The mother has no idea where she begins and ends and where the child begins and ends. The child is then perceived as being an extension of the mother. If the child is an extension of the mother and not separate, the child's own needs may be ignored and dismissed. As a result of this, the child ends up being enmeshed in the mother and used to fulfill her needs. Here the mother tries to control her child's emotional needs by using extreme methods to curtail freedom of choice.

BARRIER TEN: Catholic Guilt
The term **Catholic guilt** is used to describe the feeling of remorse or conflict that can occur when a person raised as a Catholic has engaged in behavior their religious faith has declared wrong or sinful.

People who were raised in the Catholic faith are given very clear messages about which types of behaviors are acceptable and which are not. Homosexuality, or same-sex love, is forbidden. This is not to say that people raised in a different faith do not feel guilt about these choices. Still, Catholic childhood religious indoctrination may cling to us throughout our lives. Catholic guilt may influence our behavior and cause undue remorse for our actions even when we are no longer practicing Catholics. We are reminded of childhood lessons about sinning against God and the fear of committing a mortal sin that will doom us for eternity.

BARRIER ELEVEN: Loving a Woman
The first lesbian relationship can be a first step toward overt bisexuality and may be a turning point in a person's life, especially if it is the first sexual relationship, the one that lays the foundation for future sexuality. If this attachment is disrupted, it can result in feelings of sexual confusion, disillusion, and anger toward the person or event that caused the disruption.

The narcissistic parent won't accept a child's life choices if they signal a departure from what the parent envisioned for her/him. Rather, the child is forced to become "one with" the narcissist until there is no perceived difference (on the part of the narcissistic parent) between the parent and the child. A narcissistic mother wants to shape her daughter into her own image and to become an instrumental extension of herself. The narcissistic mother will attempt to perpetuate her adult daughter's dependence to the point where she is not permitted to develop her own identity.

BARRIER TWELVE: Marriage as a Solution
Internal homophobia. From the youngest of ages, we are steeped in a society that scorns the odd and encourages the average. Until recently society sent a clear message to be like everyone else, be heterosexual. Men

should want women and women should want men. Even in this more liberal society, heterosexism is still a system of attitudes, bias, and discrimination in favor of opposite-sex sexuality and relationships. This may include the presumption that everyone is heterosexual or that opposite-sex attraction and relationships are the norm and therefore superior.

Internalized homophobia refers to negative feelings toward oneself because of homosexuality. It causes severe discomfort or disapproval of one's own sexual orientation. The label of internalized homophobia is sometimes applied to conscious or unconscious behaviors. This can include extreme repression and denial coupled with forced outward displays of hetero normative behavior for the purpose of appearing or attempting to feel "normal" or "accepted."

BARRIER THIRTEEN: Married, but Loving Another Woman
A double life becomes destructive when this lie takes on a life of its own, according to Dr. Saliha Afridi,* former clinical psychologist in the Human Relations Institute in Chicago, and currently of The Lighthouse Community Psychology Clinic in Dubai. While many individuals may carry on living a double life for years, this lie especially impacts on relationships. If and when we present ourselves as doing or being something we are not, we are creating deceit in the relationship. This can be devastating to a relationship because we are not living our truth, so we are not happy. Being truthful to oneself sometimes hurts other people and may throw a relationship off-balance. There can be collateral damage or pain to the family because of the loss of a dream. The question remains: Was being authentic worth it?

BARRIER FOURTEEN: Finding a Father for My Lover's Child
Mental health professionals and religious authorities in the sixties called homosexuality perverted, immoral, and sick.

For a homosexual parent the fear of losing one's children in a custody battle was a very real issue. It was challenging for a lesbian couple who desired a child.

In those days in Mexico the only way to conceive was to have sex with a man whether she liked it or not. Choice of a man to father one's child could be a difficult decision. It was important for the child's sake to know the sperm donor and his genes.

BARRIER FIFTEEN: An Emotional Conflict
In our culture, it is generally assumed that a person is either heterosexual (the default assumption) or homosexual (based on appearance or behavioral clues). Because bisexuality doesn't fit into these categories, it is often denied or ignored. When it is recognized, bisexuality is often viewed as being part heterosexual and part homosexual, rather than being a unique and complete identity within itself.

Many people still think that claiming a bisexual orientation is gay or lesbian, and not all bisexuals have come to terms with their sexual identity.

Sexual orientation is primarily defined according to one's feelings of sexual attraction and not one's behavior. Some persons with a bisexual orientation make a conscious decision to confine their sexual activity to person(s) of one gender and still be considered a bisexual by themselves and others.

Bisexuals are in many ways a hidden population. There isn't much research on the subject of bisexuality, and as yet it is not possible to determine how common it might be.

A bisexual person is capable of having equal and simultaneous deep, committed relationships with more than one person because one's identity as bisexual is constant.

BARRIER SIXTEEN: Betrayal

Betrayal at any stage of the social cycle results in extreme biopsychosocial distress far beyond the event itself. It disrupts the person's established mental model by which he or she views, understands, and responds to his or her environment and life events, destabilizes the co-occurring psychological contracts by which one trusts, and negates important aspects of viable strategies by which the person copes with life events. – **Hensley 2009a, 2009b, 2009c**

A lover's betrayal, particularly in the case of same-gender love, may result in avoidance of future same-sex relationships. Trust is broken and the disappointment so acute that the ability to love another person of the same sex may be lost.

Psychological Trauma

Psychological trauma results from an event or events so egregious that they offend the mental model by which a person views, understands, and responds to his or her environment and violates his or her psychological contract(s) with others. This violation results in biopsychological distress that interferes with the person's ability to adaptively interact with others.

BARRIER SEVENTEEN: Late-Life Recognition of Sexual Orientation

Because of conditioning and because women are told they can be sexual only in relation to men, some gay and lesbians don't become aware of their sexuality until later in life when they fall in love with somebody of the same sex. This may happen after being married for years in a heterosexual relationship.

Until recently women were doubly oppressed by a system that rejected homosexuality and accepted women only in certain roles, i.e., as wives and mothers..

The combined effects of homophobia and sexism means that women are less likely than men to realize their homosexuality, to act on the feelings, or to come out.

Other lesbians, because of internalized homophobia, are aware of their true feelings for women, but they believe the myth "it's only a phase" and think they will grow out of it or hope that by getting married and having children they can suppress their feelings.

Some lesbians stay in marriages for the sake of their children or out of fear of losing family and friends, and have lesbian relationships without ever accepting they are probably bisexual and attracted to both the same as well as the opposite sex.

BARRIER EIGHTEEN: A Powerful Man
"Women's bisexuality an 'identity,' not phase" by **Sharon Jayson*** *USA Today*

Bisexuality among women isn't just a phase, according to new research that followed seventy-nine non-heterosexual women for a decade and found that bisexual women continued to be attracted to both sexes over time.

Being bisexual is a distinct orientation, not a temporary stage, says the study by Lisa Diamond, an associate professor of psychology and gender studies at the University of Utah. It was published in the January 2008 issue of *Developmental Psychology*, a journal of the American Psychological Association. Diamond conducted face-to-face interviews around New York State, when the women (who identified themselves as lesbian, bisexual, or unlabeled but not heterosexual) were ages eighteen to twenty-five. She then spoke with them by phone every two years.

"These findings are therefore more consistent with the model of bisexuality as a stable identity than a transitional state," the study says.

Diamond suggests that most women possess the capacity to experience sexual desires for both sexes, under the right circumstances. She found that bisexual women were more likely than lesbians to switch between describing themselves as bisexuals and unlabeled rather than to identify themselves as lesbian or heterosexual.

The study also debunks the stereotype that bisexual women aren't able to commit to monogamous relationships because they're always thinking about their desire for the other gender.

BARRIER NINETEEN: A Different Reality
Innate bisexuality (or predisposition to bisexuality) is a term introduced by Sigmund Freud based on work by his associate Wilhelm Fleiss that expounds all humans are born bisexual but through psychological development (which includes both external and internal factors) become monosexual, while the bisexuality remains in a latent state.

There is modern scientific consensus as to how biology influences sexual orientation.

Research into how sexual orientation may be determined by genetic or other prenatal factors plays a role in political and social debates about homosexuality and also raises fears about genetic profiling and prenatal testing.

BARRIER TWENTY: Leading a "Straight Life"
In 1995 Harvard Shakespearean professor Marjorie Garber* made the academic case for bisexuality with her *Vice Versa: Bisexuality and the Eroticism of Everyday Life*, in which she argued that most people would be

bisexual if not for "repression, religion, repugnance, denial, laziness, shyness, lack of opportunity, premature specialization, failure of imagination or a life already full to the brim with erotic experience albeit with only one person or only one gender."

Alfred Kinsey was the first to create a scale to measure the continuum of sexual orientation from hetero to homosexuality. Kinsey studied human sexuality and argued that people have the capability of being hetero or homosexual even if this trait does not present itself in the current circumstances.

BARRIER TWENTY-ONE: A Heterosexual Woman
BARRIER TWENTY-TWO: The Complexities of Loving Another Woman
BARRIER TWENTY-THREE: Different Directions

Two significant differences distinguish lesbian relationships from others. First, both partners are women; gender-related, intrapsychic dynamics will characterize the partnership. Second, the relationship bears the strain of illegitimate status in the eyes of the dominant culture. The partnership must find ways of coping with stigmatization. Both of these factors lend weight to the tendency of intimate relationships to move toward merger.

The complex mother-daughter connection may endow women with a greater relational capacity than men. As a result, women may have difficulty experiencing themselves as separate and a greater tendency toward psychological merger in intimate relationships.

Although merger occurs in all types of relationships, lesbian relationships may have a greater tendency toward fusion because of these factors that distinguish them from other relationships.

In the early stages of a relationship, merging of cells is pursued. Both partners are clearly separate individuals but with a pull toward coming together. Touching, deep eye contact, and lovemaking are primary means of facilitating merger. Later in the relationship, if enmeshment replaces the ebb and flow of connection and separation, the two individuals may develop merged identities. Individual differences may be smoothed over so thoroughly that one or both persons abandon whatever parts of their self that does not fit with the other. The denial of differences may exist only when they are together; at its extreme, one person is unable to think or act in ways the other would not, even when they are apart.

Sometimes in a heterosexual relationship a woman may feel unsatisfied in her greater capacity for emotional relating, and in fact this is a complaint that heterosexual women frequently present in couples therapy. Conversely, in lesbian relationships there are two women now with greater relational capacity but also a greater pull toward merging and loss of boundaries. The relationship may be more deeply satisfying in the beginning; it may be inhibiting to autonomy later. – **Beverly Burch,** *Psychotherapy and the Dynamics of Merger in Lesbian Couples*

BARRIER TWENTY-FOUR: A Different Life

Bringing a child into the world is a great responsibility. Children that are the result of same-sex relationships must have a strong foundation for a better chance of a successful and happy life.

Being open and free about parenthood and their relationship will help the children adjust to the situation and be self-confident.

Occasionally when parents split up, children may be lost to one or other of them. The child is the one who suffers the consequences because one of her parents and part of her family are not accessible to her. She is taken away from the environment in which she could develop and thrive, and half her identity is missing.

Unfortunately when the couple splits there are always consequences for the child, especially if that child loses the security of a family where she/he felt loved and safe.

Sometimes an innocent life is brought into this world for the wrong purpose in mind, and this can have a long-term impact on the innocent life. The couple might think that children can be an anchor that would bring deeper ties to the relationship; most of the time this doesn't happen. This is a false anchor.

BARRIER TWENTY-FIVE: Repeated Patterns

Emotional memory converts the past into an expectation of the future, without our awareness, and that is both a blessing and a curse. It is a blessing because we rely daily on emotional implicit memory to navigate us through all sorts of situations without having to go through the relatively slow, labor-intensive process of figuring out, conceptually and verbally, what to do; we simply know what to do and we know it quickly. It is easy to take for granted the amazing efficiency and speed that we access, and we are guided by a truly vast library of implicit knowing. Yet our emotional implicit memory is also a curse because it makes the worst experiences in our past persist as felt emotional realities in the present and in our present sense of the future.
– **Bruce Ecker, Robin Ticic, and Laurel Hulley,** *Unlocking the Emotional Brain*

BARRIER TWENTY-SIX: Separating Self From Mother

Differentiation of self is one's ability to separate one's own intellectual and emotional functioning from that of the family.

Differentiation is the process of freeing yourself from your family's processes to define yourself. This means being able to have different opinions and values than your family members but being able to stay emotionally connected to them. It means being able to calmly reflect on a conflicted interaction afterward, realizing your own role in it, and then choosing a different response for the future. Those with generally higher levels of "self-differentiation" recognize they need others, but they depend less on others for acceptance and approval. They do not merely adopt the attitudes of those around them but acquire and maintain their principles thoughtfully, not because they are caving into relationship's pressure. – *Differentiation of Self (Bowen's Theory)*

References

Aeronaves de México – Airline established 1934. Nationalized 1959. Became Aeromexico 1972

Afridi, Dr. Saliha – American-Pakistani clinical psychologist, The LightHouse Arabia

1995 International Conference of Women – Fourth World Conference on Women, Beijing

Buscaglia, Leo – (1924-1998), "Dr. Love." American author, motivational speaker

Chapman University – largest private university in Orange County, California

Civil Rights Act – (July 2, 1964) civil rights legislation ended racial, ethnic, national, religious, and gender discrimination, racial segregation in schools, at the workplace and by public facilities

Clinton, Hillary Rodham – (b. 1947) American politician, 67th US Secretary of State, Senator for New York, wife of President Bill Clinton, First Lady of the United States 1993-2001

Corín Tellado – María del Socorro Tellado López (1927 – 2009) Spanish writer of romantic novels

del Rio, Dolores – (b. 1905 – d. 1983) Mexican film actress, Hollywood star

Diamond, Lisa Ph.D. – University of Utah, Developmental Psychology, Health Psychology, Author

Edelman, Marion – (b. 1939) American activist rights of children. Founder Children's Defense Fund **Equal Rights Amendment (ERA)** Proposed amendment to the United States Constitution designed to guarantee equal rights for women.

Freud, Sigmund – (1856 – 1939) Austrian neurologist known as the founding father of psychoanalysis.

Hill, Anita – (b. 1956) American attorney, academic, professor social policy, law and women's studies

Jueves de Excelsior – Supplement to Excelsior newspaper, launched 1917

Landmark – Self-improvement, personal development course. Origins Werner Erhard, *est* training.

L'Armée du Salut – International evangelical movement founded 1865, follows the precepts in the Bible

Las clases del cha-cha-cha – 1955 Mexican hit song, dance composed by Sergio Marmolejo García

Love Is a Many-Splendored Thing – 1955 love song written by Sammy Fain and Paul Francis Webster

LAGPA – Lesbian and Gay Psychotherapists Association

Mexicana de Aviación – Founded in 1922, this airline was Mexico's oldest

Maslov, Abraham – (1908-1970) American psychologist, created Maslov's hierarchy of needs

Moore, Thomas – contemporary philosopher, author

Nietsche, Friedrich – (1844-1900) German philosopher, author

Oaxaca – state in Southwestern Mexico

Phantom of the Opera – (1988 – to date.) Musical, stage show adapted from Gaston Leroux's novel.

Reagan, Ronald – (b. 1911 – d. 2004) 40th President of the United States (1981–1989). Before that, 33rd Governor of California (1967–1975), and a radio, film and television actor.

Rebel Without a Cause – 1955 movie starring James Dean, Natalie Wood

Roosevelt, Eleanor – (1884 – 1962) longest-serving First Lady of the United States (1933 – 1945) during her husband Franklin D. Roosevelt's four terms in office. Human and women's rights advocate.

Sanborns – large restaurant, retail, pharmacy and department store chain. First Sanborns located in 16th century House of Tiles, La Casa de los Azulejos, a major Mexico City tourist attraction

Singin' in the Rain – 1952 movie starring Gene Kelly, Donald O'Connor, Debbie Reynolds

Steinem, Gloria – (b. 1934) American feminist, journalist, and social and political activist who became nationally recognized as a leader of, and media spokeswoman for, the women's liberation movement

The Hunger Project – An organization committed to the sustainable end of world hunger.

The Well of Loneliness – 1928 lesbian novel by British author Radclyffe Hall

Thomas, Clarence – (b. 1948) Associate Justice of the Supreme Court of the United States

Un Mundo Maravillose – fictional name of film

Bibliography

1   Sexual Fluidity: Understanding Women's Love and Desire – Lisa Diamond (Author)
    First Harvard University Press, 2009

2   Oddly Normal: One Family's Struggle to Help Their Teenage Son Come to Terms with His Sexuality – John Schwartz (Author)
    Gotham Books. 2012

3   Dear John, I Love Jane: Women Write About Leaving Men for Women – Candace Walsh (Author/editor); Laura Audre (Editor); PhD. Lisa Diamond (Foreword)
    Seal Press, 2010

4   An Unquenchable Thirst (A memoir) – Mary Johnson (Author)
    Spiegal & Grau, (2013)

5   The Bisexual Option: A Concept of One Hundred Percent Intimacy – Fred Klein (Author)
    Arbor House, 1978

6   Older Man Younger Man: A Love Story – Joseph Dispenza (Author)
    CreateSpace Independent Publishing, 2011

7   Double Life: A Love Story from Broadway to Hollywood – Alan Shayne and Norman Sunshine (Authors)
    Magnus Books 2011

8   The Last Nude – Ellis Avery
    Riverhead Books, 2011

9   The Invitation – Oriah Mountain Dreamer
    Harper Collins, 1999.

10 Unlocking The Emotional Brain: Eliminating Symptoms at Their Roots Using Memory Reconsolidation – Bruce Ecker, Robin Ticic & Laurel Hulley (Authors)
    Routledge, Taylor & Francis 2012

11 The Power of Now: The Guide to Spiritual Enlightenment – Eckhart Tolle (Author)
    Namaste Publishing Inc. 1997

12 A New Earth: Awakening to Your Life Purpose – Eckhart Tolle (Author)
    Namaste Publishing 2006

13 Soul Mates: Honoring the Mysteries of Love and Relationships –
Thomas Moore (Author)
HarperCollins, 1994

14 Untied: A Memoir of Family, Fame, and Floundering – Meredith
Baxter (Author)
Crown Archetype, 2011

15 Unbearable Lightness: A Story of Loss and Gain – Portia de Rossi
(Author)
Atria Books, 2010.

16 The Courage to Heal: A Guide for Women Survivors of Child
Sexual Abuse – Ellen Bass (Author) Laura Davis (Author)
HarperCollins, 1988

17 Magnificent Mind At Any Age: Natural Ways to Unleash Your
Brain's Maximum Potential – Daniel G. Amen, M.D
Three Rivers Press, 2008

18 Getting the Love You Want: A Guide for Couples – Harville
Hendrix, Ph.D. and Helen La Kelly Hunt, Ph.D. (Authors)
Atria Books, 2003

19 The Healing Power of Play: Working with Abused Children –
Eliana Gil (Author)
Guilford Press, 1991

20 The Four Agreements: A Practical Guide to Personal Development
– Don Miguel Ruiz
Amber-Allen Publishing 1997

21 The Mastery of Love: A Practical Guide to the Art of Relationship.
A Toltec Wisdom Book – Don Miguel Ruiz
Amber-Allen Publishing, 1999.

22 Loyalty To Your Soul: The Heart of Spiritual Psychology – H.
Ronald Hulnick, Ph.D. Mary R. Hulnick, Ph.D. (Authors), Neale
Donald Walsch (Foreword)
Hay House, 2010

23 The Meaning of Matthew: My Son's Murder in Laramie, and a
World Transfixed – Judy Shepard
Plume, 1999.

24 Staring At The Sun: Overcoming the Terror of Death – Irving
Yalom
Jossey-Bass, 2009

25 Myths/Realities of Bisexuality – Sharon Forman Sumpter, p.12-
13 of Bi Any Other Name: Bisexual People Speak Out – edited by
Loraine Hutchins and Lani Kaahumani.
Boston:Alyson 1991

Acknowledgments

My gratitude to my co-author Penelope James for her invaluable help with this book. We established a deep connection due to her knowledge and understanding of both the American and Mexican cultures, both of which have influenced my life.

My children are unfailing in their love and support. I am blessed to have them in my life.

My friends and authors, Ellen Snortland and Joseph Dispenza gave me valuable feedback and contributions.

My appreciation to Cathy Law who called for greater clarity with her insightful comments, and to my other beta readers, Rachel Connolly and Betty Statton.

My wonderful therapist Mary Clark Ph.D. encouraged me to tell my story to create more awareness and a better understanding of bisexuality.

My friend and assistant, Maureen Beck, for her help and encouragement.

For their skill and professionalism, I thank editor, Marsh Cassady, who helped give form and coherence to the book; Jacqueline Logue for her scrupulous copyediting; and Marty Safir for his commitment to deliver outstanding cover art and book design, and for his guidance through the publication process.

My thanks to my dance studio, Culture Shock, where I constantly renew my passion for dancing.

My gratitude to my adopted country, the United States of America, for providing a home where I am free to be myself and accept my bisexual identity.

Made in the USA
Charleston, SC
20 September 2013